# World Wisdom
## The Library of Perennial Philosophy

The Library of Perennial Philosophy is dedicated to the exposition of the timeless Truth underlying the diverse religions. This Truth, often referred to as the *Sophia Perennis*—or Perennial Wisdom—finds its expression in the revealed Scriptures as well as the writings of the great sages and the artistic creations of the traditional worlds.

*Universal Aspects of the Kabbalah and Judaism* appears as one of our selections in the Perennial Philosophy series.

## The Perennial Philosophy Series

In the beginning of the twentieth century, a school of thought arose which has focused on the enunciation and explanation of the Perennial Philosophy. Deeply rooted in the sense of the sacred, the writings of its leading exponents establish an indispensable foundation for understanding the timeless Truth and spiritual practices which live in the heart of all religions. Some of these titles are companion volumes to the Treasures of the World's Religions series, which allows a comparison of the writings of the great sages of the past with the perennialist authors of our time.

Cover:
A *shiviti* or meditative plaque,
by Solomon ben David Attias, 19th century

# Universal Aspects

## of the

# Kabbalah
# & Judaism

### by

# Leo Schaya

### Edited by
## Roger Gaetani

### Foreword by
## Patrick Laude

World Wisdom

Universal Aspects of the Kabbalah and Judaism
by Leo Schaya
© 2014 World Wisdom, Inc.

Library of Congress Cataloging-in-Publication Data

Schaya, Leo, 1916-1986.
[Works. Selections]
Universal aspects of the Kabbalah & Judaism / by Leo Schaya ; edited
by Roger Gaetani ; foreword by Patrick laude.
     pages cm. --  (The perennial philosophy series)
  Includes bibliographical references and index.
  ISBN 978-1-936597-33-8 (pbk. : alk. paper)
 1. Cabala--History. 2. Judaism.  I. Gaetani, Roger, 1954- editor. II. Title.
III. Title: Universal aspects of the kabbalah and Judaism.
  BM526.S314 2014
  296.1'6--dc23

                                        2013048238

Printed on acid-free paper in the United States of America

For information address World Wisdom, Inc.
P.O. Box 2682, Bloomington, Indiana 47402-2682
www.worldwisdom.com

# CONTENTS

# EDITOR'S PREFACE

World Wisdom is pleased to present this edition of key writings by the Perennialist writer Leo Schaya. World Wisdom's series of books on the "essential writings" of major Perennialist/Traditionalist authors is greatly complemented by the addition of these articles from Schaya, an author who devoted so much of his work to Jewish esoterism as a particular lens through which we might contemplate the universal Mysteries.

Leo Schaya (1916–1986) was a close associate of Frithjof Schuon and was much influenced by the thought and writing of Schuon, René Guénon, and Titus Burckhardt. Yet, Schaya's own writing also drew very heavily upon the Hasidic traditions of his Eastern European Jewish ancestors. It is this current of esoteric Jewish thought coursing through an intellect expanded by the *Sophia perennis* that gave Schaya much of the raw material and the particular direction of his writing.

Schaya's work is important to the body of Perennialist writings for several reasons. The first is his extensive treatment of Jewish esoterism, as well as its texts, primarily the *Zohar*, and its practices, which receive only occasional mention elsewhere in the works of other Perennialist writers. The second is Schaya's style, which sometimes borders on the ecstatic, thus mirroring the writings of the great Kabbalists; this aspect of his writing is examined in the excellent "Foreword" to this volume by Patrick Laude. Third, Schaya had a powerful attraction to the inner meaning of sacred symbols, and although all writers of his school of thought share this tendency, Schaya often chose to write expansively upon one or several related symbols. Finally, Schaya made significant contributions to the body of scholarly studies that reveal the capacity of an integral tradition, in this case Judaism, to serve as a vehicle through which we might perceive the universal realities that underlie all authentic traditions. According to a central Perennialist principle, it is in the nature of things that these pure realities exist beneath the clothing of the various traditions, and it is a goal of Perennialist writings to illuminate those underlying realities. Leo Schaya often summoned forth the words of both Jewish scripture and Kabbalah to give voice to those truths known to esoterists and metaphysicians of many other traditions.

Some readers will object that they find much of Schaya's writing to be too complex and challenging. Others will consider some of it too speculative for their tastes. Still others may find the departures from pure metaphysics into mystical realms unsettling. There is a certain validity to all these objections. Certainly, it would be useful for a reader of Schaya to have a background in comparative religion, the Perennial Philosophy, and Kabbalah in particular, but this is not essential for those willing to forge ahead directly into his work: many terms are explained a number of times and from different perspectives, some of which are likely to be familiar to many readers. We have also included a glossary to assist with many of the terms encountered in this book. No doubt, having a good dictionary of world religions at hand might be useful in many cases. However, it is also quite possible that a reader will be, even for just a few moments, caught up in the current of images and symbols and learn something of the awesome Reality of the Holy One (blessed be He) by a means of understanding that operates at a different level than that of the discursive mind. The Sufis, the Islamic mystics of whom Schaya writes in the final chapter, call this a *dhawq*, a "taste" of direct knowledge.

This brings us to an observation of a different sort that many readers make upon reading Schaya. They sense a powerful spirituality behind the words. They *experience* his words as much as understand them. It is not difficult to imagine Leo Schaya sitting in a circle with others in a synagogue, delving deeper and deeper into the mysteries of a passage from scripture. Yet, Schaya never sought nor claimed the status of a *tzadik* (a teacher of the Mysteries), and in none of the included articles did he write about his own spiritual life. Even so, it is inescapable that a mind so attracted to the outpouring of the Divine into all creation and a soul so immersed in describing that mystery to others could have existed in a state of exile from spiritual sustenance. We must respect Schaya's decision not to make his own spiritual life the focus of our attention, but we are also justified in discerning that there must have been a knowledge more profound than mere scholarly learning underlying his words.

Towards the very end of his life, Leo Schaya turned to more purely metaphysical and philosophical writings, but in this collection we have chosen to focus mostly on his works which used Judaism and its esoterism, Kabbalah, as their point of departure. Many of Schaya's articles were published in French Traditionalist journals of the day, and some of these were translated and published in the British journal *Studies in Comparative Religion*, starting in 1971. The present collection contains all of Schaya's articles published in *Studies*, since all of these pertain to our title *Universal Aspects of the Kabbalah and Judaism*. Through the generosity of the Traditionalist publisher Sophia Perennis, we have also been able to include some chapters from Leo Schaya's much-acclaimed book *The Universal Meaning of the Kabbalah*. These were selected because they illustrate certain essential aspects of Schaya's thought. In assembling this book, we also came across a previously unpublished paper of Schaya's which was written for and presented to a German-speaking audience in 1982, titled "The Worldview of the Kabbalah." It is a recapitulation of certain themes that frequently found their way into Schaya's work, but it also contains much that he covered for the first and only time in this article. In addition, it has a conversational character that many readers will find attractive. The final chapter comes from a paper titled "Contemplation and Action in Judaism and Islam." In this masterful talk Schaya very clearly demonstrates how two different spiritual traditions approach one and the same divine Reality to formulate doctrine and to engage in profound spiritual practice.

We have included a list of sources, biographical notes, a glossary, and an index at the back of this book to assist further research and understanding. For those interested in more details on Schaya's life and work, the "Biographical Notes" section concludes with some suggestions for further reading.

There are people who deserve our thanks for their assistance with this book. James R. Wetmore of Sophia Perennis has been very kind to let us use some of the included chapters. Gerhard Giesse did a wonderful job with some very challenging translating work. We very much appreciate Patrick Laude's insightful and balanced "Foreword" and his willingness to contribute to this volume. World Wisdom has been, to say the least, extremely patient and encouraging in the collection and editing of *Universal Aspects of the Kabbalah and Judaism*. Their decision to produce a book of this sort in this day and age is not only a tribute to the legacy of Leo Schaya's work, but also a tribute to the efforts of those behind the scenes who continually pursue the Good in their daily life and work.

To the readers of this book, we also extend our thanks, for ourselves and for the late Leo Schaya. It is very likely that in some way you will be touched by his words, and this was his primary reason (as it is our own) for publishing his work. He would be pleased to know that readers still turn their minds to the expansive realms of the One Reality.

Roger Gaetani

# FOREWORD

Among the names of writers associated with what has come to be known as the Perennialist perspective, i.e. the view that there is a universal source of sapiential wisdom underlying all religious traditions, Leo Schaya's is no doubt one of the lesser-known names in the English-speaking world. Indeed, only one book from Schaya's opus, *L'Homme et l'Absolu selon la Kabbale* (Man and the Absolute According to the Kabbalah), first published in 1957, has been translated into English and reissued three times under the title *The Universal Meaning of the Kabbalah*, in a translation by Nancy Pearson. There are several reasons for this relative obscurity of Schaya's works, not the least being the complexity of the task of translating his texts, as well as his primary focus on Judaism, a tradition that is rarely perceived as being especially conducive to an exposition of the *Sophia perennis*. Schaya is, indeed, the only major Perennialist author who hailed from a Jewish religious background.

Leo Schaya, or Ariel Lev Schaya, was born in Basle, Switzerland, on May 30, 1916. His immediate family had lapsed in closely following the religion of their forefathers, although Schaya counted rabbis and *Hasidim* among his ancestry.[1] In accordance with the spiritual realism of the Semitic religions, Schaya pursued an intense personal life of spiritual work and scholarly endeavors while at the same time maintaining a successful and demanding business career in order to support his family.

Leo Schaya's entire corpus deals with the world of Semitic monotheism, with an emphasis on Kabbalah and, secondarily, on Sufism. However, his contributions to a wide range of traditional studies are also considerable. Alongside his professional activities, his own writing, and his active personal spiritual life, Schaya was still able to undertake a number of impressive scholarly activities with great energy and considerable productivity. From 1977–1984 he served as editor-in-chief of the celebrated French Traditionalist journal *Études Traditionnelles*, which had highlighted the works of René Guénon, Ananda Coomaraswamy, and Frithjof Schuon. In addition, Schaya was the founder of a new Traditionalist journal, *Connaissance des Religions*, serving as its editor-in-chief until his death in 1986.

---

[1] Paul Fenton, "Journal d'un voyage spirituel au Maroc en 1950," *Horizons Maghrébins*, Toulouse, 2004.

As suggested above, the Jewish tradition is no doubt the one that would seem, *prima facie*, least likely to provide an adequate language for the exposition of what Schaya, together with Guénon, Coomaraswamy, Schuon and others, would refer to as the *Sophia perennis*, or the *Religio perennis*; that is, the non-formal, eternal wisdom that underlies all the spiritual traditions of humankind. There are several reasons for this difficulty. Firstly, the specificity of the Chosen People may be deemed to resist any attempt at finding a universal meaning within the Covenant because it is so exclusively defined as binding the One God to His one people. Secondly, inasmuch as the *Sophia perennis* stresses a message of metaphysical Unity akin to Advaitin non-dualism and to the Sufi concept of *wahdat al-wujūd* (Unity of Essence), the Jewish insistence on the incommensurability between the human and the Divine would seem to be radically antithetical to the premises of this message. Thirdly, and more generally, it has been argued, particularly by Frithjof Schuon, that the language of Semitic monotheism—due to its tendency to overlook or marginalize the notion of "relativity *in divinis*"[2] and the centrality of the Intellect—does not lend itself to the direct and hence complete expression of universal metaphysical reality.

However, the works that Leo Schaya devoted to the Hebrew tradition dispel, or at least qualify, the first two of the assumptions above. Schaya does this by underlining the Adamic and Abrahamic—and therefore universal—foundation of the Jewish tradition. He also highlights the central importance within Judaism of the exclusive affirmation of Divine Reality, which acts as the metaphysical key to the doctrine of Unity and its spiritual consequences. The third point may remain an unresolved area of ambiguity and weakness in Schaya's later books, but we will not delve into this complex question in the current context inasmuch as no such excerpts are included in the present anthology.

For Schaya, it is clear that what most fundamentally defines Judaism lies in its own "affirmation of the pure and supreme Reality," an affirmation which forms the foundation of all humankind's realization of its highest spiritual destiny. Schaya identifies this realization with *Yobel*, or Jubilee, "the 'universal' or 'divine state' . . . the state of supreme illumination and identity, of total union with God." However, Schaya

---

[2] For detailed explanations of this metaphysical concept, see the writings of Frithjof Schuon, for example, in *Logic and Transcendence* (Bloomington, Indiana: World Wisdom, 2009), pp. 75–76, 88n, and 90; or *Form and Substance in the Religions* (Bloomington, Indiana: World Wisdom, 2002), pp. 150, 207–209, and 249.

was intimately shaped by the Jewish outlook and was well aware of the limitative implications of its predominant formal perspective of religious "fear" or awe. In its Jewish manifestation, this perspective rejects any forms of idolatry because they create a confusion between the finite and the Infinite. It also does not allow for explicit expressions that might approximate the Christian "deification" or the Hindu "deliverance" as ways to describe the most elevated possibilities for spiritual realization. But Schaya gives us an essential key to understanding how Jewish spirituality finds its way to the same universal possibility for the human spirit from within its doctrinal framework. He leads us to comprehend that while it is true that in Judaism "the fear of God predominates," an alternative path to expressing the same spiritual reality opens up when the idea of sanctification is substituted for that of deification.

Judaism's uncompromising affirmation of the Unicity of the Absolute and its correlative duty of sanctification are no better expressed than in the admonition once given by Leo Schaya to young seekers in search of spiritual instruction: "We are unconditional devotees of the Absolute!" (*Nous sommes des inconditionnels de l'Absolu!*) Leo Schaya was indeed, in spiritual temperament, an unconditional pilgrim of the Absolute endowed with an intense mystical love for the One. This spiritual aspiration could not be better illustrated than by the long spiritual retreat he undertook as a young man as he embarked on the spiritual path; it ended after no less than nineteen days and nights when his friend and spiritual mentor Frithjof Schuon enjoined him to return to the world.[3]

Consequently, there is a definitely mystical and even ecstatic dimension in many of Schaya's writings, and this places him, perhaps, in a somewhat "ex-centric" position in the world of Perennialism, a world in which conceptual and verbal sobriety is by and large a function of intellectual discernment. Such a mystical bent has its beauties and undeniable power, as well as its occasional pitfalls. The former are illustrated, for example, by the inspired pages Leo Schaya devoted to the Divine *Sefirah Tif'eret*, or Divine Beauty, as in this passage:

---

[3] As an illustration of how Schaya's spiritual experience informed his intellectual insight, we offer the following reflection that he once shared with some friends regarding a striking mystical paradox. He noted that while spiritual practitioners alternately experience withdrawal from the world (the Sufi *khalwah*) and radiation in the world (*jalwah*), they might rather consider their experience in the world, due to its oppressive limitations, as a kind of *khalwah*, and the Name of God, along with the spiritual retreat during which it is invoked, as a *jalwah*, due to its limitlessness and its liberating grace.

The essential principle of divine beauty (*Tif'eret*) is the identity of the absolute (*Ayin*)—which excludes all that is not itself—and the infinite (*Ein Sof*)—which includes all that is real; it is the unity of the more-than-luminous darkness of Non-Being with the dazzling plenitude of pure Being, the supreme and most mysterious of unities, which is revealed in the saying (Song of Songs 1:5): "I am black, but beautiful. . . ."[4]

This mystical tendency is also discernible in some of Schaya's most eloquent pages on the Supreme Name, in which many sentences resonate with a mystical love of the Invocation:

Just as letters, when pronounced, return to their origin—the silent world of the uncreated and creative Word—so do animate beings or subtle "waves," having issued with the "primordial sound" from the divine silence and having vibrated through the heavens as far as here below, then return from their terrestrial end-point toward their celestial point of departure, from which they have never been separated and which is itself in permanent union with God.[5]

At times, Schaya's writing seems to be an attempt at encompassing the widest possible portion of the inexpressible, or rather at suggesting the latter through a recurring profusion of mystical expression which can approach hyperbole; it is as if the author had wanted to embrace mystically and lyrically the Divine with an ever-extending garland of words in order to suggest Its inconceivable greatness. This is so true that some of Schaya's elder readers and associates are said to have cautioned him against a certain temptation to say everything, a tendency that is, on the other hand, a beautiful testimony to his mystical thirst for, and love of, the Word.

Finally, it bears stressing that the works of Schaya constitute, as argued by Robert G. Margolis,[6] a bridge between the worlds of Judaism and Islam. Schaya was not only a scholar of Kabbalah and Judaism who was deeply attuned to the world of the Psalms, but he was also inti-

---

[4] *The Universal Meaning of the Kabbalah* (Hillsdale, New York: Sophia Perennis, 2005), p. 43.

[5] See Chapter 7, "The Great Name of God", p. 118.

[6] Robert G. Margolis, "At 'The Meeting of the Two Seas': An Introduction to Leo Schaya and His Writings," *Ajames*, no. 13, 1998, pp. 389–418.

mately connected to the world of Islamic mysticism, as testified by his remarkable study *La Doctrine Soufique de l'Unité* (The Sufi Doctrine of Unity), first published in 1962, and written in the intellectual current of Ibn 'Arabī or the *Advaita Vedānta*. It is considered to be one of Schaya's best books by some of his most eminent readers. This spiritual connection is also expressed in the beautiful diary that he wrote during his travels in Morocco in 1950. The personal account of his very moving meeting with the venerated Sufi master the Shaykh at-Tādilī in El Jadida is particularly eloquent in this respect. In it, Schaya recounts how the Shaykh at-Tādilī commented for him on the traditional Islamic saying (*hadīth*) in which the Prophet of Islam declares, "O how I would like to see my brothers of the end of times!" The Shaykh affirmed that Schaya and his fellow travelers were indeed "the lovers of God of the latter times" who accepted the religion without seeing the Prophet. It is also in the context of his meeting with the Shaykh at-Tādilī that Schaya beautifully evokes the non-dual Selfhood in which a Master and a disciple are one: "I am thou! Thou art Me!"; he mentions this while narrating with arresting emotion how the Shaykh blessed Schaya's own search for the spiritual goal, a blessing more precious than "a mountain of gold."

Enough has been said to suggest that the texts herein judiciously selected by Roger Gaetani from among Schaya's most accessible works, offer a splendid testimony to the author's inspiring focus on the One.

Patrick Laude

# CHAPTER 1

# Some Universal Aspects of Judaism[1]

Like all revealed religions and traditions, Judaism contains aspects which give it its special character and which constitute by definition its own way of affirming the Absolute. Its particularity involves the laws and rites specific to Israel, determined to a large extent by that nation's ethnological relationship with God, by the vocation of the "Chosen People" and by their sacred history. But if we examine the "doctrine" (*Torah*) of Judaism closely, as revealed by the Bible—or more precisely by its first part, known to Christians as the Old Testament—as well as by its traditional exegeses, exoteric and esoteric, we will uncover the universal foundation by which the Jewish religion is linked to all other genuine religions. This foundation, this common essence, is the real affirmation of the pure and supreme Reality, an affirmation through which man consciously binds himself to the only True and Real, an attachment destined to spiritualize man and finally reintegrate him with the Divine Absolute.

## Universal Aspects of Monotheism and Messianism

In Judaism, this unitive affirmation of the Absolute takes on the monotheistic form which the Bible traces back to Abraham and, through Shem, Noah and their ancestors, to Adam, the first man. This monotheism was restored and crystallized by way of the Sinaitic theophany in the form of Mosaism, which came into being to save Jewish souls of every generation, starting with the one which Moses led, and to unite spiritually the elite[2] amongst them with the One—the ultimate monotheistic aim. Now, if this salvation and union could have been realized in principle in all post-Mosaic epochs, the Jewish prophets who have extended and revitalized Mosaism have in particular proclaimed the coming at the end of time of him who will bring the "lost tribes of Israel" back to the city of God and, with them, all non-Jews who

---

[1] Editor's note: This article originally appeared in English as a chapter in the book *The Unanimous Tradition* (Colombo: Sri Lanka Institute of Traditional Studies, 1991), edited by Ranjit Fernando. We have added the section headings and reformatted portions of the essay.

[2] Editor's note: The author uses the word "elite" here to refer to the most holy, or sanctified seekers after God in those faiths, those who have attained the highest spiritual stations.

might wish to follow them in such a return to and union with the One who is actually present in the mystical Jerusalem. It is here a question of the coming of him who in Psalm 2 is called both the "Anointed" (*Mashiach*, Messiah) and the "Son" (*Ben*) of God. To the monotheism of Israel is thus joined the other fundamental and universal aspect of its religion: messianism.

That monotheism and messianism are by nature truly universal springs from their universalization by Christianity and Islam. It was Islam that universalized Semitic monotheism to the highest degree by making it return, through its Abrahamic main-stem, to its Adamic or primordial root. In fact, Islam freed monotheism from the necessity for ethnic "election"; that is, from the need to belong to a "chosen" people in order to unite with the One. It also freed it from a worship dedicated to trinitarian and messianic intermediaries between humanity and the absolute Divinity. It allows every man to make contact with the one and universal God without any of these preliminary conditions. As to Christianity, its *credo in unum Deum* ("I believe in one God") implies the affirmation of the Trinity, and in particular of the "son incarnate," an affirmation completed in practice by recourse to the intercession of the Virgin Mary. It also involves the belief that Jesus of Nazareth, conceived by the Holy Ghost and born of the Virgin Mary, was crucified and, having risen from the dead after his descent into Hell, ascended into Heaven, whence he will come again to judge the living and the dead. Finally, it involves the belief that the "son of God," according to the Psalm already cited, is also the Messiah (*Mashiach*), the "Anointed," or in Greek *Christós*. The Christian religion, whilst universalizing the monotheistic faith of Israel, thus eminently represents the universalization of its messianism, which is etymologically what the term "Christianity" means.

Christianity itself testifies everywhere in the Gospel to its having been proclaimed, and to a certain extent foreshadowed, by Judaism; and the Koran reveals that Islam came into being in order, amongst other things, to confirm the truth and saving power, not only of the Mosaic but also of the Christian revelation, both of them, in essence, at one with the pure monotheism of Abraham, which the Islamic message itself insistently calls to witness. If the Koran makes any criticism of Jews and Christians, it is precisely in respect of their deviations from the simple affirmation of the One made by Abraham. Unlike Judaism, Islam, without in its own heart interposing any messianic screen whatever between God and man—whom it calls upon to unite directly with that God—identifies Jesus of Nazareth with the Messiah (*al-Masīh*) proclaimed by the Jewish prophets, and furthermore, with the "Word" (*Kalimah*) and the "Spirit" (*Rūh*) of God, "directed at Mary," the Virgin whom "no man has touched" (see Koran 4:171; 3:47). But it does this without sharing the Christian doctrine of the "son of God" and his "incarnation," thus cautioning Christians against the "divinization" of the man Jesus and his mother, as well as against a trinitarianism deviating into tritheism (see Koran 23:91; 4:171). Finally, the Koran (4:157) insists on the fact that the "crucified one" was not "with certainty" Jesus, that is to say in his "reality" or divine nature which is the "Word" and "Spirit" of God, directly conveyed by his inner and incorruptible body, that of the transfiguration and resurrection. His mortal and crucified body was that which according to the esoteric interpretation of the Koranic text "resembled" the inner and divine reality of Jesus. Besides, as we have just seen, this body which directly provided the vehicle for his human nature was not regarded by Islam as a "divine incarnation," but as a simple "manifestational support" (*mazhar*) of God, whose absoluteness does not permit being made relative by a "localization" (*hulūl*) in the flesh.

Therefore, Jewish monotheism and messianism, though fundamentally adopted by the independent revelations, direct or "vertical," of Christianity and Islam, have at the same time been adapted by them in different ways according to the varying needs of the immense human groups which they might reach before the end of time. To these different "variations on the same theme," which are twofold (monotheism complemented by messianism) and by nature universal, are added those which relate to the cosmology and anthropology of the Torah, two more doctrinal aspects whose universal character has in turn been revealed through their universalization by Christianity and Islam. It is this that was attested—despite the customary exclusivism of the Jews which treated these religions as simple "modifications" or deviations from Judaism—by the great spiritual authorities of Israel, like Maimonides (Rabbi Moshe ben Maimon, 1135–1204 C.E., called the "Eagle of the Synagogue"), who wrote in *Yad Hasaqa* ("The Strong Hand"): "Thanks to these new religions, the whole world is filled with the idea of a Redeemer-Messiah, and the words of the law and the Commandments; these words have spread to distant islands and amongst numerous peoples . . . all are now occupied with the Torah. . .". In fact, if the New Testament is regarded as an extension of the Old Testament, together constituting the Bible which in its entirety was "confirmed" by the Koran, the conclusion may be reached that a great part of the human race is "occupied with the Torah." On every page of the Gospel are echoed the words of the Pentateuch, the Prophets, and the Hagiographs of Israel—thus its entire Holy Scripture—as also in the Koran from beginning to end.

Before mentioning in this category of ideas the essential aspects of Mosaic cosmology and anthropology, universalized by Christianity and Islam, let us return for a moment to the fundamental truth that unites the three Semitic religions, namely, the monotheistic faith which, according to them all, goes back through Abraham, Shem, and Noah to Adam. In Judaism, it is affirmed by the opening words of the Decalogue: "I am YHVH,[3] thy God, which have brought thee out of the land of Egypt, out of the house of bondage. Thou shalt have no other gods before Me" (Exod. 20:2–3). This very statement by the one God, together with the rejection of "other gods," is repeated many times in the Torah, finally denying in Isaiah (45:5–6) reality to all that man—through his *idola mentis*—regards as being outside of Him who in truth alone is real: "I am YHVH and there is none else, there is no God beside Me. . . . That they may know from the rising and the setting of the sun, *that there is none beside Me*" (*ki-efes biladai*).

Here we have the ultimate spiritual conclusion of monotheism, which Jewish esoterism—the *Qabbalah* or direct "reception" of divine truth—takes literally, not by postulating as do the pantheists that everything is God, but by affirming that everything is in God, the Infinite (*Ein Sof*) who, as we have just seen, has revealed Himself in the words, "There is none beside Me." Thus, all is in Him, either essentially and absolutely in His pure transcendence or in the ontological and prototypic state of His causal Being which is that of the Creator, or, yet again, as a created and transitory form in His cosmic omnipresence.

Islamic monotheism reaches the same conclusion at the heart of its esoterism—*Tasawwuf* or Sufism—starting with the credo revealed by the Koran, the *Shahādah* or "testimony" rendered to the one Divinity, universal and absolute, which begins with the words: "There is no divinity but God (*Allāh*)"—(*Lā ilāha illā 'Llāh*, 47:19). That first part of the

---

[3] The Tetragrammaton YHVH represents, in Judaism, the sacrosanct name of God; it is not translatable literally, but is derived from *HaYaH* or *HoVeH*, "being" or "reality," and signifies the Divine Essence, at once transcendent and immanent, or the total-reality of God. Conforming to the Jewish usage, we will transcribe this name without vocalization, its pronunciation being forbidden to Israelites for more than two thousand years "because of their sins," excepting initiates who in every age represent the "chain of esoteric tradition" (*shalsheleth ha-qabbalah*) and alone know how to enunciate the word according to the rules of incantationary learning going back to Moses. Vocalizations like *YeHoVaH* and *YaHVeH* do not, by themselves, give the key to that learning; like other known vocalizations, they only indicate the different aspects or manifestations of the sole Divine Essence.

*Shahādah* is spiritually interpreted by the Sufis as: "There is no reality but the divine Reality," which comprises all realities, whether uncreated and eternal or in created and transitory form. Thus all is in the one God, the only Real. And if things in their created and finite state are distinguished from the Infinite in order to affirm it to the extent of becoming extinguished in it, they are in their essence uncreated and infinite, eternally one with Him whose "unity is without association" (*wahdahu lā sharīka lahu*). It is the Absolute One, attested elsewhere in the Koran by the revelation: "Say: He, God, is one" (*Qul Huwa 'Llāhu ahad*, 112:1) which also constitutes, *mutatis mutandis*, the content of the credo of Israel: "Hear, O Israel, YHVH, our god, YHVH is One" (*Shema Israel* YHVH *Elohenu* YHVH *Ehad*, Deut. 6:4). This credo was confirmed by Jesus in the Gospel who when he was asked: "Which is the first commandment of all" answered: "The first of all the commandments is, 'Hear, O Israel: The Lord our God is one Lord'" (Mark 12:28–29). On another occasion Jesus effaced himself before the one God, saying: "Why callest thou me good? There is none good but one, that is, God" (Mark 10:18).

These are the two characteristic forms of the monotheistic confession and spirituality, to be found alike in the Gospel, the Torah, and the Koran: that is, either the pure and simple affirmation of the "One God," or His affirmation through the denial of any "other god" and even of all other reality. This last affirmation of God as the only True and Real has led the elite of the three monotheistic faiths to the same end in their respective spiritual paths, even though these might vary in their methods of approach to the One and union with Him—a conclusion which the Christian mystics call *unio mystica* or *theosis*, the Kabbalists call *devekuth* (unitive adhesion) or *yihud* (union) [with God], and the Sufis call *tawhīd* (unification) or *ittihād* (union) [with the One].

## Multiple Aspects of Being in Judaism, Christianity, and Islam

As to variations in approaches to the One, we have seen that they are the product firstly of differences in Jewish, Christian, and Muslim ontology or theology, differences which nevertheless do not affect the basis of their common monotheistic faith: the absolute or supra-ontological unity of the Divine Essence. Their different ontological or theological views—those concerning the one and the same causal Being of God and His relations with His created effects, human beings in particular—are determined by their varied revelations, Mosaic, Evangelic, and Koranic: the diversification of the spiritual and universal manifestation of the One, which Judaism contains in germ in its simultaneously monotheistic and messianic metaphysics.

5

Thus, with regard to monotheism, Islam, like Israel, while insisting on the absolute unity of the Divine Essence, nevertheless affirms the multiple aspects of its one Being, called by the two sister religions His "Names" (*Shemot* in Hebrew, *Asmā'* in Arabic) or His "Attributes" (*Middot* in Hebrew, *Sifāt* in Arabic), or in Jewish esoterism His "Numerations" (*Sefirot*) or first self-determinations. Concerning the latter, which number ten, a prefiguration of the Christian Trinity may be found in the three supreme *Sefirot*, the triple transcendent unity of God insofar as it rests in itself, whereas in the other seven *Sefirot*, which are of an onto-cosmological nature, we discover the Trinity in that it descends towards the cosmos, which is either to be created or is already created.

Amongst other things to be discovered in the ten sefirotic numerations of the Kabbalah, which Jewish mystics contemplated long before Christianity came into existence, are notions of the "Father" (*Aw* or *Abba*) and the "Mother" (*Em* or *Imma*), as well as the "Son" (*Ben*) and the "Kingdom" (*Malkhut*), the divine immanence which in the revelatory state is also known as the "Holy Spirit" (*Ruah ha-qodesh*). And if we include—besides the Jewish idea of the *Memra* or "Word" of God— the scriptural relation between the "Son" and the "Anointed" or Messiah, to which we have already referred, it can be seen how Judaism already contains not only the metaphysics of the Names or Attributes of God, later characteristic in its own way of Islamic monotheism, but also—and above all in the esoteric or Kabbalistic domain—the trinitarian and messianic doctrine proper to Christianity. Hence the following statement which dates from the Christian Middle Ages: *Moysis doctrina velat quod Christi doctrina revelat.*[4]

## Universal Aspects of Jewish Cosmology

Now, following this final glance at the Mosaic prefiguration of Christian and Muslim metaphysics and theology, let us briefly examine Jewish cosmology and anthropology, whose universal nature has also been confirmed by their adoption in the New Testament and the Koran.

So far as cosmology is concerned, we know that the biblical idea of Genesis or God's "creation of the heavens and the earth" was perpetuated by the two non-Jewish monotheistic faiths, and correlatively the

---

[4] "The teaching [or doctrine] of Moses conceals what the teaching of Christ reveals." The doctrine of *Sefirot* has been explained extensively in my *The Universal Meaning of the Kabbalah* (London: George Allen & Unwin, 1971; revised and corrected editions, Secaucus, New Jersey: University Books, 1972 and Baltimore, Maryland: Penguin Books, 1973). (Editor's note: A more recent edition is by Sophia Perennis, 2005.)

division of the universe into celestial, terrestrial, and infernal levels; so also the angelology of the prophets of Israel, the triple structure—corporeal, psychic, and spiritual—of man, as well as his eschatological destiny, which on the collective level implies the resurrection of the body and the Last Judgment.

Individual eschatology is set in relation to the deeds committed by man in his life, deeds dictated by his reason (or lack of it) and free will, either in conformity or nonconformity with the divine Truth and Will, which from the beginning offered him a paradisal existence fed by the "Tree of Life" while forbidding him the mortal fruit of the "Tree of the Knowledge of Good and Evil." Having rejected what God had offered him by eating the "forbidden fruit," man lost his paradisal access to Eternal Life and was driven from Eden. But, though He condemned man to death, God in His infinite mercy restored to him that paradisal access on the "cursed earth" in a purely spiritual form, and completely in the beyond, on condition that he should thenceforth choose the good and abstain from evil: "See, I have set before thee this day life and good, and death and evil . . . choose life, that thou may live. . ." (Deut. 30:15, 19).

All these sayings from the Torah concerning the original perfection of man, his fall and its consequences, as well as the choice between good and evil with its eschatological repercussions—that is to say, life after death either in paradise or in hell—were continued and universalized by both the Gospel and the Koran. Similarly, we find in them once more the universal commandments of the Decalogue, to which is added: ". . . love thy neighbor as thyself" (Lev. 19:18). Lastly, the spiritual methods of the Christian and Muslim elites (who like their Jewish counterparts seek the Absolute "here and now"), while diverging in their forms—whether rigorously ascetic or a mild integration of psycho-physical elements in the pure spirit—require the same affirmation of the One "with all thine heart, and with all thy soul, and with all thy might" (Deut. 6:5) in order to attain final union with Him.

Thus, the fundamental truths of a metaphysical nature, and their application on cosmic and human levels as given in the Torah, have been spread throughout the world in one way or another by Christianity and Islam. In the revelation made to Israel these have been thrown into relief by the dialogue between the "Eternal and His people"; in the Gospel by the Message and the gift of the "Son of God" to this people and to "all the nations of the earth"; and in the Koran by its confirmation of the earlier revelations and its correction of deviations in their application. However, these fundamental truths have been emphasized in the Koran chiefly by an untiring call to the polytheistic Arabs to turn to *Allāh*, the one God.

The doctrine of Israel is "judaically" monotheist, and it is messianic only in an eschatological and triumphant sense of the word; Christianity is centered upon the universal Messiah, pre-eschatological and suffering as well as eschatological and glorious; and Islam is the universal and absolute monotheism.

A further comparison (also non-exhaustive, but nevertheless elucidating a few characteristic features of the monotheistic triad) might be one in which Judaism is seen, symbolically, as man—personified in Moses—ascending towards God while raising the fallen world with him so as to unite everything with the One at the summit of the Mountain of Illumination, whereas with Christianity, on the other hand, God descends into the world, incarnate as man, to bear his sins, to atone for him, to be assimilated by him, until "man becomes God." In Islam, man is obedient to the One until his extinction in Him who is "God in Heaven and God on Earth"—He being the only real, the spiritual total-reality in which everything that seems to be "other than Him" is finally absorbed.

In these successive and complementary revelations of Semitic monotheism—accompanied by messianism—there is an undeniably logical sequence, a secret law obedient to eternal Providence and ruling over a great part of our world for nearly two millennia. It is from the "little point *Yod* (')"—the smallest letter in the Hebrew alphabet, and the ideogram of both YHVH and Israel—that in the Near East emerged the universalization of Judaic monotheism and messianism, realized in the Occident mainly by Christianity and in the Orient primarily by Islam. Such is the evidence of a Judaism comprising universal aspects which, passing beyond their own frontiers, have become religious factors of world dimension and of essentially infinite reach.

### The Universality of Judaism and Non-monotheistic Religions

The universal nature of Judaism is revealed in other ways when it is compared with the non-Semitic religions usually regarded as not monotheistic: those called "polytheist" or "natural" or even "atheist." Looked at superficially, these religions do not appear to have any relation to monotheism, either spiritually or historically; but if we eliminate the erroneous views expressed by many Westerners with regard to these religions, their essential relation to monotheism—and even to messianism—is revealed in one way or another.

Thus, if we refer to the Torah, the Gospel, and the Koran, all three of which, apart from the divine, "vertical," or direct origin of their respective revelations, trace their monotheistic—and messianic—belief through Abraham, Shem, and Noah to the first man, we shall see that Judaism and the two other Semitic religions are spiritually and historically connected with the roots, both of Hinduism—through its self-identification with the "perpetual tradition" (*Sanātana Dharma*)—and of Buddhism, whose "eternal law" (*Akālika Dharma*) was that of the "old road taken by the wholly awakened ones of old" and revealed afresh by Gautama Siddhartha. This is also true, amongst others, for the Chinese "Old Way," the "True doctrine of *Tao*" which according to Chu-li, "has always existed in the world and has never perished; except that, this doctrine, having been confided to men, some of them broke it while others maintained it scrupulously. That is why its fate in the world is to be sometimes brilliant and sometimes obscure."

According to the Torah itself, at the time of the Tower of Babel and therefore after the Flood, all humanity "was of one language and of one speech" (Gen. 11:1). This "language" according to Kabbalistic exegesis, signifies the "unanimous tradition" that descends from Adam, the first receiver of the revelation of the One, a revelation which was "saved from the waters" by Noah's material and spiritual Ark. It was handed down as a renewed and universal "alliance" between God and man by Noah's three sons, Shem, Ham, and Japheth who together with their father and mother, their wives, and the animal pairs were the sole survivors of the Flood. These three patriarchs of post-diluvian man passed on this "language" to the various races and peoples that descended from them (see Gen. 6–10). Now the latter, according to the Bible, formed, until the time of Babel, "a single people" (Gen. 11:6) despite their different ancestors, having "one language," that is to say one tradition known to Jewish exegesis as Noachism (the Hebrew form of Noah being *Noach*).

Thus, according to the Torah, all humanity was still united by a single traditional and monotheistic culture, although it was diverted by its immanentism and its magic—so the Kabbalah attests—to the point of opposing the divine transcendence. Human unity, strengthened by having usurped certain immanent powers of God, sought to rule the world in an autonomous fashion in its own name, thenceforth ignoring its dependence on the divine unity, transcendent and immanent, an infinite unity to which man is summoned to conform and unite himself spiritually.

This is what, according to the Kabbalah, is meant by the words of the men of Babel: "Go to, let us build a city, [a worldly city founded not on theocracy but on autocracy][5] and a tower, whose top may reach unto heaven [this "tower" signifies a "counter-ascension" to heaven, that is to say a magical over-reaching of natural human means, of which the "top" or principle is a usurpation of the powers of heaven], and let us make us a name [by the "science of letters," a name which represents this principle and constitutes the universal key which permits—by way of this onomatological magic—the aforesaid usurpation and, consequently, the autocratic domination of the world] lest we be scattered abroad upon the face of the whole earth [a dispersal that signifies the breaking of the "magic circle" of that human unity, which believes itself protected by the circle and thereby capable of holding the divine unity in check]" (Gen. 11:4). Then the sole One, Himself confirming that in these conditions "nothing would be restrained from them, which they have imagined to do" (Gen. 11:6), decided to go down to men in order to break the magic circle of a false human unity: "Go to, let us go down, and there confound their language, that they may not understand one another's speech. So YHVH scattered them abroad from thence upon the face of all the earth. . ." (Gen. 11:7–8).

In other words, human unity, initially traditional, by raising such a revolt against the divine Unity, compelled the latter to break it into ethnic fragments, dispersed over the entire earth and henceforth opposed one to another; and this through a lack of understanding caused by the confusion, or more precisely by the differentiation of their "language" or single tradition into several "languages" or divergent traditions, but with a foundation that remains unanimous thanks to its divine essence. Indeed, the transcendent One's "descent" is seen as His own multiform revelation come to institute a plurality of religions or traditions in response to the deep needs of the various races and ethnic groups descended from Noah's three sons, and taking the place of the single primordial tradition that goes back to God's revelation to Adam.

According to the Bible, then, this is the starting point on earth of the multitude of traditions, revealed simultaneously and later successively, but each having, from a trans-historical viewpoint, its direct root in Heaven. They perpetuate and renew the doctrine of primordial man like so many rays that every day spread afresh the light of the rising sun, symbol of eternal light or wisdom, the *Sophia perennis*. This wisdom, articulated by the spiritual language of the first man, has remained fundamental to the diverse post-Babel "languages" or traditions. It comes down to us through the millennia, through various and

---

[5] Throughout this essay square brackets signify interpretive insertions by the writer.

complementary expressions, each form of which is at the same time the synthesis of the others, and humanity always has this common spiritual language, despite differences of idiom or formal concept. This universal language constitutes the secret link that unites the entirety of religions: doctrines Jewish and non-Jewish, Semitic and non-Semitic. Judaism, as we have seen, calls this link "Noachism," that is to say the primordial and universal religion of the absolute One, as revealed to Adam and perpetuated by Noah and his three sons, themselves prefiguring the multitude of religions after Babel.

Therefore, we repeat, it is through comparative metaphysics, cosmology, and anthropology that we are able to discover, behind the traditional forms (though antinomic in appearance) the link that is permanently established by the proper and primordial affirmation of the one and only Absolute. When we examine these forms thoroughly in order to make spiritual "translation" of their contents—whether such forms be abstract or clothed in symbolism—equivalent meanings are disclosed and it becomes clear finally that the doctrine of the only True and Real is the common basis of all genuine revelations. The distinction between the monotheistic and non-monotheistic religions is thus shown to be improper; we ought rather to speak of the Semitic triad and of the non-Semitic forms—or to use biblical language, Hamites and Japhetites—born of Noachism, the unique affirmation of the Absolute.

Although the triad we call monotheist insists on the divine unity, it nevertheless affirms, in one way or another, the multiple aspects of the One. In Judaism and Islam, as we have seen, these are especially His "names" or "attributes," and in Christianity it is "a single God in three persons," with whom are associated other mediatory aspects, such as the Holy Virgin. And even as in Christianity all the mediatory aspects between God and man are synthesized in Christ, who is at once "Son of God" and "Son of Man" (i.e., the archetype of man manifesting himself through human nature) or Man-God, in Judaism and Islam all the divine names and attributes are summed up, from an esoteric viewpoint, in the universal mediator called by the Kabbalah "Principial Man" (*Adam Qadmon*) or "Man above" (*Adam ilaah*), and by the Sufis "Perfect Man" or "Universal Man" (*al-Insān al-kāmil*).

The female aspect of this universal mediation between God and the created is regarded by Judaism as His *Shekhinah* or "Real Presence," and by Islam as His *Sakīnah* or "Great Peace," which He "causes to descend into the hearts of the faithful" (the term "Real Presence" is found literally in the Name *al-Hudūr*). In Christianity, as already stated, this same presence gives birth here below to the Christ who incarnates it and is consequently its perfect dwelling-place—a presence which is also personified and conveyed by his human mother, the perfect manifestation of "virginal femininity" and of the "merciful motherhood" of God.

## Universal Aspects of Judaism, Taoism, and Buddhism

Semitic monotheism, therefore, does not exclude a plurality, essentially one, of aspects through which the one and only Absolute is revealed and adored, just as in those religions mistakenly regarded as "polytheist" or "natural" or even—like Buddhism—as "atheist" or "based on nothingness." Clearly it is only when awareness of the one True and Real has been lost, and its aspects are disassociated from the unanimous essence and glorified as autonomous divinities, that monotheism (understood in the broadest sense of the word as the affirmation of the one and only Absolute on which all universal relativity depends) can be said to have degenerated into polytheism.

As for the idea of natural or even atheistic religions, this is, in both cases, a simple contradiction in terms, for a genuine religion cannot be "natural" in the sense of excluding the supernatural, nor atheistic in the sense of denying the Absolute. On the contrary, it is the intelligible and salvific link between relative man and the Absolute, being therefore itself supernatural and essentially absolute and therefore revealed by the Absolute and not the product of simple human thought, having as its object its own objectified and relative nature.

If a non-theistic (not "atheistic") religion exists, such as Buddhism, it is because the link between the relative and the Absolute is revealed there not under the aspect of a divine cause of existence, but under that of the Buddha-nature (*Buddhatā*) which frees man from existence—an existence full of suffering—and leads him to absolute Reality. *Nirvāna* ("Extinction"), or *Shūnya* (the "Void"), is not nothingness, but on the contrary it is that absolute and beatific Reality in which all relative existence is destined to be reintegrated. The same is true of *Ayin*, or the "nothingness" of Jewish esoterism, which describes this reality as "non-being" since it is actually a kind of supra-being that is both absolute and impersonal; it is the supra-essential and supra-intelligible essence of divine "Being" (*Ehyeh*; *Yesh*; *Havayah*), which is intelligible, causal, and personal.[6]

---

[6] Editor's note: The author is demonstrating that this state of existence cannot actually be considered "being" since it transcends all categories and concepts that we use to understand all other things that exist. Thus, "Nothingness" or "Void" become ways to

While this is the object of the "adoration of God by the mind" and of human faith—an adoration characteristic of Jewish exoterism—the final object of esoteric or Kabbalistic contemplation proceeds not only to the "surpassing" or "annihilation of human reason" but to the "cessation of existence" (*bittul ha-yesh*, which corresponds to the Buddhist *bhavanirodha*), the spiritual absorption, either transitory or definitive, into the "nothingness" of all nothingness, namely the absolute Reality. Whenever this Kabbalistic absorption into the Absolute is transitory and the Kabbalist returns to his relative existence, this return implies the instant restoration of his being, of his mind, and of all his individual faculties. But more important, he is thenceforth filled with the "luminous flux" of the causal and intelligible Being—of his own illumination, which rises finally to the more than luminous darkness of the "nothingness" or supra-intelligible non-being, for according to the Kabbalah, "Wisdom comes from the Nothingness," that is, from the Absolute.

The supreme principle in Judaism is the unity of "nothingness" or absolute Beyond-Being,[7] with causal Being acting as the origin of the relative. The same applies to the one Principle of contemplative Taoism, which goes back to the pure spirituality of the ancient Chinese Tradition and is distinct from popular and religious Taoism. The latter has as its supreme object the divine and causal Being under one or another "lordly" aspect or name, while the contemplative Principle has no proper name, because of its ineffable absoluteness, and is known symbolically as the "Way" (*Tao*) which leads to it.

But *Tao* is not only "non-being." It is a single Principle having two aspects, one which is supra-ontological and the other which is ontological: *Wu-ki*, the "Non-summit" or non-beginning, the absolute non-cause or non-manifestation, the Beyond-Being; and *Tai-ki*, the "Great Summit" of the cosmic edifice, the beginning or the cause of relative

---

describe that which defies our rational minds. This apophatic approach to conceiving the divine Essence is universally used in the esoterisms of other traditions such as in Christianity, Islam, Hinduism, Buddhism, etc. Here the divine "Being" refers to the personal God who creates, legislates, and "speaks" to humanity, but not to the Essence beyond that Being.

[7] Editor's note: In English translations of Schaya's work, the term "Super-Being" or "Supra-Being" is often used. For the sake of clarity and uniformity, we have used the term "Beyond-Being" throughout this volume wherever the equivalent term was used in Schaya's French or German original writings. Those familiar with the sermons of Meister Eckhart will recognize that the distinction in Schaya's writings between Being and Beyond-Being is the same made by Eckhart between God and Godhead.

existence, the universal being, also called *Tai-i*, the "Great Unity" of all existing things. The contemplative way of the Taoist leads to the spiritual realization of this "Great Unity," a realization which implies the union of the principles at once opposite and complementary which govern the universe. These are "Heaven" (*tien*), the active principle, and "Earth" (*ti*), the passive or receptive principle, which the Taoist must unite in himself by conforming to their respective properties or laws: the *yang*, active, masculine, positive, and luminous, and the *yin*, passive, feminine, negative, and dark.

We are reminded of the conformity required by Jewish spirituality to the positive and negative laws of the Torah, issuing respectively from the "grace" (*Hesed*) of God—which is His masculine aspect, affirmative or luminous—and "judgment" (*Din*), or His "terrible power" (*Geburah* or *Pahad*), His feminine, negative, or dark aspect. This conformity is the *sine qua non* of union with the One. And, just as the supreme aim of Jewish spirituality is the "nothingness," the supreme aim of purely spiritual Taoism is situated even beyond the "great unity" of all things, in their non-beginning, *Wu-ki*. It is at the heart of the deepest, contemplative "Non-action" (*Wu-Wei*) that the perfect Taoist is absorbed into his non-causal absoluteness, which is that of all things; and though he "descends again," this "non-action" will be reflected in his "non-active activity" (*wei-wu-wei*) at the core of a relative existence henceforth completely dominated by the Absolute. Furthermore, the non-active activity is also an essential element of the way that leads to this total and supreme non-action, which is none other, as already mentioned, than non-beginning itself, *Wu-ki*.

Like Judaism's "nothingness," this non-beginning relates to the Buddhist state of extinction (*Nirvāna*) or the void (*Shūnya*), the cessation of relative and painful existence through the "awakening" (*Bodhi*) in the supreme and absolute reality. In this reality, which surpasses all differentiation and multiple spiritual ways, the Taoist becomes "Transcendent Man" (*Shen-jen*), whose absolute condition then precedes (for in the "re-descent" it is followed by) the earthly condition of "True Man" (*Chen-jen*) situated at the spiritual center of this lower world, a center found within himself from which he dominates, spiritually, all human existence including his higher prolongations. Moreover, between the transcendent Absolute and the earthly relativity of man there is the intermediary or "mediator" state of Heaven, towards which contemplative man rises in order to realize not only these higher prolongations of human existence but to surpass them and become a "heavenly" man in the transposed sense of the word, that is to say, a reality which "is no longer a man" but the "Great Unity" (*Tai-i*) of Heaven and Earth. Furthermore, the "way of Heaven" (*Tien-tao*) on which he has embarked and which is finally identified with the entirety of the "Middle Way" (*Tchung-tao*)—the spiritual axis of all reality—draws him, as we have said, even beyond the "Great Summit" (*Tai-ki*) of Heaven and Earth to the "Non-summit" (*Wu-ki*) or Beyond-Being. That is why on descending again from that supreme state by this very Middle Way—which corresponds to the "Middle Column" (*Amida-di-Netsiuta*) of Jewish esoterism—the contemplative is called not only "True Man" (*Chen-jen*) but also "son of Heaven" (*Tien-tse*) and "Transcendent Man" (*Shen-jen*). "In the body of a man there is a man no more," says Chuang-tzu: "infinitely small is he to the extent by which he is still a man, infinitely great is he to the extent by which he is one with heaven."

Now these three aspects of universal man are also found in Jewish esoterism, beginning with "Transcendent Man" (*Adam ilaah*) or "Principial Man" (*Adam Qadmon*), whose body is none other than the unity of divine aspects of ontological and supra-ontological order, since his "hidden brain" is *Ayin* ("Non-Being" or "Beyond-Being"). This unity of divine aspects, symbolized in an anthropomorphic fashion by the principal limbs or organs of the human terrestrial body, is also symbolized on the cosmological level, amongst others, by the infinite ocean of the Divine Reality before its separation into "upper waters" and "lower waters" (see Gen. 1:6–7), that is to say before its "waves" or manifestable possibilities have passed from their non-manifested or immobile state to their manifested or mobile condition. At the "eternal moment" when this separation, and thereby this manifestation took place, the lower or cosmic waters were "gathered together into one place and the dry land appeared" (see Gen. 1:9). This "one place" (*maqom ehad*) is that of the immanent "One" (*Ehad*), "gathering together" or concentrating all his waters or manifestations into an "instantaneous crystallization" which is the dry land, the "body," the "form," or the universal and luminous sphere of the *Shekhinah* or divine omnipresence. But the *Shekhinah*, being in itself supra-formal and infinite, is distinguished from its form or from this spiritual and universal body, called *Metatron*, which in its revelations to humanity (that is, to the prophets and the saints) takes the "likeness of an appearance of a man, [who is] above [the earth and even the celestial throne], on high [at the supreme level of creation]," as stated in Ezekiel (1:26). Ezekiel continues:

And I saw as it were a shining surface [or a "burning eye," *ein hashmal*] as the appearance of fire within and around it, from the appearance of his loins and upward, and from the appearance of his loins and downwards, I saw as it were the appearance of fire and it had brightness round about. As the appearance of the bow [or rainbow: the luminous and spherical form of the *Metatron* which in other respects takes sometimes the shape of celestial man, sometimes that of the supreme angel— a rainbow] that is in the cloud [or formless "immanence of God"] in the day of rain [when his "waters" or revelatory manifestations descended upon the earth to purify and illumine men], so was the appearance of the brightness round about [of *Metatron*]. This was the appearance of the likeness [heavenly and universal: *Metatron*] of the glory [or immanence] of YHVH [the transcendent essence of God, or "Transcendent Man"] (Ezekiel 1:27–28).

According to the Kabbalah, "Enoch, who walked with God and who was no more, for God took him" (see Gen. 5:24) was not only raised living into Heaven—like the prophet Elijah much later (see 2 Kings 2:1–18)—but transformed into the totality of celestial man: *Metatron*. Inversely, the creation of terrestrial man was like a divine descent, Adam being created in the "image of God" (see Gen. 1:26–27), of God who is at once transcendent and immanent, or in the image of "Transcendent Man" and his spiritual and universal manifestation, *Metatron*, taking the form "of an appearance of man," that of celestial man. That is why primordial and terrestrial man (*Adam ha-rishon*) was in the beginning perfect, and after his fall was called upon to seek his lost perfection and, in a sense, more than that. For God "sent him forth from the Garden of Eden to till the ground from whence he was taken" (Gen. 3:23), that is to say until he recovered in himself the Edenic earth or the paradisal state, not in its first perfection, which was passive and corruptible, but in its ultimate perfection, which is active and incorruptible. According to Judaism, this perfection will be personified in the highest degree by the Messiah.

This Kabbalistic doctrine of the three bodies, or the transcendent, heavenly, and primordially earthly states of man—symbolized by the three Hebrew consonants in the name *ADaM*—corresponds to the doctrine of the *Mahāyāna* school of Buddhism relating to the *Trikāya* or "triple body" of the Buddha. This "body" may be identified in the first place with the pure transcendence of the Buddha: it is the *Dharmakāya* or transcendent "Body of Truth," which is itself manifested as the *Sambhogakāya*, or heavenly "Body of Beatitude" and universal compassion; and finally as the *Nirmānakāya*, the "Body of Transformation" of this truth or beatitude—or compassion—into the earthly appearance of the Buddha, a pure and perfect body, which also makes possible his transformation into his own celestial, universal, and transcendent reality.

There are very many definitions or descriptions of the *Trikāya*, but we cannot deal with them all here; we will restrict ourselves to the following, the first of which recalls in a striking way the symbolism of the Adamic body: "The *Dharmakāya* is symbolized . . . by an infinite ocean, calm and waveless, from which rise mists, clouds, and a rainbow symbolizing the *Sambhogakāya*; these clouds, lit by the rainbow's glory, condense and fall as rain symbolizing the *Nirmānakāya*."[8] We should add that the *Nirmānakāya* is the primordial and incorruptible body that is concealed in our perishable body and conveys in it the spirit. "With our physical (and corruptible) body we take refuge in the body of transformation or body of incarnation of the Buddha (*Nirmānakāya*)," said Hui-neng (628–712 C.E.), and he adds: "our physical body might be compared to a hostelry, that is to say a temporary habitation: therefore we cannot take refuge there. It is in our own nature (inner, spiritual, and universal) that the *Trikāya* of the Buddha can be found, and it is common to all."[9] It is the total-reality envisaged and realized through archetypal man, like the triple body of *ADaM*, whose name has indeed the same numerical and consequently spiritual value (that is, 45) as that of the divine total-reality, YHVH, when these letters are written out fully in this way: *YVD HA VAV HA*. The Buddha came to show the way to the realization of the *Trikāya*, which coincides with the way to escape from an existence that is painful because of "ignorance" (*avidyā*) and a "thirst" (*trishnā*) for that existence.

Buddhist truth is conveyed by universal compassion, whose salvific rays are personified by "all the Buddhas" and the Bodhisattvas (or future Buddhas), who themselves take the vow not to enter into the supreme and final *Nirvāna* before all beings have been saved:

---

[8] *Tibetan Yoga and Secret Doctrines*, ed. Dr. W. Y. Evans-Wentz, from the French translation by M. La Fuente (Paris, 1938).

[9] From the French translation by L. Houlmé, *Houei-Neng, Discours et Sermons* (Paris, 1963).

I have taken that vow that all beings shall obtain purity and omniscience; my practices are destined to procure for them omniscience; it is not for myself at all that I seek Liberation. . . . I accept all pain for all beings so that they may emerge from the indefinite number of transmigrations and from the vale of suffering; for all beings I will experience all pain in all the worlds, in all the worst destinations, until the end of future periods, and it is for them that I will ceaselessly cultivate the roots of good. For it is best that I should experience alone all suffering and that the beings shall not fall into Hell. In Hell, among the animals, in the Kingdom of Yama, in all difficult places, I shall make a hostage of my body and will ransom all things in the worst destinations" (*Mahāparināmanasūtra*).

In Buddhism, therefore, we find the very essence of the soteriology of messianism including the role of the salvific "body," not only that which the Bodhisattva offers as "hostage" for the salvation of all beings, but also—and above all—the body of the Buddha which, as *Trikāya*, gives itself totally and inwardly to every Buddhist as his "own nature," while outwardly assuming form and substance in sacred images or sculptures as objects for contemplation and veneration of the delivering splendor of the Truth. In exoteric Judaism, the body of man only occasionally appears in anthropomorphic symbolism applied to God; in esoterism it constitutes the object of spiritual contemplation and the realization of "Principial Man" (*Adam Qadmon*) with repercussions on the physical plane, where contemplative man regains, in the very heart of his mortal body, his primordial body, which is Edenic and incorruptible. Indeed, the contemplation and spiritual realization of the "body" of principial or transcendent man and that of its cosmic and heavenly manifestation, *Metatron*—which occurs in a "vision" while descending into the depths of the heart, a descent which is simultaneously an ascent towards the "chariot" (*merkabah*) or "throne" (*kisse*) of the immanent Divinity—this contemplation and vision, supported by penitence and an obedience to the Commandments, and deepened by the mysteries of the Torah, "frees men from the [four corporeal] elements from which they were made [after the original sin]" (see *Zohar, Bereshith*, 27a). It also, and in an inner fashion, gives to them their terrestrial, paradisal, and imperishable body, which serves as a vehicle for the bodies or higher aspects of the universal Adam.

Finally, in Christianity, the soteriological function assumed by the body of the Messiah or Christ, the "Word made flesh," the incarnate and teaching truth—the living and divine archetype of man, which must be contemplated and imitated—is not only that of a hostage for the salvation of all beings but that of the redeeming universal sacrifice; his expiatory death eminently perpetuated by the sacraments of Baptism and the Eucharist allows every man who receives them to participate in this salvific body and to commune with it, even so far as to become it himself spiritually. For, according to the words of the Apostle Paul: "Ye are the body of Christ" (1 Cor. 12:27), and "Christ is all, and in all" (Col. 3:11) so that all Christians can in principle reach "the unity of the faith, and the knowledge of the Son of God, thus becoming a perfect [or spiritually complete] man, with the measure of the stature of the [universal] fullness of Christ" (Eph. 4:13).

Now, like the body of universal man as envisaged by those other traditions of which we have spoken, according to Christian tradition the body of Christ also implies a *triplex modus corporis*.[10] The three aspects of the Body of Christ or *Triforme Corpus Christi*, although they cannot be identified entirely with those of integral man as viewed respectively by Judaism, Taoism, and Buddhism, nevertheless join these in a global sense. In descending order, it is firstly a matter of the *Corpus Mysticum*, the mystical and ecclesiastic body of which Christ is the "head" or principle, at once transcendent and immanent—or divine and human—who unites in himself all the "members" of the Church, each of whom for his own part is called upon to become in spirit the entirety of that body. Next is the *Corpus sacramentale* or *eucharisticum*, that of the Transubstantiation, which through the Communion makes possible for all members this transformation into the totality of the Christly body. The last is the *Corpus natum* of the Son, begotten by the Father and born, through the operation of the Holy Spirit, of the Virgin Mary; this is intrinsically his glorious and incorruptible body which, extrinsically and sacrificially, "assumes" the mortality of the body of fallen man. In other words—inversely—although he might be outwardly the suffering and crucified body, inwardly he is the *Corpus gloriosum* of Christ transfigured on Mount Tabor.

If the crucified Christ is an essential object of Christian contemplation, the "glorified" Christ is another, joining not only the image of the Buddha, but before that, and more directly, the description in Ezekiel quoted above (1:26–27) concerning the "likeness as an appearance of a man, above on high [the divine throne]," a form surrounded

---

[10] See Jean Borella, "Du mystère des plaies du Christ," *Études Traditionnelles*, No. 460 (Paris, 1978).

by "fire" and a "brightness round about," like "the appearance of a bow [rainbow]." In fact, this symbolism occurs again in Revelation (4:2–3), where Christ is moreover surrounded by the Tetramorph, described in Ezekiel (1:5–14), which we shall not discuss here. Occasionally, the circumference of Christ's halo is presented in Christian iconography not in the form of a rainbow but of a mandorla or "almond," which in Judaism symbolizes the "kernel of immortality." For *luz*, the "almond tree," also means, etymologically, the "vital element" or the "quintessence," and in the Jewish tradition designates, furthermore, an indestructible bone in the human vertebral column which will survive until the resurrection of the dead so as to give birth to the glorified body. But in Ezekiel's vision, as in the Apostle John's, celestial man is surrounded by a rainbow whose colors symbolize the divine qualities of his spherical and universal body. In other words, at the center of this macrocosmic body is manifested the microcosmic "likeness of an appearance of a man," that is the celestial and individual prototype of the terrestrial human body—the anthropomorphic image of the "Middle Column," or the central axis around which all worlds revolve. This individual prototype, which detaches itself from the spiritual and universal sphere of "man on high," is not only the symbol of the transmutation and extrinsic particularization of universal man into individual man, but also that of the man who "represents" God and who, as His more perfect image or symbolic form, dominates all forms of existence created through it. Viewed from below, it is also the image of terrestrial man, raised up and transfigured firstly as celestial man, then in his own spherical irradiation or glory which symbolizes or prefigures his transformation or spiritual totalization as universal man. This irradiation or halo surrounding the "likeness of an appearance of a man" and encircled by a rainbow, therefore finally signifies, at one and the same time, the spiritual and universal sphere of macrocosmic man manifesting in his heart microcosmic man considered as the "image of God"—at first celestial, then terrestrial—and inversely the glorified body of terrestrial man raised to heaven and transformed there into the universal body.

To return once more to Buddhism, this transformation is that of the *Nirmānakāya*, the earthly "body of transformation," transfigured as *Sambhogakāya* or celestial "body of beatitude"; now this celestial body, synonymous with "rainbow body," is said to be the highest body obtainable by the *yogī* (a Sanskrit term transposed from Hinduism in order to designate here the Tibetan Buddhist consecrated to *yoga*, the spiritual "union" with absolute Reality) while still in *samsāra* (the circle of existence) and comparable to the glorified body of the *Christós* which the disciples had seen on the Mount of Transfiguration. In this "body of glory" the yogic Master is said to be able to exist for eons, having the power to appear or disappear at will in numerous spheres of existence throughout the entire universe (as Christ showed after his resurrection, and as Jewish tradition attests in the case of the prophet Elijah, who was raised to Heaven, coming back to earth again many times through the centuries in order to reveal the "mysteries of the Torah" to the élite).[11]

## Universal Aspects of Judaism and Hinduism

We cannot conclude this survey of the fundamental and universal aspects of Judaism—so far as they appear not only in other Abrahamic religions but also in non-Semitic traditions—without briefly mentioning Hinduism. We have seen how the Jewish doctrine of *Adam Qadmon* is to be found everywhere, and how, in particular, it appears in Christianity in the aspect of "God made man" or "Word made flesh," sacrificing himself for the redemption of the created, and coming at the end of the world in the form of the Messiah. In Hinduism, according to the *Rig-Veda* (10:90), the supreme principle, *Brahma*, appears as universal man or *Purusha*, who is sacrificed at the beginning, so that by his sacrifice or "sub-division" all worlds and beings were created. We should add, however, that this symbolism likewise joins by direct analogy that of *Adam Qadmon*, whose universal manifestation implies the creation; and so also that of Christ as the "Word," by which, according to John (1:3), "all things were made."

In Hinduism, according to the *Purusha-Sukta* in the *Rig-Veda*, the manifest universe—embracing the three worlds, corporeal, subtle, and spiritual—represents only one "quarter" of *Purusha*, while the other three "quarters" are related to his transcendence, which is symbolically the "fourth" world. The same division of the total-reality into four parts—its sub-division into four "worlds" or "states"—is found in the *Maitri Upanishad* (7:11), where *Purusha* is *Ātmā*, the "Self"—at once transcendent and immanent—of everything that exists, and which is itself identical with *Brahma*, the only Real and All-Real. Here we are involved with the "four states of *Ātmā*. The greatest [or highest] of these is the fourth (*Turīya*). In the other three states *Brahma* lives with one of His *pāda* ["foot" or "quarter"]; He has [the other] three quarters [or feet] in the last [*Turīya*]." This signifies that *Brahma*, *Ātmā*, or *Purusha* comprises, in His transcendence or non-manifestation, the three

---

[11] *Tibetan Yoga and Secret Doctrines.*

worlds of His manifestation; He is their infinite and absolute essence, which is equally true of *Adam Qadmon* who is identical with the highest level of the "four worlds" of the Kabbalah, to wit, the transcendent "world of emanation" (*Olam-ha-Atsilut*), the undifferentiated reality of which is *Ayin*, the "nothingness" or the Absolute, which corresponds to the Hindu definitions of *Turīya*.

But even though, or because, this world nevertheless implies every possibility of manifestation in a state of absolute undifferentiation, these are intellectually projected by the Kabbalists in meditation, starting from the state of differentiated manifestation and ending with the heart of the supreme and undifferentiated world, which thus becomes in their eyes, and at the same time, the world of the transcendent archetypes of all things, united in the archetype of archetypes, the divine "Being" (*Ehyeh*) united with "Non-Being" or "Beyond-Being" (*Ayin*).

Here—*in divinis*[12]—the first emanation of "Being" or of the archetypes which He comprises, also takes place, and this is why this transcendent level of the total-reality is called the "World of Divine Emanation." But the Kabbalists insist on the fact that "everything there is one," that "everything there is God, and God is everything there." They use this same definition for the first spiritual and cosmological manifestation of the transcendent world, which is itself the "descent" of the divine immanence, comprising in potentiality all the archetypes of the created, ready to pass immediately to the act of creation operating within itself.

In this transition to the creative act—thus immediately before the celestial and earthly universe is created—the immanent Divinity, which is itself formless, at first takes spiritual and universal "form" or "body" as *Metatron*, the divine man, cosmic, omniscient, and all-powerful, called among other names YHVH *qatan*, the "little YHVH," that is to say the transcendent and invisible Essence in its immanent aspect, likely to become the object of the spiritual vision of earthly man. This is therefore celestial man in his universal aspect, within which his individual shape is released, the man who, before this individuation, then "around" it, is (to use that famous Hermetic formula) a luminous "sphere whose center is everywhere and whose circumference is nowhere."

---

[12] Editor's note: The term *in divinis* means, literally, "in or among divine things." Thus, the author is here being careful to distinguish that this emanation is occurring in a metaphysical realm that is still within the vast realm of the Divine and not properly in the realm of lower things, or manifestation. This important distinction emphasizes that although this emanation is, of course, a kind of "manifestation," it occurs at the highest level of manifestation, the level at which, because of its proximity to the Divine, any existence or emanation must still be considered to be "among divine things."

This purely spiritual sphere of the divine immanence or omnipresence which the Kabbalah calls *Olam ha-Beriyah*, the "world of [proto-typic] creation," corresponds to the third Hindu world called *Prajñā*, "He who knows" [all in His cognitive unity]. "He is the Lord (*Īshvara*) of all; He is the origin and the end of the universality of beings," says the *Māndūkya Upanishad* (5:6). Then, in the Kabbalah, comes the world of the first differentiated manifestation of the immanent Divinity, at the center of which His Universal "form," *Metatron*, appears as individual celestial Man, surrounded by all celestial creation; it is *Olam ha-Yetzirah*, the subtle "World of Formation" of beings and things, the world of spirits, angels, and souls, which corresponds in the Hindu world to *Taijasa*, the "luminous" world where everything that will be found on earth is "pre-distinguished" or "pre-differentiated" (*pravivikta*).

We have just seen in fact that terrestrial man is prefigured in heaven by the first individual manifestation of Universal Man, at the center of the luminous sphere which is the inner aspect of the celestial and earthly macrocosm. The Hindus symbolize the light of this sphere by gold, reminding us on the one hand of the Latin etymology of *aureola* ("golden color") and on the other hand of the fact that in Hebrew the word *aur* (pronounced *or*) signifies "light." In the Hindu pantheon, the heavenly Lord, *Brahmā* (the creative manifestation of *Brahma*, the Absolute), is Himself compared to the "golden embryo" (*Hiranyagarbha*) which encloses itself in its own luminous sphere like an "egg," *Brahmanda*, the celestial and terrestrial "Egg of the World." This is reminiscent of the verse in Psalms (104:2): "Who coverest thyself with light as with a garment: who stretchest out the heavens like a curtain."

Finally, the terrestrial world is called by the Kabbalah *Olam ha-Asiyah*, the "World of [sensory] Fact" where *Adam Qadmon*, after his manifestation in heaven is "created" and "shaped" as the "first man" (*Adam ha-rishon*) in the earthly paradise. There his primordial and glorious body, made of "ether" (*Avira*, corresponding to the *Ākāsha* of Hindu cosmology), is coextensive with the entire corporeal universe, such that "its light fills the world from one end to the other." This is, in Hinduism, too, the world of the terrestrial manifestation of the "Universal Man," *Vaishvānara*, a world known by his very own name, just as *Olam ha-Asiyah*, which, as Adam's world, is called *Adamah*, the "earth."

Just as *Adam Qadmon* or *Adam ilaah* ("Transcendent Man") is thus immanent in the three manifested worlds and rules them from the "Middle Column," of which he is the personification, so *Purushottama*, the "supreme *Purusha*," is immanent in the three worlds which represent His manifested "quarter" or "foot." Thus, though He is in

Himself their transcendent Essence, He is also the immanent One, universal and indestructible, who dwells in them and penetrates them to the point of being Himself considered—only under an extrinsic aspect which does not in the least affect His undifferentiated reality, immutable and imperishable—as "cut up" or "shared out" amongst all manifest and destructible things. Thus the *Bhagavad Gītā* (15:16–18) speaks of two aspects of *Purusha*,

> the one destructible and the other indestructible; the first [extrinsic] is divided between all beings, the second [intrinsic] is [the] immutable [Immanence of *Purusha*]. But there is [still] another [aspect of] *Purusha*, the highest [*uttama*, transcendent] called [consequently] *Purushottama*, [the supreme *Purusha*] or *Paramātmā* [the "Supreme Self" of all that exists], who, as imperishable Lord, penetrates and supports the three [manifest] worlds. As I pass beyond the destructible [extrinsic aspect] and even the indestructible [Immanence in all things], I am celebrated in the world and in the *Veda* by the name *Purushottama* [the transcendent *Purusha*].

Nevertheless, it is *Purushottama* or *Paramātmā* who by His manifestation or immanence is "incorporated" (*sharīra*) in the three worlds; and by the light of this symbolism, arising from the corporeal, the spiritual world is called *kārana-sharīra*, the "causal and universal body," while the subtle world of individualities is that of the "subtle body," *shūkshma-sharīra*, or *linga-sharīra*, and the terrestrial world that of the "crude body," *sthūla-sharīra*.

Thus, contrary to Judaism, Christianity, and Buddhism, and certain branches of Muslim esoterism, too, which transpose the symbolism of the body to the transcendent Principle, Hinduism reserves it for the three manifested worlds, the fourth (*Turīya*) being in itself "indefinable" (*alakshana*), "beyond thought" (*achintya*), and consequently "beyond description" (*avyapadēsha*). The doctrine of integral man therefore arises here, not under a triple aspect or as a "triple body," but through a quaternary, that of the four worlds, which is also to be found in Judaism as we have seen. The same holds true of esoteric Islam, where the "Perfect Man" or the "Universal Man" (*al-Insān al-kāmil*) is identified with the combination of the four worlds, beginning with *ʿālam al-ʿizzah*, God's transcendent "World of Glory," followed by *ʿālam al-jabarūt*, the divine and immanent "World of Power," then by *ʿālam al-malakūt*, the celestial "World of Royalty," and finally by *ʿālam al-mulk*, *Allāh*'s terrestrial "World of Possession."

But to pass from comparative anthropology and cosmology to Hindu metaphysics, *Ayin*, the "Non-Being" or "Beyond-Being" of Judaism is found there as *Brahma nirguna* or "non-qualified" *Brahma*, while *Ehyeh*, the Being, corresponds to *Brahma saguna*, the "qualified" *Brahma*, who is *Sat*, "Being," or *Sachchidānanda* (*Sat-Chit-Ānanda*), "Being-Consciousness-Bliss." Contrary to the false idea that the Hindu tradition is polytheistic because of its multitude of divinities, these correspond to the multitude of divine aspects and their spiritual and cosmic manifestations to be found in Jewish monotheism, summarized under the name of the Universal Cause, *Elohim*, literally "the gods," a name which designates the unique God-Creator throughout the first chapter of Genesis. On this subject Jewish esoterism has this to say:

> This Name has been transmitted [in its universal reality] to beings of this earth below; it has been given in shares to the leaders and to the angels charged with governing other peoples [while the name YHVH designates the Divine Essence, insofar as it has revealed itself, directly or through *Elohim*, especially to Israel]. . . . All the principalities and powers appointed to the nations of the Gentiles—all are included in this Name [or in the reality of *Elohim*], even the objects of idolatry [through which the idolaters unknowingly adore the only Real, the unique God] (*Zohar*, *Mishpatim*, 96a).

Similarly the *Bhagavad Gītā* (9:23) reveals—without taking into consideration idolaters—the following words of Krishna, personifying Vishnu and through Him the one God: "Those who piously adore other gods, of whom they are faithful followers, [in truth they] adore Myself alone [though] not knowing the appropriate rites." Whoever these Hindu gods might be, and by extension the gods of other religions, they are regarded—as in the passage quoted above from the *Zohar*—as so many aspects of, or approaches to the "One who is without nuances" in Himself, but who "might appear by secret intent under various colors, the effect of His multiple power" (*Shvetāshvatara Upanishad*, 4:1–4).

That the whole "multitude of [Hindu] gods" (*vishvēdēva*) may be reduced in fact to the "One without another" (*ekamevādvitīyam*) results not only from the explicit affirmation that "the worshipful Divinity of resplendent beings is unique" (*mahaddevānam asuratvan ekam*), but in an exhaustive fashion—too long to be quoted here *in extenso*—by the *Brihad-Āranyaka Upanishad* (3:9), which reduces the "three-thousand-three-hundred-and-six gods" of the Hindu pantheon to "That which is called *Brahma*," the Absolute, which transcends all its particular aspects. Similarly, Sri Shankarāchārya, the great spokesman of Hindu spirituality, summarizes this in the following passage from *Viveka-Chūda-Māni* (464): "Alone in *Brahma*, the One without another, the infinite *Brahma*, without beginning or end, transcendent and changeless; in Him there is no trace of duality." Is there any need to emphasize the identity between this and the following statement concerning Judaism: "He is one without another" (*hu ehad we-en sheni*, which corresponds to the Islamic formula quoted at the beginning of this essay, *wahdāhu lā sharīka lahu*)?

In truth, alone is YHVH, alone is *Brahma*. And if we descend from the supreme truth of Judaism and Hinduism—from *yihud*, the "union" which unites all things to YHVH, or the *advaita*, the universal "non-duality" of *Brahma*—to the soteriology of messianism, we find it once more in the descent of the *Avatāra* or divine incarnations, coming successively to bring saving light to humanity. Invoking their very Names is—together with the contemplative incantation of the sacred monosyllable *AUM* (pronounced *OM*), each letter of which symbolizes in ascending manner one of the three manifested worlds and their entirety, the non-manifested fourth—one of Hinduism's ways to salvation and spiritual deliverance. The same is true, in Buddhism and Christianity, of the names of Buddha and Jesus—the latter being sometimes accompanied by the name of Mary—while in Islam the name of *Allāh* is invoked, or one of His "most beautiful Names" (*Asmā' al-husna*). Similarly, in Judaism is invoked one of the Names of the Divine Essence, YHVH, according to the words of the Psalmist (145:18): "YHVH is nigh unto all them that call upon Him, to all them that call upon Him in truth," or those of the prophet Joel, referring particularly to those living through the terrible events of the end of time: "whosoever shall call on the Name of YHVH shall be saved" (2:32).

What is fundamentally true of Judaism is also true of all genuine religions and traditions: there is but one Absolute, one Real, one God, the basis of all the revelations and their formal antinomies, the basis of all apparent dualism. As Ananda Coomaraswamy has expressed it in a simple but limpid phrase: "God is an Essence without duality."[13]

*Translated by Malcolm Barnes*

---

[13] Ananda K. Coomaraswamy, *Hinduism and Buddhism* (New York: Philosophical Library, 1943), p. 10; French edition, *Hindouisme et Bouddhisme* (Paris, 1949).

## CHAPTER 2

# The Meaning of the Temple[1]

In order to obtain a comprehensive understanding of Jewish doctrine concerning the Temple of Jerusalem, it is necessary to refer not only to the descriptions given in the Bible, but also to the oral tradition; this includes both the Talmudic and rabbinical writings, which proceed from the outward to the inward meaning of the revealed word, and the Kabbalah, the purely inward doctrine. It is obviously impossible here to consider all the scriptural texts referring to the Temple, and the numerous commentaries dealing with them; it will be sufficient for our present purpose to touch on only a few essential aspects, and to observe how these proceed from the purely spiritual doctrine and lead to an "inward vision" of the sanctuary.

The Temple in Jerusalem has the same fundamental meaning as the Tabernacle, its movable prototype. It is God's "dwelling" (*mishkan*) or the holy place of His "indwelling" (*Shekhinah*) in the midst of Israel. "And I will dwell among the children of Israel, and will be their God. And they shall know that I am YHVH,[2] their God, that brought them forth out of the land of Egypt, that I may dwell among them: I am YHVH their God" (Exod. 29:45–46). God wished to live in the "sanctuary" (*miqdash*) in order to be known; in it His Presence was to appear, speak, command: "There I will appear to thee, and I will commune with thee from above the mercy seat, from between the two cherubims which are upon the Ark of the Covenant, of all things which I will give thee in commandment unto the children of Israel" (Exod. 25:22). These words were addressed to Moses, and applied not only to the Holy of Holies within the Tabernacle, but also to that of the Temple, which Solomon called an "oracle" (*d'bir*), for it was here that was revealed God's "word" or "command" (*dibrah*) and thus also the "prophetic message" (*dibber*).

Moses erected the Tabernacle for God's "indwelling" (*Shekhinah*) and Solomon erected the Temple for God's "Name" (*shem*). Thus their

---

[1] Editor's note: This article originally appeared in English in *Studies in Comparative Religion*, Vol. 5, No. 4, Autumn, 1971.

[2] In accordance with Jewish custom, the Tetragram is not vocalized. Its pronunciation is no longer known and it has been forbidden to the Jews, for spiritual reasons, for about two thousand years.

two works were essentially one, just as God is truly present in His Name, this being precisely His "indwelling" or "habitation."

The most sacred duty of the high priest consisted in the invocation of the Name of God. He called upon Him, and the *Shekhinah* was revealed. God Himself spoke of the indwelling of His Name in the Temple of Jerusalem: "Since the day that I brought forth My people out of the land of Egypt I chose no city among all the tribes of Israel to build an house in, that My Name might be there; neither chose I any man to be a ruler over My people Israel: But I have chosen Jerusalem, that My Name might be there; and have chosen David to be over My people Israel" (2 Chron. 6:5–6). And Solomon, who handed down these words of God, added: "YHWH said to David my father: Forasmuch as it was in thine heart to build an house for My Name, thou didst well in that it was in thine heart: notwithstanding thou shalt not build the house; but thy son which shall come forth out of thy loins, he shall build the house for My Name" (2 Chron. 6:8–9). That God Himself dwelt therein is evident from, amongst other things, the following passage which refers to the Temple: "I will perform My word with thee, which I spake unto David thy father: and I will dwell among the children of Israel, and will not forsake My people Israel" (1 Kings 6:12–13).

The Tabernacle had provided the Presence of God with no permanent habitation, for it was set up after the model of His heavenly "vehicle" (*merkabah*), in which He would lead His people through the wilderness to the fixed "center of the world," Jerusalem. The oral tradition tells us that in the wilderness the bearers of the Ark of the Covenant were miraculously carried by it as by a vehicle. Not only did they feel no weight, but they soared with it like angels, penetrated by the light of the holy Ark and raised to prophetic vision. . . When God's vehicle came to rest, it was His throne; but the true earthly image of His throne, the fixed habitation of God here below, was not the Tabernacle, but the Temple. For this reason the latter alone is called God's "house" (*beth*) or His "Lower Throne." In themselves His vehicle and His throne are one and the same universal center; but here below it is the Temple alone which "solidifies" the latter. In it is found—according to the Talmud (*Yoma*, 54b)—the "foundation stone" (*eben shetiyah*), around which the earth was created and on which the whole world rests. Thus the Kabbalah (*Zohar*, *Terumah*, 157a) also says that the Holy Land is the center of the world, Jerusalem is the center of the Holy Land, and the Holy of Holies is the center of Jerusalem. Onto this central point all good and all nourishment descended for distribution to the entire world.

The Presence of God itself descended into His earthly dwelling, and in it appeared, spoke, listened, forgave, and blessed, so that Israel and all mankind might be raised up to Him:

> Moreover concerning the stranger, which is not of Thy people Israel, but is come from a far country for the sake of Thy great Name, and Thy mighty hand, and Thine outstretched arm; if he comes and prays in this house: then hear Thou from the heavens, even from Thy dwelling place, and do according to all that the stranger calleth to Thee for; that all the peoples of the earth may know Thy Name, and fear Thee, as doth Thy people Israel, and may know that Thy Name was invoked upon this house which I have built (2 Chron. 6:32–33).

Thus did Solomon pray at the consecration of the Temple. The Chosen People were the intermediary between all peoples and the Lord of the worlds, just as the high priest was the intermediary between Him and His people. All Israel was a "kingdom of priests": its mission consisted in "being holy" in the likeness of Holy God and thereby sanctifying the whole world; in following the Commandments; in inner purification and spiritual realization; and in the total surrendering of the heart. Of these inward operations the sacrifices and prayers of the Temple were but the outward and visible expression. Without inward conversion the offering made in the sanctuary was not accepted by the *Shekhinah*. The oral tradition describes the clear signs of God's hearkening or anger in the Temple. From the center—the Holy of Holies—proceeded not only blessings and the light of grace, but also lightning and punishment.

Israel was "chosen" in order to espouse the indwelling (habitation) of God and thus to unite what is above with what is below, "the *Shekhinah* with the Holy One, may He be blessed." This union of the Presence of God—and, in it, of all existence—with His infinite Majesty constituted the exalted mystery of the "center of the world." This mystery, also called the "union of the Name"—the Name which contains both the hidden essence and the universal manifestation of God—was first performed in the Tabernacle through the mediation of Moses and Aaron, and then through the successors of the high priest in the first and second Temples. After their destruction "the *Shekhinah* accompanied Israel into exile." God destroyed both Temples, just as He had destroyed the first two Tables of the Law by the hand of Moses, because of Israel's sins. He punished His people very harshly, but did not forsake them, and everywhere that they went glorifying His Name, the "scattered sparks of the *Shekhinah*," shone forth brightly and led back those illumined to the original sun. Yet Israel would never again possess a visible center until the messianic rebuilding of the Temple foretold by the prophets.

Although the Temple represented the fixed house of God or the fixed center of the world, it was itself only a "pattern" and not yet the definitive descent of the heavenly throne, sanctuary, or Jerusalem on earth. This "will not be built by human hands, but by God Himself" as the indestructible center of the messianic kingdom. Solomon's prototype—or rather, his anticipated image—of this divine center was as such destructible, yet not completely so, for in it an invisible spiritual "river" was crystallized and flowed forth towards all the directions of space, its vibration continuing until the final achievement of its goal. This is "the river of Yobel flowing from the supreme Eden," the universal messianic redemption.

The spiritual stones, crystallized out of the river Yobel, were never destroyed. They are indestructible, and await their final use. Thus it is said in the Kabbalah (*Zohar, Pekudei*, 240b), that it must not for a moment be imagined that the stones serving as a foundation for Zion and Jerusalem had fallen into the hands of alien peoples. In reality they had all been hidden and preserved by the Holy One, blessed be He, so that no single one is wanting; and when He will again raise up Jerusalem, these foundation stones will return to their original places "set round with sapphires." These are the stones of the Higher Throne, which in the Heavenly Jerusalem reflect the uncreated light streaming out from God. For the "pattern" of the earthly sanctuary is to be found in heaven, and the eternal prototype of the heavenly pattern is in God Himself. "Let them make Me a sanctuary, that I may dwell among them. According to all that I show thee, after the pattern of the Tabernacle, and the pattern of all the instruments thereof, even so shall ye make it" (Exod. 25:8–9).

This pattern or prototype of the earthly sanctuary has, as has been said—following the Kabbalah (*Zohar, Terumah*, 159a)—two overlapping aspects: one heavenly and one divine. God revealed to Moses, in the vision of the heavenly Tabernacle and its objects, the supra-formal, eternal prototypes of His earthly dwelling-place, which are based on the ten *Sefirot*, the synthetic "enumerations" of His infinite qualities. He allowed Moses to be present at the "service" of *Metatron*, the Heavenly Man and Prince of the Angels. *Metatron* is the lord of the heavenly Tabernacle, in which the sacrificial mystery is performed by the

Archangel Michael as "high priest." But beyond that, hidden in God's Reality itself, there is yet another "Tabernacle," whose "high priest" is the "Divine Light."

These three hierarchic aspects of the universal dwelling-place of God have their image here below in the tripartite division of the sanctuary: the "divine" Holy of Holies, the "heavenly" Holy, and the "earthly" outer court. Here the outer court of the Temple symbolizes the "earthly paradise." Here below God dwells in the darkness of the Holy of Holies, for "above" also His absolute essence rests in eternal invisibility, from out of which His shining Being and its indwelling reveal themselves. The light of His indwelling radiates from the Holy of Holies to the Holy, and shines upon the seven-branched candlestick, just as above God descends from His infinity in order to sit in state above the seven heavens as Lord of the worlds, in the radiant crown of the seven all-determining, all-illumining aspects of His countenance. Finally, the outer court, like the whole earth, serves as a permanent point of departure for the return of man to God: it is the "footstool for His feet" before which man must prostrate himself in awe, and before which the altar, on which all bodily things are offered, is set up, as is the water basin in which all souls are purified in order to appear before Him. "Woe unto the soul that does not purify itself: it shall be purified in the 'river of fire' (*nahar dinur*)!"

"Thus saith YHWH, the heaven is My throne, and the earth is My footstool: where is the house that ye build unto Me? and where is the place of My rest?" (Is. 66:1). God dwells in the immeasurable, He is omnipresent and because of this He is to be found in the smallest space, as He Himself has said, according to oral tradition: "If I will, I can dwell in a space of the extent of twenty boards to the North, twenty to the South, and eight to the West. More than that, I can descend and enclose my *Shekhinah* in one square cubit" (*Exodus Rabbah*, 34:1). His infinite Presence rests in the Holy of Holies, His immense heavenly world in the Holy, and the whole inward Reality of the physical universe in the outer court of His earthly dwelling.

Thus here, in the outer court, the earthly is sacrificed on the brazen altar, and the fleshly soul (*nefesh*) is purified in the water of the sacerdotal basin. Only thus purified may the soul enter the Holy, and, once penetrated and filled with the Spirit, it assumes the nature of the spiritual soul (*ruah*). Then is revealed to it the seven-armed candlestick, the sacred Face of God in His seven universal properties, with which the soul is clothed. Now the soul itself shines in the sevenfold light of God, and becomes shewbread[3] for all creatures. Man is completely purified, illumined, spiritualized, and sanctified and transmits the light of life and of salvation thus received to all those who earnestly seek it. One with God's entire creation, man's sanctified soul (*neshamah*) rises like incense from the golden altar of his heart and presses through the most inward curtain of his being to the Holy of Holies within it. Here, over the sacred Ark of its intimacy with God, the soul finds the redeeming cover of the reconciliation of all duality. The two cherubim are united in the Presence of the One, in whom the soul recognizes its eternal life and its own union with Him. Henceforth the soul is called the eternally "living" (*hayah*), the "one and only" (*yehidah*). The faith of Israel is realized: *Ehad*, "One."

The Temple has been destroyed, but not the path of purification, illumination, and union that lay concealed in it. Nor was His Name destroyed, "Who is near to all who call upon Him in truth." The path begins with "conversion"; it is a permanent "conversion," a turning back to God. The entire work of the Spirit has to do with conversion or return, and this is why the masters of Israel teach as follows (*Leviticus Rabbah*, 7:2): "Why is it that when someone is converted, it is accounted of him as if he had been lifted up to Jerusalem, had rebuilt the Temple, erected an altar, and carried out all the sacrifices prescribed by the Law? Because, according to the following passage (Ps. 51:17), 'the sacrifice which most pleases God is an extinguished spirit. . .'."

That which must be extinguished in the human soul is the vain, the false, the ungodly, that which is not really man's own, but which clings to him like a darksome "shell" (*qlipah*). When this is extinguished, the spirit rises once again to its own original being, which is completely filled with God. The whole man arises anew as a temple of God, a source of blessing for the world.

---

[3] Editor's note: "Shewbread" (or "show-bread") refers to the twelve loaves of bread which, by biblical command, were replaced every Sabbath "before the Lord" on a special table beside the incense altar and the lamp-stand (the seven-branched candlestick) in the holy place. This area of the Tabernacle of ancient Israel was permitted only to priests and was separated from the Holy of Holies (which contained the Ark of the Covenant) by a heavy curtain or veil. In Hebrew, the term for the bread means, literally, "bread of the Presence."

# CHAPTER 3

# The Mission of Elias[1]

## Elias' Ascension

And it came to pass, when YHVH would take up Elias into heaven by a whirlwind, that Elias went with Elisha from Gilgal. And Elias said unto Elisha, Tarry here, I pray thee; for YHVH hath sent me to Bethel. And Elisha said unto him, As YHVH liveth, and as thy soul liveth, I will not leave thee. So they went down to Bethel. And the sons of the prophets that were at Bethel came forth to Elisha, and said unto him, Knowest thou that YHVH will take away thy master from thy head today? And he said, Yea, I know it; hold ye your peace. And Elias said unto him. Elisha, tarry here, I pray thee; for YHVH hath sent me to Jericho. And he said, As YHVH liveth, and as thy soul liveth, I will not leave thee. So they came to Jericho. And the sons of the prophets that were at Jericho came to Elisha, and said unto him, Knowest thou that YHVH will take away thy master from thy head today? And he answered, Yea, I know it; hold ye your peace. And Elias said unto him, Tarry, I pray thee, here; for YHVH hath sent me to Jordan. And he said, As YHVH liveth, and as thy soul liveth, I will not leave thee. And they two went on. And fifty men of the sons of the prophets went, and stood to view afar off: and they two stood by Jordan. And Elias took his mantle, and wrapped it together, and smote the waters, and they were divided hither and thither, so that they two went over on dry ground. And it came to

---

[1] Editor's note: This article originally appeared in English in *Studies in Comparative Religion*, Vol. 14, Nos. 3 and 4, Summer-Autumn, 1980. It is a revised version of the essay "The Eliatic Function," which appeared in the 1979 Winter-Spring edition. In that earlier essay, Schaya introduces the essay like this: "In an article headed 'Le "mystère" juif et la "vertu" d'Elie,' Jean Reyor referred briefly to the problem of the survival of Judaism in connection with the spiritual influence of the prophet Elias. A quarter of a century later we ourselves dealt at length with this Jewish 'mystery' in our article 'The Sinaitic Theophany According to the Jewish Tradition.' We propose now to examine the function of Elias (Elijah), not only with reference to Judaism but also in its universal aspect. In order to do this we will begin with the scriptural passage which tells both of Elias' ascension to heaven and of the investiture of his immediate spiritual successor, Elisha."

pass, when they were gone over, that Elias said unto Elisha, Ask what I shall do for thee, before I be taken away from thee. And Elisha said, I pray thee, let a double portion of thy spirit be upon me. And he said, Thou hast asked a hard thing: nevertheless, if thou see me when I am taken from thee, it shall be so unto thee; but if not, it shall not be so. And it came to pass, as they still went on, and talked, that, behold, there appeared a chariot of fire, and horses of fire, and parted them both asunder; and Elias went up by a whirlwind into heaven. And Elisha saw it, and he cried, My father, my father, the chariot of Israel, and the horsemen thereof. And he saw him no more: and he took hold of his own clothes, and rent them in two pieces. He took up also the mantle of Elias that fell from him, and went back, and stood by the bank of Jordan; And he took the mantle of Elias that fell from him, and smote the waters, and said, Where is YHVH God of Elias? and when he also had smitten the waters, they parted hither and thither: and Elisha went over. And when the sons of the prophets which were to view at Jericho saw him, they said, The spirit of Elias doth rest on Elisha. And they came to meet him, and bowed themselves to the ground before him. And they said unto him, Behold now, there be with thy servants fifty strong men; let them go, we pray thee, and seek thy master: lest peradventure the Spirit of YHVH hath taken him up, and cast him upon some mountain, or into some valley. And he said, Ye shall not send. And when they urged him till he was ashamed, he said, Send. They sent therefore fifty men; and they sought three days, but found him not. And when they came again to him, (for he tarried at Jericho,) he said unto them, Did I not say unto you, Go not? (2 Kings 2:1–18).

With these words of Elisha, the Scriptures show that Elias could no longer be found because he had in fact been taken up into Heaven.

### Elias Comes Down Again from Heaven

But according to Judeo-Christian tradition the Prophet Elias (or Elijah)—whose immediate spiritual successor was thus Elisha—was not only raised alive into Heaven but has since come down again many times in secret and continues to reveal himself on earth in mysterious fashion. Thus it is that in Judaism he is invisibly present at the circumcision of every male child eight days after his birth and at every

Passover meal celebrated by families; moreover he manifests himself visibly to certain spiritual persons in order to initiate them into the Mysteries of Scripture. For the majority of Israel his presence signifies the blessing which comes down directly from heaven and, for the elite, more particularly an influence that brings enlightenment. His manifestation is destined, in a world approaching its end, to vivify the study and observance of the Law of Moses and, in particular the spiritual realization of his Mysteries. This is touched upon hermeneutically in the closing passage of Malachi (4:4–6):

> Remember ye the law of Moses, my servant, which I commanded unto him in Horeb for all Israel, with the statutes and judgments. Behold, I will send you Elias the prophet before the coming of the great and dreadful day of YHVH: And he shall turn the heart of the fathers to the children, and the heart of the children to their fathers, lest I come and smite the earth with a curse.

**Moses and Elias**

The scriptural passage quoted above is rich in significance; it indicates the respective missions of Moses and Elias: that of Moses refers above all to the "Law" or "Doctrine" (*Torah*)—the Pentateuch; that of Elias concerns the "Prophet" (*Nebim*)—and, by extension, the "Hagiographies" (*Ketubim*) as well; these revelations as a whole constitute the Old Testament. The Law of Moses embraces the entirety of Israel's exoterism and esoterism; its texts are recalled and elaborated—and augmented with accounts of sacred history after Moses—by the Prophets and Hagiographies (these latter consisting of the Psalms, Proverbs, Job, the Song of Songs, Ruth, Lamentations, Ecclesiastes, Esther, Daniel, Ezra, Nehemiah, and Chronicles). As for Elias the Tishbite, he bequeathed no prophetic writing but he appears, as we have just seen, in the book of Kings—among the prophets he represents the type of the "hidden master" who initiates the elite of Israel into the esoteric and universal wisdom of the Torah. In other words, in the passage from Malachi quoted above, "Moses" signifies the exoteric law of Israel which implies esoterism, whereas "Elias" is the enlivening of exoterism by esoterism explained to the elite and realized by them. Finally, "Elias" means not only esoterism and its influence upon Jewish exoterism but also esoterism in its universality, which links the Mysteries of the Torah to those of all the genuine traditions of East and West.

## Elias, Forerunner of the Messiah

By his universality, Elias goes beyond his significance for Israel alone and joins that unanimous Tradition which, according to a doctrine found in most religions, goes back to the revelation made by God to the first man. This revelation, which is expressed in the Jewish esoteric exegesis of the Bible (Gen. 11:1) as the "one language," or the primordial tradition of mankind, was diversified as a result of the confusion of spirits at Babel; it was made manifold in various parallel "tongues" or traditions, and then in those which succeeded one another down through history and which then frequently came to exist side by side. Each of these traditions served, in its own fashion, simply to renew the first and universal revelation of the One, being destined to come together in that revelation's full and final restoration with the ultimate theophany. This will be none other than the "Messiah of Glory," awaited not only by the faithful of the three Abrahamic religions but also, in one way or another, by those of the majority of living religions. With the Messiah, or "Anointed" of God (*ha-Mashiach* in Hebrew, *al-Masīh* in Arabic, *Christós* in Greek) there will come down from heaven the new, unanimous Tradition of mankind which Elias is destined to prepare as the direct forerunner of the Savior; he himself comes down from heaven to "pave the way" for the Messiah, whereas Moses—or Mosaicism—made more particularly the "announcement" of the Anointed one's coming. This "announcement" and this "preparation" respectively were confirmed, for Christianity, among other things on Mount Tabor where Jesus in his Transfiguration revealed himself in his future glory to three of his disciples:

> And after six days Jesus taketh Peter, James, and John his brother, and bringeth them up into an high mountain apart, and was transfigured before them: and his face did shine as the sun, and his raiment was white as the light. And, behold, there appeared unto them Moses and Elias talking with him. Then answered Peter, and said unto Jesus, Lord, it is good for us to be here: if thou wilt, let us make here three tabernacles; one for thee, and one for Moses, and one for Elias (Matt. 17:1–4).

This Gospel story reinforces the importance attributed by Malachi to Elias, side by side with Moses and with regard to the Messiah. In fact when God, after exhorting Israel to observe the Law of Moses, adds through the mouth of Malachi: "Behold I will send you Elias the prophet before the coming of the great and dreadful day of YHVH," He reveals thereby that Elias must come down again to the earth both to revivify the Path of Moses and to prepare for the coming of the Messiah; for the "day of YHVH" will inaugurate the future Reign of the Messiah; according to the traditional exegesis he will open up the transition of the present cycle of humanity into the Messianic Reign understood in its perpetual fullness—a passing that implies the end of our world, the resurrection of the dead, and the last Judgment. Whereas evil, suffering, and death reign in this world, in the world to come, which will be "a new heaven and a new earth" (see Is. 65:17; Rev. 21:1), "there shall be no more death, neither sorrow, nor crying, neither shall there be any more pain" (Rev. 21:4). In this new world, which will be like a single city of spiritual peace and union—called the "New Jerusalem" (Rev. 21:2)—*every* man will be an incorruptible sanctuary in the image of him who is the New Man *par excellence*, the Messiah, the living and midmost Temple of the One who will be truly present; they "shall see His Face" (Rev. 22:4) and this unanimous beatific vision, that is unity or spiritual peace, will be prepared by Elias the ever-living prophet, according to the common tradition of Israel and Christianity. Judaism even affirms that Elias' preparatory task will include the resurrection of the dead whereas, according to the Christian perspective, it is the Messiah who will not only judge the dead but also bring them to life.

## The Universal Role of Elias

In order to announce to the world the spiritual peace which the Messiah will establish forever when "the first things shall have passed away," Elias will raise his voice so loud, as the end of time draws close, that it will be heard, according to Jewish tradition, from one end of the world to the other. This means that Elias' mission will not be confined to Israel, but will extend to all peoples and thus to all religions. Such is, moreover, the sense of the words of Scripture quoted above: "And he shall turn the heart of the fathers to the children and the heart of the children to their fathers, lest I come and smite the earth with a curse," that is to say, the end will not come without the last men that are open to truth and grace being saved by their respective traditions and prepared for the advent of the Messiah. In fact the relationships between "fathers" and "children" here signify the revealed and salvational traditions, the authentic religions, which open up the door of eternal salvation to believers and to such of them as have a thirst for the absolute, and give access to the ultimate spiritual deliverance of union with the One. The "*heart* of the fathers" is the inward, central, essential aspect of the traditions—their esoteric, spiritual, universe kernel—as well as the teachings, methods, and influences that flow out from them. The "*heart* of the children" is their spiritual receptivity—their inward acceptance and reception of what is given them by their "fathers" or their respective traditions. This acceptance and reception is translated in Hebrew by the term *qabbalah*, which has become synonymous quite specifically with the esoteric tradition of which the prophet Elias is the invisible Master, who comes down by secret into this world, not only towards the end but each time, since his ascension, that tradition needs to be brought alive again from within. But towards the end as we have just seen, this descent of Eliatic instruction and influence will become general; it will become so, in principle, through all the "fathers," all the intrinsically orthodox religions. Elias "will proclaim peace" between them, that is, he will reveal their *essential and transcendent unity* which, on the final advent of the Messiah, and only then, will make itself manifest in a new, *unanimous form* of affirmation of the One. "On that day, YHVH shall be one [the Divine Essence will reveal itself to all mankind as the only real Presence] and His Name [the mode of His affirmation] shall be one [for all the believers in the world]" (Zech. 14:9).

### The Function of Elias Delegated to Others

A particular aspect of the universal function of Elias is the fact that it can be exercised by persons other than himself. His mission, emanating from him by way of his universal influence, can in fact be performed not only by himself but also by delegation, with the concurrence of elite representatives of the various religions; each of them comes to revivify his own religion—whilst, it may be, also stimulating the others—from the "heart," the spiritual essence of the tradition. This essence is to be identified with the transcendent and universal reality of all religions; it shows itself as the unique truth underlying metaphysics, cosmology, and the doctrine of man as these are explained throughout the various religions; it reveals itself as the unity within their multiplicity without however confusing their forms which are, let us insist, destined to be maintained as they stand until the ultimate advent of the Messiah. Thus, Elias signifies not only a particular prophet sent to Israel but a universal function susceptible of being exercised by several persons both within Judaism and within the other traditions whatever names be given them to the unique heavenly source of the "Spirit that bloweth where it listeth." The possibility of his manifold personification emerges, among other things, from the Gospels which identify John the Baptist with him who "crieth in the desert and prepareth the way of the Lord" (Matt. 3:3; Luke 3:4–6; John 1:23). He who is first thus designated by Isaiah (40:3) is—according to Jewish tradition—the forerunner of the Messiah, the prophet Elias. John the Baptist refused to be identified with Elias; however he declared himself to be the one of whom Isaiah spoke and, by this seeming contradiction, he made it precisely clear that, without being Elias in person, he exercised the Eliatic function for his own period and in his own orbit. The Gospel confirms, in fact, that it is he who goes before the Messiah on his first coming; and Jesus, after the beheading of John the Baptist, continues to prophesy the return of Elias, this time for the period preceding the *parousia* (the Second Coming of Christ): "Elias truly shall first come, and restore all things" (Matt. 17:11).

### Elias, *al-Khidr*, and the *Mahdī*
Islamic tradition recognizes, for its part, a spiritual tradition corresponding to that of Elias and affirms that it is exercised notably by two personages each having his own sphere of activity. We are not speaking here of Elias himself, who is mentioned in the Koran by the side of Jesus (6:85) and in the struggle against the worshippers of Baal (37:123–132); it concerns in the first place *al-Khidr* or *al-Khādir*, the "green one" or the "verdant," who bears in the esoteric tradition of Islam the same fundamental characteristics as Elias, at least those that bear upon his function as the "ever-living" spiritual Master who comes down suddenly from a world above the earth in order to manifest himself in secret to him who thirsts for the Absolute. He is above all the Master of the spiritual solitaries, the elite beings to whom he reveals himself as an ocean of initiatic and universal wisdom, an inexhaustible source of enlightenment, a conserver and giver of eternal "water of life." As for the other personage who reflects Elias in Islam, he it is who will come at the end to establish once and for all what the Judeo-Christian tradition calls the "Reign of the Glorified Messiah": this is *al-Mahdī*, the "guided by God." He resembles Elias not insofar as he "prepares" the advent of the Messiah, but in so far as he "accompanies" him in his eschatological task. In fact, according to Muslim tradition, the *Mahdī* will reveal and realize in detail everything that Jesus "the Messiah, Son of Mary" will cause to come down from heaven; it names this revelation and realization the "Book of Divination and of the Sum of all Things" (*Kitābu'l-Jafrī wa'l-Jāmi'ah*). According to the esoteric exegesis of the Koran attributed to al-Qāshānī, this "Book will be read [its contents will be manifested] as it is in reality [and not by a simple verbal exposition], by him [the *Mahdī*] alone." This Book "embraces that which has been [from all eternity, that is, the "Eternal Decree" or

the eternal archetypes of things] and that which shall be [manifested from this "Decree," that is, the "assigned Destiny" of things]—the Book that was pledged—as surely coming [and whose manifestation will, on the one hand, reveal the Archetypes or Metaphysics and, on the other unroll the eschatological or Messianic events]—This is in accord with the saying of Jesus—on whom be Peace: 'We bring you the Descent (*at-Tanzīl*) of the Word, but its Interpreting (*at-Ta'wīl*) [the "real" Interpretation or the earthly realization of this Descent] is the *Mahdī* who, at the end of time, shall come with it.'"

## The Book of Elias

Here, then, we find again the role of Elias insomuch as he "must come to re-establish all things" when the present world passes over to the future world. According to the Judaic perspective, he will re-establish all things, spiritually to begin with and, in the first place, within Israel. He will begin by explaining to the children of Israel everything in the Law of Moses that has become unclear to them because of their transgressing that Law, with the result that their Temples were destroyed and they have been dispersed and persecuted throughout the world. Even their traditional exegesis of the Law has been impregnated by this lack of clarity, this uncertainty of spirit, as emerges notably from the Babylonian Talmud where many interpretations of the Scriptures are found to be without any conclusion and to end with the enigmatic word *Teiqu*, written *TeIQuV*. This word is composed from the initial letters of four words forming the sentence: *Tishbi Ietarets Qushioth Veyabaoth*, meaning "The Tishbite (Elias) will resolve the difficulties and problems"; that is to say, all traditional and spiritual problems that remain pending for lack of valid explanation will receive an answer through Elias when he comes to prepare the advent of the Messiah.

Elias will resolve not only the problems arising from these incomplete passages in the Talmudic exegesis, but will cause Israel to know the perfect and definitive interpretation of the Divine Word revealed by the Torah of Moses; moreover, he will set the ultimate revelation of the Torah's content into such an unfolding that all the world shall "see" and "live" the eschatological prophecies of Scripture. This revelation of Eternal Truth and this actualization of the Messianic prophecies constitute the contents of the "Book of Justice" (*Sefer ha-Yashar*) which Elias must bring with him and which corresponds to the Book of the *Mahdī*. According to Jewish tradition, the entire Torah of Moses amounts to no more than a single line of the *Sefer ha-Yashar*, which means that this Book, by virtue of its being not "scriptural" but "operative" in nature, will be the veritable final accomplishment of Scripture, the "realization" which by definition goes immeasurably beyond the "letter." At the same time, Judaism tacitly places the remaining "lines" of this "Book" at the disposal of all the Divine revelations, whatever they may be, each one formulating or announcing in its fashion the same Eternal Truth and the same Destiny of man and the world. The "Book" of Elias is the integral Wisdom of the unanimous Tradition and the eschatological Manifestation of the one and only Principle. For the Jews, Elias represents the transition from their traditional exclusiveness to the universality which they too possess, since they affirm that the Tishbite will raise his voice so loud to announce spiritual peace that it will be heard from one end of the earth to the other; and the Doctors of the Law teach that "the righteous of all nations have a portion in the life to come" or, again, that "all men who are not idolaters can be considered Israelites."

### Elias, Builder of the New Jerusalem

This said, the "Book of Elias," in comparison with which the "Torah of Moses" amounts to no more than a single line, is itself no more than a foretoken of the "Torah of the Messiah," the spiritual reality of which is that of the "New Alliance" in the full sense of the term, namely the future state of perpetual union between mankind and God. Elias must re-establish all things in the name of, and for the sake of, that spiritual "peace" which the Messiah will bring once and for all: it will be crystallized forever in the New Jerusalem "founded by—or for—peace," according to the etymology of *Yerushalem* or *Yerushalaim*. Elias came down, and has come down for centuries, to the world below to prepare, with the concurrence of those he inspires, this final state of humanity. He reveals, little by little and more intensively and generally towards the end, the spiritual and universal essence, the transcendent unity of all the authentic religions. It is as if the radiant city were being patiently built by putting one luminous stone after another into place. The motivating power of this task can be called the "Eliatic flow," at least in the orbit of Judeo-Christian Tradition, whereas other traditions will each use their own terms to describe this same universal flow. According to the terminology of Jewish esoterism, this flow belongs to the "river of highest Eden," the "river of Yobel" or "great Jubilee," which is final Deliverance. Revelations calls it the "river of water of life, clear as crystal" (Rev. 22:1); it will be crystallized in "precious stones," the unquenchable lights of the New Jerusalem. The new City of God and men will be in fact like a single immense crystal, whose myriad faces will blaze—as

Revelation says (21:18–21)—like jasper, sapphire, chalcedony, emerald, sardonyx, sardius, chrysolite, beryl, topaz, chrysoprasus, jacinth, amethyst, and pearl. Bathed in the light of "pure gold," all these "stones" will be so many aspects of the single "foundation Stone" of the World, the single Divine Presence revealing itself to all future humanity.

### The Eliatic Flow in Our Own Age

Faced with this eschatological doctrine, in which Elias and the spiritual flow that bears his name play a leading role, one may ask how much this has to do with humanity in our own day. The traditions declare that we are now in the last age. But it would go far beyond the framework of this present article to go into the details of traditional criteriology concerning the cycles of mankind. In any case we do not intend to concern ourselves with the duration of this last age; it suffices for us to look at things as they present themselves unambiguously to us today. We can perceive, among other things, that mankind is facing its own total destruction by monstrous material means that it has forged for itself with the concurrence of its vaunted scientific progress: it has virtually brought the world close to its end. Even if, according to the traditions, it is not man but God who will bring our world to its close, this destruction will be, according to the Scriptures, His response to the very Promethianism or "Satanism" that has led mankind to its present situation and which will not cease to add further to its provocations against Heaven.

The present situation shows to anyone who can see, that the "hard shell" created by materialism, and which is tending to imprison our world more and more to the point of stifling all life, is beginning to "crack." It is as if fissures were opening up in the earth's foundation, through which infra-human and chaotic influences were seeping out. These malefic influences seem to be spreading not only as bestial forces overturning everything that modern civilization thought it had set up once and for all to replace ancient traditional cultures, but also as pseudo-traditional or pseudo-spiritual currents misleading a younger generation that is starved of the real nature of things—the True and the Real. Fortunately, any world that continues to exist implies a certain balance by definition, no matter how precarious; when the terrestrial globe—to take up the thread of our symbolism—begins to crack, it brings about, according to traditional teachings, not only fissures "below" but "above" as well. From the upper fissures which represent so many apertures of the Good and of Grace opposing the evil surging up from the depths, there streams down a spiritual light that is able to illuminate the "hearts of the children" of Adam and lead them to the "hearts of the fathers," the spirituality of the traditions.

This spirituality appears, despite the contrary currents launched by the "Adversary," to be making headway; one notes at the outward level, among other things, the growing interest in comparative religion, in the metaphysics of East and West and the various authentic paths leading man to the absolute. But it is important, as far as contemporary literature on this unanimous spirituality is concerned, to distinguish very carefully between what really expresses the truth revealed by the traditions—such as the works of Frithjof Schuon—and what is only a very inadequate, or even completely false, approach to it. The true "Eliatic flow" will grow stronger, according to the Scriptures, as the world's darkness grows deeper, until the final moment. Then

> . . . your sons and your daughters shall prophesy, your old men shall dream dreams, your young men shall see visions. And also upon the servants and upon the handmaids in those days will I pour out My spirit. And I will shew wonders in the heavens and in the earth, blood and fire and pillars of smoke. The sun shall be turned into darkness and the moon into blood before the great and terrible day of YHVH come. And it shall come to pass that whosoever shall call on the name of YHVH shall be saved (Joel 2:28–32).

# CHAPTER 4

# The Sinaitic Theophany According to the Jewish Tradition[1]

## The Theophany

In the third month, when the children of Israel were gone forth out of the land of Egypt, the same day came they into the wilderness of Sinai. For they were departed for Rephidim, and were come to the desert of Sinai, and had pitched in the wilderness; and there Israel camped before the mount. And Moses went up to God, and YHVH[2] called unto him out of the mountain, saying: "Thus shalt thou say to the house of Jacob, and tell the children of Israel; Ye have seen what I did unto the Egyptians, and how I bare you on eagles' wings, and brought you unto Myself. Now therefore, if ye will obey My voice indeed, and keep My Covenant, then ye shall be a peculiar treasure unto Me above all people, for all the earth is Mine; and ye shall be unto Me a kingdom of priests, and a holy nation. These are the words which thou shalt speak unto the children of Israel." And Moses came and called for the elders of the people, and laid before their faces all these which YHVH commanded him. And all the people answered together, and said "All that YHVH hath spoken we will do." And Moses returned the words of the people unto YHVH. And YHVH said to Moses: "Lo, I come unto thee in a thick cloud, that the people may hear when I speak with thee, and believe thee forever." And Moses told the words of the people unto YHVH. And YHVH

---

[1] Editor's note: This article originally appeared in English in *Studies in Comparative Religion* in two parts: Vol. 16, Nos. 3 and 4, Summer-Autumn, 1984, and in Vol. 17, Nos. 1 and 2, Winter-Spring, 1985.

[2] The Tetragram YHVH is often transcribed in the vocalized forms *YeHoVaH* or *YaHVeh*, implying variants each of which has a particular spiritual meaning. But for more than two thousand years the pronouncing of this Name has been forbidden to the Jews, except for an elite of initiates who, through all time, represent the (uninterrupted) "chain" of the (esoteric) Tradition (*shelsheleth ha-qabbalah*), and who are the only ones to know how the Tetragram is pronounced according to the sacred rules of the incantatory science which has been orally transmitted from the time of Moses up to the present.

said unto Moses: "Go unto the people, and sanctify them to-day and tomorrow, and let them wash their clothes. And be ready against the third day, for the third day YHVH will come down in the sight of all the people upon Mount Sinai" (Exod. 19:1–11).

YHVH Himself would come down upon Mount Sinai, and He "rejoiced more than any other day since the creation of the world,"[3] for "on that day, the words: 'The Lord doth reign, and cloth'd is He with majesty most bright; His works do show him cloth'd to be, and girt about with might' (Ps. 93:1) were explained."[4] He wished to reveal Himself through His Ten Supreme Aspects, the ten *Sefirot* or "Enumerations" which synthesize His Infinite Attributes, investing them with the "ten Words" or "Commandments" which "contain the essence of all the Commandments, the essence of all the mysteries of heaven and earth, the essence of the ten Words of the creation [which can be found in the first chapter of Genesis]."[5] It was as if God were recreating the world spiritually by revealing the purpose of its existence, the One and Universal Being, the aspects of which are the archetypes of all things; archetypes which are crystallized in the Torah; it is as if creation had no proper foundation before Israel received the Torah and as if only on that day "was the world duly and completely established, heaven and earth received their proper foundation, and the Holy One was known everywhere and exalted above everything."[6]

In the beginning, His ten Words of creation were at first impressed into pure and universal substance, the "primordial Ether" (*Avir Qadmon*) and then into the subtle substance of heaven and the solidified matter of earth, from which all that was created was brought forth. On Mount Sinai, His ten revealing Words "were [at first] engraved in the [first] stone Tablets [which were still completely transparent, as they issued directly from the "primordial Ether," the substance of the "tree of Life"] and all that was hidden became visible to the eyes and perceived by the minds of all Israel: everything became clear to them. At that moment, all the mysteries of the Torah and all the hidden things of heaven

---

[3] *Zohar*, 2:94a.

[4] Ibid.

[5] Ibid. The first of the creating Words is the first of Genesis: *Bereshith* ("In the beginning"); the nine others are the words that are repeated nine times in Gen. 1:3–29: "and God said. . . ."

[6] Ibid.

and earth were opened up to them and revealed, for they lived face to face with the Splendor of the Glory of their Lord. Never before, since the Holy One created the world, had such a revelation of Divine Glory taken place. Even the crossing of the Red Sea was not comparable. On that day the Israelites were discharged and purified from all earthly imperfections, and their bodies became as bright-shining as the radiant garments which clothe the angels [formless spirits] on high in order that they may carry out the mission entrusted to them by their [Divine] Master. In these raiments [which, being subtle, clothe the angels and which correspond here on earth to bodies that clothe souls] they entered the [heavenly or earthly] fire without fear, as is written of the angel who appeared to Manoah (Judg. 13:20): 'When the flame went up toward heaven from off the altar, the angel of the Lord ascended in the flame of the altar.' Thus, as we said, when the Israelites were freed from all carnal impurity, their bodies became luminous like stars and their souls became resplendent like heaven: they were made fit to receive the [Supreme] Light. In that state [of primordial and angelic purity] the Israelites saw the Glory of their Lord...,"[7] "... and amongst them, there were no more blind, or crippled, or deaf: all the people saw [see Exod. 20:18]; all the people stood [see Exod. 19:17]; all the people heard [see Exod. 24:7: "... all that the Lord hath said will we do, and be obedient"]."[8] Israel had regained the primordial and paradisical state, when

> It came to pass on the third day in the morning, that there were thunders and lightnings, and a thick cloud upon the mount, and the voice of the trumpet exceeding loud; so that all the people that were in the camp trembled. And Moses brought forth the people out of the camp to meet with God; and they stood at the nether part of the mount. And Mount Sinai was altogether on a smoke, because YHVH descended upon it in fire; and the smoke thereof ascended as the smoke of a furnace, and the whole mount quaked greatly. And when the voice of the trumpet sounded long and waxed louder and louder, Moses spake, and God answered him by a voice. And YHVH came down upon Mount Sinai, and YHVH called Moses up to the top of the mount; and Moses went up (Exod. 19:16–20).

[7] Ibid.

[8] *Zohar*, 2:82b.

And "Moses received the Torah from the top of Mount Sinai" (*Mosheh qibbel Torah mi-Sinai*) says the Talmud in the "Sentences of the Fathers" (*Pirkei Avot*, 1:1); this lapidary phrase summarizes the most important idea in Judaism: the direct reception of the revelation of the One, destined for Israel and, in certain measure, for the entire spiritual posterity of Abraham. The word *qibbel*, "he received"—as in the term *qabbalah*—is derived from *qabbel*, which means "to receive," but also "to welcome" and "to accept," and implies also the idea of being "face to face with" or "in the presence of" (*haqbel, qabbal*); here, it indicates direct reception of divine revelation by the man who is ready to accept it, to welcome it, standing before the Revelation's very source, in His very Presence, which brings enlightenment and redemption. This perfect human receptacle appears above all in Judaism in the person of Moses, whom the Talmud, in the above-mentioned passage, connects forever with the Kabbalah, the direct "reception" of divine revelation. This revelation, though taking place at a certain moment in history and leaving its traces "drawn by the finger of God" on the Tablets of Testimony and later in the Book of the Torah, surpasses time and space, the Commandments, the teachings and narratives of the Bible, letters, language, and human reason; it grants man direct knowledge of Him who reveals Himself. This immediate and unifying knowledge exists in the eternal present; it is the permanent and universal knowledge of the only True and the only Real, of which Moses was a perfect receptacle, not in order to possess it for himself alone, but in order to make it accessible to the whole of Israel.

"All the Israelites saw the Glory [or the real Presence] of their Lord face to face on Mount Sinai," says the *Sefer ha-Bahir*;[9] and it specifies that "the souls of all the past, present, and future generations of Israel—whether incarnate or not—were present there . . . as is written [concerning the renewal of the Covenant in Moab, after forty years in the desert, at the end of Moses' mission, which the Kabbalah associates with what took place earlier on Mount Sinai]: 'Neither with you only do I make this covenant and this oath; but with him that standeth here with us this day before YHVH our God, and also with him that is not here with us today' (Deut. 29:14–15). And each [of the souls of Israel] saw [the Divine Presence on Mount Sinai] and received the Words [the Torah] according to his degree [of spiritual receptiveness]."[10] Thus, the Israelite generations of Sinai were united with those of the past and the

---

[9] The "Book of Light," part of the *Sefer ha-Zohar* (Book of Splendor), 2:82b.

[10] *Zohar*, 2:83b.

future, by a spiritual uplifting which—as we have said—transcended time, space and all that is corporeal, so that the "entire people," with Moses as guide, were united in a heavenly union with the One. "When the Holy One, blessed be He, revealed Himself and began to speak, all beings everywhere were moved with great fear and the souls of the Israelites left their bodies . . . and ascended to the Throne of the [divine] Glory, there to remain forever. Then the Torah addressed the Holy One, blessed be He, and said: 'Is it for naught that Thou didst create me two thousand years before the world? Is it for naught that I contain words such as: "Each of the children of Israel. . ." [etc., meaning that the Torah contains laws which concern only Israel]? Where, then, are the children of Israel?' Immediately [after this plea by the Torah] the bodies of the children of Israel received back their souls, which had fled to the Divine Splendor, for the Torah [itself] brought each soul back to its place; it took each soul and gave it back to the body to which it belonged and which was its proper dwelling. This is what is meant by the words (Ps. 19:8): 'The statutes of the Lord are right, and do rejoice the heart [or make the soul return] (*meshiboth*).'"[11]

It was through the Torah that the souls of the Sinaitic generations returned to earth and the souls of past and future generations accompanied them as far as the "Heavenly Land" where they remained to attend the revelation of the Decalogue. This "Heavenly Land" was none other than the true Presence of God Himself, His *Shekhinah*, which "stood over Mount Sinai."[12] Then the words that came from the mouth of God, His "[luminous] voices, took shape and form in the threefold darkness [which reigned at that moment according to the Scripture, where three different terms are used to describe it: "gloom," "clouds," and "darkness," symbols of threefold substance: the "primordial Ether" and the heavenly and earthly substances which are derived from it and which veil the Divine Being who is truly present; His sounding lights or "voices," in order to become "words," detached themselves from the "inner darkness" or "primordial Ether"], so that they became visible,"[13] as is written: "and all the people saw the thunderings, and the lightnings, and the noise of the trumpet, and the mountain smoking" (Exod. 20:18). But at what exact moment in the scriptural account did the souls of the children of Israel leave their bodies to be united with God, and at what moment did they descend to earth to receive

---

[11] *Zohar*, 2:82b, 84–85b.

[12] *Zohar*, 2:81a.

[13] Ibid.

all the words of the Decalogue? In fact, this revelation consisted of two phases, the first summarizing "all the words" into one word, the second expanding them beyond that initial summarizing word. The first word of the Decalogue, which summarizes all the others, is *Anokhi*, as it is written in the text which can be read as follows: "And God spake all these words, saying: I (*Anokhi*). . ." (Exod. 20:1–2). It was this first word introducing the Ten Commandments—the Divine Name that had already been revealed to Moses at the burning bush—which, when the Israelites "heard and saw it at the same time" in a vision of its Divine Contents, called forth the separation of their souls from their bodies and their re-absorption into *Anokhi* Himself, into the "I" or "Self" that is Supreme and alone Real. At that moment, Israel penetrated the Mystery of supreme Wisdom; for "*Anokhi* embraces all the sacred names, and all the commandments of the Torah . . . . *Anokhi* is the Mystery of everything, the Synthesis of all the [sacred] letters [which, in their turn, symbolically synthesize the infinity of the Eternal Archetypes] and [out of the Synthesis] all the mysteries in heaven and on earth. It is *Anokhi* which contains the mystery of the reward of the Just, . . . *Anokhi* which contains the hidden, most recondite Mystery of all [the Supreme Identity of the human essence—the essence of all beings, all things, all the words of Scripture—and the Divine Essence]. . . ."[14]

When the souls of Israel left their bodies, they resumed their heavenly and spiritual existence in order to be reunited with the formless and ontological "Body" of Him who revealed Himself: *Anokhi*. Each "part" or "limb" of His "Body" is one of His fundamental Aspects: but in reality, His "Body" is infinite, without parts, and His aspects are indivisible, eternally fused without confusion of their respective roles. These are eternal archetypes of His words and commandments, as well as their receptacles, which are human souls. "When [the word] *Anokhi* [and, thereby the Divine Self] was uttered, it comprised all the commandments of the Torah, which [long before] had been united in the 'Body' of the sacred and supreme King. Indeed, all the commandments are united in the one 'Body' of the King, some in His 'Head,' others in His 'Trunk,' others in His 'Arms' or His 'Feet,' and none of them ever actually leave the 'Body' of the King to be separated from it or lose touch with it. That is why one who disobeys even one of the commandments of the Torah, sins against the 'Body' of the King Himself [and, thus, against His real divine essence]."[15]

---

[14] *Zohar*, 2:90b, 91a (*Sithré Torah*).

[15] *Zohar*, 2:85b.

The "Body of the King" is none other than the eternal human archetype, "transcendent Man" (*Adam ilaah*) or "principial Man" (*Adam Qadmon*) through whom the One reveals Himself to humanity and each principal member or organ of whom is a fundamental divine aspect, a *Sefirah*, a "Numeration" or ontological Determination of God. Let us recall that there are ten *Sefirot*; the three highest, namely, *Keter*, *Hokhmah*, *Binah* (Crown, Wisdom, Intelligence) symbolically form the "threefold Head" of the "King"; the following two, *Hesed* and *Din* (Grace and Judgment), are His "Right Arm" and His "Left Arm"; *Tif'eret* (Beauty) His "Trunk" or His "Heart"; *Netsah* and *Hod* (Victory and Majesty) form His "Right Thigh" and His "Left Thigh"; *Yesod* (Foundation), His "Reproductive Organ"; and *Malkhut* (Kingdom), His "Feet" or His "feminine Aspect," His *Shekhinah*, His Immanence or His real Presence. This divine "Body" with its ten aspects was revealed on Mount Sinai, as the archetype of the human being, who contains them in a latent state and is called upon to realize them. But apart from that, each human being has a particular archetype, which is a "unique" mode of one *Sefirah* which reflects, however, all the other *Sefirot*, so that all the divine aspects are assembled in one particular way in each human soul. And this applies to each living being and each existent thing, to each divine word and each commandment; in reality, all of these are the inseparable members of the one Divine "Body"; in fact, all of them have only one common Essence: *Anokhi*.

The revelation of *Anokhi* was the revelation of the one and only Essence of all things, the divine Unity in all that is. That is why every soul present had to be united with the One, without wishing, or being able, to be separate from Him. And that is why it was necessary that God should pronounce a second word in order that Israel should descend again to the earth and receive His revelation "from outside" and "from below." But God Himself needed to "descend" with His Torah and with Israel, since otherwise neither His words, nor the souls destined to receive them, would have been able to descend and be separated outwardly from Him. This is clearly confirmed by Scripture: "And the Lord came down upon Mount Sinai. . ." (Exod. 29:20). "He came down from one level to another, from one crown [or second cause] to another, until He was attached to that [heavenly] earth [which hung over Mount Sinai and which was His very *Shekhinah*]."[16] This is the mystery of the second Sinaitic word: YHVH (which comes after *Anokhi*: "*Anokhi* YHVH, I am YHVH. . ."), this word, this Divine

---

[16] *Zohar*, 2:86a.

Name, being the supreme means of grace for the terrestrial union of Israel with God, having been already revealed to Moses at the burning bush (see Exod. 3:15). Indeed, as *Anokhi* is the Name of the Divine Essence which "raises" all that is up to itself, and which integrates everything with the supreme and universal Self, YHVH is the Name of the Essence which reveals all that is, by "lowering" Itself into all existence, thus enabling the human being to find It and to realize It in his innermost being, here on earth: "YHVH descended from one level to another...."

Each of the four letters of His Name summarizes a fundamental world of His Infinite Reality, and each of those hierarchically superimposed worlds comprises, in its turn, innumerable degrees of reality. The first letter, *Y*, which has the numerical value of ten, represents the ontological world of the ten *Sefirot, Olam ha-Atsilut*, the "World of divine and transcendent Emanation"; the second letter, *H*, designates the Immanence of the ten *Sefirot* in *Olam ha-Beriyah*, the purely spiritual and prototypical "World of Creation," which is situated between divine Transcendence and the actual creation; the third letter, *V*, designates the divine Immanence in *Olam ha-Yetzirah*, the celestial "World of Formation" (of which hell is the shadow); and the fourth letter, *H*, symbolizes the Presence of God in *Olam ha-Asiyah*, the earthly "World of Fact." Thus, the four letters of the name YHVH represent the descent of YHVH Himself, from the supreme level of His Reality to the level of His Immanence here on earth. At the same time, they indicate the archetype of that descent within the supreme World, which means that they summarize the ontological degrees of the ten *Sefirot* themselves: *Y* (Hebrew letter *Yod*: י) summarizes *Keter-Hokhmah*; *H* (Hebrew letter *He*: ה) summarizes *Binah*; *V* (Hebrew letter *Vav*: ו) has the numerical value of six and represents the six following *Sefirot: Hesed-Din-Tif'eret-Netsah-Hod-Yesod*, and the last *H* (Hebrew letter *He*: ה) designates the last *Sefirah, Malkuth*. The revelation *in divinis*, or the purely ontological descent of these four "letters," letters which summarize the ten sefirotical degrees that are the archetypes of the Ten Commandments, is also the descent of "transcendent Man": he descends from the Absolute or from "Non-Being," *Ayin*, and is identified with Divine "Being," *Ehyeh*. This becomes clear when we write the four letters of the name YHVH (יהוה) vertically. This is the image of the "descent of YHVH," of the ten *Sefirot* which are His aspects, and also of "Man above"; it is the descent of the common Archetype of the four worlds, of man, and of the Ten Commandments which summarize the Law in its entirety.

At the moment when God pronounced His Name YHVH, the souls of the Israelites—which were united with Him—returned to earth with Him and His Torah in order to "hear and see" all His words and to fulfill them on earth. It is in this descent from the supreme state of "holy union"—a state in which the One reveals Himself to Himself and to all that is in Him, and in which "the Holy One, blessed be He, manifests Himself in all His Glory"—that His Revelation branched out into: the "One who revealed Himself"; the people who "received" and "accepted" His Revelation; and the manifold revelatory degrees and symbols, thus all the words and illuminations of the Torah and "all the mysteries contained in Scripture and entered into by Israel." But before going through the manifold aspects of the One in their varied "colors" or "qualities," Israel, emerging from the One, saw only the One, His real Presence alone, His unique Glory in all the worlds that He held together, from above to below. The great Kabbalistic Master Moses de Leon describes this in the *Sefer ha-Rimmon*:

> Every single thing is linked to another, down to the last link in the chain, and the veritable Essence of God is both above and below, in both heaven and earth, and nothing exists outside Him. That is what the wise mean when they say: "When God gave the Torah to the Israelites, He opened the seven heavens for them, and they saw that there was nothing there but His Glory [or Presence]; He opened the seven worlds ["or earths"] for them and they saw that there was nothing there but His Glory; He opened the seven abysses [or "hells"] for them and they saw that there was nothing there but His Glory." Meditate upon these things and you will understand that the Essence of God is tied to these worlds and that all forms of existence are tied to one another, but that they are all received from the Existence and Essence of God.

## The Ten Commandments

Just as in the beginning, the One came down Himself with all things proceeding out of Him, so that He would exist through all levels of creation. He then "came down upon Mount Sinai. . . . He descended from one level to another. . . ." He descended with Israel in His Name YHVH, which comprises His whole Revelation and the Revelation of all things; in His Revelation, His Torah, lies His All-Reality: "The Torah is the Name of the Holy One, Blessed be He," and "God and His

Name are one."[17] God took the form of His Name and, from the beginning, His Name took the form of all the world, beings, revelations, the words of the Torah and all the souls that were destined to receive and fulfill those words; He took the form of all Israel, which is the "portion of the Lord himself" (Deut. 32:9): the "sacred Community of Israel," his *corpus mysticum*, is one with the *Shekhinah* on earth, which is the "last *H*" of YHVH.

Thus, when they heard the second divine word, "YHVH," the children of Israel saw not only the One in all the worlds, but also the One shining in all His revelatory clarity in their own hearts; that is why the One could say to Israel: "For this commandment which I command thee this day, it is not hidden from thee, neither is it far off. It is not in heaven, that thou shouldest say, 'Who shall go up for us to heaven, and bring it unto us, that we may hear it, and do it?' Neither is it beyond the sea, that thou shouldest say, 'Who shall go over the sea and bring it to us, that we may hear it, and do it?' But the word is very nigh unto thee, in thy mouth, and in thy heart, that thou mayest do it" (Deut. 30:11–14). Israel, the "portion of YHVH," is the same essence as He, which is the same essence as His Word, His Name, His Revelation; by fulfilling His Words, and by realizing them to their very essence, the children of Israel fulfill their destiny and realize their own divine essence. When they "apply His Truth perfectly, they bring about holy union" here below, and through that they regain "the eternal union above" with the One, who is absolute and who revealed Himself to them as their own supreme "I," *Anokhi*, their own Divine Reality, YHVH, whom they must serve and adore as "their God," according to the third of His first three Sinaitic words: "I am (*Anokhi*) YHVH, your God (*Elohekha*). . . ."

The Lord no longer says, as He said to Moses at the burning bush: "I am the God of your father, the God of Abraham, the God of Isaac, and the God of Jacob," but "I am YHVH, *your God*. . . ," whom you know now as your own Essence (*Anokhi*) and of whom you are an integral part (YHVH) whilst at the same time you are face to face with Him in order to serve Him as your God (*Elohekha*). Indeed, *Anokhi* designates the transcendent identity of Israel with the Absolute and YHVH designates Israel's transcendent immanent identity with Him, while *Elohekha* ("your God" or *Elohenu*, "our God") is God face-to-face with Israel, who are a people who must accomplish His Will in order to experience union with Him again and again in order to realize

---

[17] *Zohar*, 2:90b.

His Kingdom on earth. His Will is thus crystallized in the Decalogue (Exod. 20:2–17): "I am YHVH thy God, which have brought thee out of the land of Egypt, out of the house of bondage...." "I am" (*Anokhi*, literally "I") designates the Supreme *Sefirah*, *Keter*, the "Crown," Being itself and Beyond-Being, the Absolute—for in the letters of *Anokhi* is concealed *Ayin*, "Non-Being" or "Beyond-Being," and *K*, the first letter of *Keter*. YHVH also means *Keter*, but in the sense that He reveals Himself by degrees, from his first Emanation, *Hokhmah*, "Wisdom," from which all the other sefirotic Emanations stream forth, to the last, *Malkhut*, the "Kingdom," or Divine Immanence. "Your God" (*Elohekha*) is *Malkhut* itself, the *Shekhinah*, the Immanence of all the *Sefirot* which have come down to the here-below, the Divinity which is truly present in Israel, His *corpus mysticum*, the "Mother below" who concerns herself with the children of Israel on earth. "She who brought you forth" designates the "Mother above," *Binah*, the divine "Intelligence," which originates from *Hokhmah*, the supreme "Wisdom," in the form of *Yobel* or eternal Deliverance: She delivers all Her children "from the land of Egypt," that is from created existence, to lead them back "out of the house of bondage" to Pure and Divine Being, the only True and Real, the One without a second. Therefore, "*Thou shalt have no other gods before Me*" for I am One and All, the sole Reality, the All-Reality, the unique Divine Essence revealing Himself in all His aspects, in all His *Sefirot*, which supplant all "gods," all secondary causes, all illusory existences outside "Him, the One with Whom nothing can be compared or associated" (*Hu ehad we-en shenī lehamshil lō lehahbirah*). "*Thou shalt not make unto thee any graven image, or any likeness... Thou shalt not bow down thyself to them, nor serve them, for I,* YHVH *thy God, am a jealous God....*"

The first two commandments concern respectively union with the One and His pure affirmation, but the third insists on the purity of this affirmation by warning against the profanation of His worship and of His very Presence which abides in His sacrosanct Name. His Name is His Affirmation proper and complete, His Worship, Revelation, and the whole Torah; His Name is Himself. "God and His Name are one." He is truly present in His Name, and He comes down from His Name to the man who invokes It in truth. To keep the Name of God holy is to unite oneself with God, whereas to profane His Name has the opposite result: to be utterly distant from Him, to fall into the darkness of the abyss. Therefore "*Thou shalt not take the Name of* YHVH *thy God in vain, for* YHVH *will not hold him guiltless that taketh His Name in vain.*"

The Divine Name must be kept holy continuously and, in principle, it unites man with God at all times. Every day of his life, man must invoke the Name which saves and delivers him, and which so fills him with the Divine Presence that It abides, remains, and acts within him as a living temple. Yet there is one day that is particularly propitious for the union of man with God, being consecrated to the revelation of His *Shekhinah*, a day when the Lord rests fully in Israel and when Israel finds complete repose in Him. This is the Sabbath: "*Remember the Sabbath day, to keep it holy. Six days shalt thou labor, and do all thy work. . . . For in six days* YHVH *made heaven and earth, the sea and all that is in them, and rested the seventh day: wherefore* YHVH *blessed the Sabbath day, and hallowed it.*"

Thus, Israel must sanctify the Divine Presence: (a) by union with the One; (b) by affirming His Oneness; (c) by the pure invocation of His Name; and (d) by contemplative repose on the Sabbath. However, Israel must also realize the Divine Presence in the neighbor, beginning with the veneration of father and mother: "*Honor thy father and thy mother; that thy days may be long upon the land which* YHVH *thy God giveth thee.*" The Scriptures promise long life in reward of the observance of this commandment. By long life the Scriptures mean eternal life. The words "upon the land which YHVH thy God giveth thee," refer to the higher region where the Divine Majesty is contemplated as if in a mirror which reflects the light. This commentary in the *Zohar* (2:93a) shows the very broad relevance of this precept; but love for parents must extend to one's neighbor in general, as is made clear in another scriptural command: "Love thy neighbor as thyself" (Lev. 19:18).

The last six commandments deal with love of one's neighbor; after the command to honor one's father and mother, the Scriptures insist that we abstain from any wrong against our neighbor. For only where wrong is absent can real good be done, the Supreme Good be actualized, and the Presence of God be realized in ourselves and our neighbors. "*Thou shalt not kill. Thou shalt not commit adultery. Thou shalt not steal. Thou shalt not bear false witness against thy neighbor. Thou shalt not covet thy neighbor's house, thou shalt not covet thy neighbors' wife, nor his manservant, nor his maidservant, nor his ox, nor his ass, nor anything that is thy neighbor's.*"

After the great Sinaitic theophany that was crystallized in the Decalogue, which is a revelation whose every word was an aspect of God Himself—from His first word, *Anokhi*, "I," to His last, *re'ekha*, "thy neighbor"—YHVH proceeded, on the express demand of the people, to speak to Moses alone, and entrusted to him, on behalf of Israel, His

Code of the Covenant (see Exod. 20:22–23:19). This was ratified, after Moses had read out the Book of the Covenant, in the sprinkling of the blood of the sacrificed animals. In fact, after he received the first Tablets of the Law, "Moses wrote down the words of God," which he "read out in the presence of the people" at the moment when the Covenant was concluded. It was only afterwards, at the end of the forty days and nights he spent on Mount Sinai before the face of the Lord, that he received the "two Tables of the Testimony," inscribed on both sides; "on the one side and on the other they were written. And the tables were the work of God, and the writing of God, graven upon the tables" (Exod. 32:15–16). But these tablets were broken because of the adoration of the golden calf. Then, when Moses gained Divine forgiveness for Israel, YHVH told him: "Hew these two tables of stone like unto the first: and I will write upon these tables the words that were in the first tables, which thou hast broken." And when Moses retreated for the second time to the mountain, where he spent another forty days and forty nights before the face of God, once more "YHVH wrote upon the tables the words of the Covenant, the Ten Commandments" (Exod. 34:1, 28).

As we have seen, however, before they were inscribed these three successive times—in the "Book of the Covenant," written by Moses, and on the first and the second "Tables of Testimony" engraved "by the finger of God"—the Sinaitic words had been revealed directly to Israel by YHVH, when "the people saw the thunderings and the lightnings, and the noise of the trumpet, and the mountain smoking" (Exod. 20:18). Israel saw what it heard: it saw the divine voices as flames or spiritual illuminations which took the shape of sacred words and letters. And "each word was divided into twenty sounds; and those sounds appeared before the eyes of Israel as seventy shining lights."[18] That is,

> Each word [that came from God's mouth] encompassed all the implications and derivatives of the Law as well as all the mysteries or hidden aspects that pertained to them; each word, indeed, was like a treasure filled with precious goods . . . each word revealed itself through its seventy aspects [which formed the basis of other aspects and interpretations], to the number of the six hundred thousand children of Israel that were present at Sinai, and even more, since all the souls of earlier and later generations were also present at the Theophany;

---

[18] *Zohar*, 2:146a.

this means that each fundamental interpretation could take the color of each receptacle of the revelation of the One. Each word received fifty minus one crowns on one side [the "right" or clement side] and the same number [or principles of exegesis] on the other[19] [the "left" or the side of rigor]. That is why each biblical law is susceptible to forty-nine arguments in one sense and forty-nine in the other. Because of this diversity of possible interpretations of each word of God, the Scriptures compare them to a fire with myriads of sparks; but it also says that each Divine Word is "like a hammer that breaketh the rock in pieces" (and frees the hidden sparks), as it is described in Jer. 23:29: "Is not my word like as a fire? sayeth the Lord; and like a hammer that breaketh the rock in pieces?"[20]

The word of God was His light that Israel "heard and saw at the same time" and from which "letters of white fire, revealing Grace, and of black fire" (which manifest rigor), hung in the air and detached themselves.[21] Then Israel saw a great light appear, that absorbed all the others,[22] being both their synthesis and their source. That source of light was the *Shekhinah*, itself emanating from the Ancient of Days, the Supreme Principle, whose Real Presence it is. From it descended the "heavenly dew" of which "two drops were transformed into precious stones. God blew on these stones, and they became two tablets [of transparent sapphire]. . . . On the back of the tablets could be read what was written on the front, and on the front could be read what was written on the back."[23] This was the substantial revelation of God through His Real Presence on Mount Sinai, the radiation of His Presence through His Light, the embodiment of His Light in His Word, and the crystallization of His Word, or spoken doctrine, and of His written doctrine; all this took place in the self-same supra-temporal moment of the great Theophany.

---

[19] The number forty-nine comes about from the seven *Sefirot* of cosmic construction, each of which is reflected in the other, so that each of them is "sevenfold"—which amounts to the forty-nine sefirotic aspects. On the other hand, each of them contains, in a different "blend," Divine Grace and Rigor; this leads to forty-nine clement or positive interpretations and forty-nine rigorous or negative interpretations.

[20] *Zohar*, 2:83b.

[21] *Zohar*, 2:84b.

[22] *Zohar*, 2:146a.

[23] *Zohar*, 2:84a, b; 85a.

This revelation of the Torah, which is both spoken and written as we have seen, is fulfilled through the conscious union of the Chosen People with Him who revealed Himself. First He revealed Himself to Israel as the "One without second"; then He showed Himself in His ten fundamental aspects, the *Sefirot*, and next in the form of the "raiment" of the *Sefirot*, the Ten Commandments, which contain the whole substance of the Torah, progressively revealed through the intermediation of Moses. And the prophecy of Moses itself is the substance of all the later revelations of the prophets and the hagiographs of Israel: "Moses had pronounced all the words of the other prophets, as well as his own [which contain the words of the other prophets], and whoever prophesied [in Israel] would only express the substance of the prophecy of Moses." Thus: "What the prophets were destined to announce to later generations, was received from Mount Sinai."[24] And the Talmud confirms: "Even that which a distinguished disciple was destined to teach in the presence of his Master, had already been said to Moses on Mount Sinai."[25] This implies that nothing which is said by a Jewish prophet or by a spiritual master or disciple interpreting Scripture according to the rules of traditional exegesis could be in contradiction with the scripts that were revealed by the intermediation of the great servant of God; nothing whatsoever could be added to it or omitted from it. The words of God, which He Himself engraved in the Tables of Testimony, were followed by Moses and constitute the Torah; and the writing of the prophets and the hagiographies followed as developments from the Torah, from the single revelations of YHVH.

### The Written Torah and the Spoken Torah

After the descent of the "Ten Commandments engraved in stone," the "Torah was written in earliest times in separate scrolls" (*Mishnah, Gittin*, 60a) and was later brought together in a single book, the Pentateuch. This is the Book of the "Torah of Moses." Tradition adds that:

> Moses wrote this book, including the parable of Balaam (Num. 22) as well as the narrative of Job. Joshua wrote his own book and the last eight verses of Deuteronomy [concerning the death of Moses]. Samuel wrote his own book, Judges and Ruth. David wrote the psalms with the [spiritual] collaboration of the ten elders, who are: Adam (Ps. 139), Heman (Ps.

[24] *Midrash, Shemot R.* 42:8; 28:6.

[25] *Yer. Pe'ah*, 2:17a.

88), Yeduthun (Ps. 39, 62, 77), Asaph (Ps. 73–83), and the three sons of Kore (Ps. 42–84 s.; 87 s.) Jeremiah wrote his own book, the Book of Kings and Lamentations. Hezekiah and his associates were responsible for the books of Isaiah, and Solomon, namely, Proverbs, the Song of Songs, and Ecclesiastes. The men of the Great Synagogue were responsible for Ezekiel, the Twelve [lesser prophets: Hosea, Joel, Amos, Obadiah, Jonah, Micah, Nahum, Habakkuk, Zephaniah, Haggai, Zachariah, and Malachi] for Daniel and Esther. Esdras wrote his own book and the genealogies of the Chronicles up to his time; Nehemiah finished the Chronicles (*Mishnah, Baba Batra*, 14b ff).

All these revelations were consigned to writing from the "written Torah" or "written doctrine" (*Torah shebikhtav*) in the broadest sense. This is the Hebrew Bible which Jewish tradition subdivides into "twenty-four books" in the following order: the five books of Moses; the eight books of the Prophets; Joshua, Judges, Samuel, Kings, Isaiah, Jeremiah, Ezekiel; the Twelve lesser prophets mentioned above, whose writings are considered as a single book and the eleven Hagiographs: Psalms, Proverbs, Job, the Song of Songs, Ruth, Lamentations, Ecclesiastes, Esther, Daniel, Ezra-Nehemiah (considered as one book), and Chronicles. The exact date when this scriptural canon was established definitively by the spiritual authorities of Israel is uncertain; it could not have been before the third century B.C.E., and there were probably discussions as late as the first century C.E. concerning the suitability for canonization of certain books, such as the Song of Songs, Ecclesiastes, Proverbs, and Esther. In the end the existing canon was consecrated by this formula: "The One and Only, Blessed be He, has said: 'I have written twenty-four books; add nothing to them. . . .'"[26]

But everything that the Lord has written, He also has spoken. He enunciated it in substance on Mount Sinai to the whole of Israel and He elaborated on it in His revelations to Moses and the other prophets, and though He insisted that no other *sacred writings* should be added to His "twenty-four books," He did not forbid *sacred exegesis*, spoken tradition, and its recording in writing. The spoken tradition goes back to His own word that is contained in the Scriptures and which can be interpreted in many valid ways that unveil His mysteries: aspects of Him who spoke and who, in His word, revealed Himself.[27] However,

---

[26] *Midrash, Bemidbar R.*, 14:4.

[27] There was, however, a school of thought in Israel, that of the Sadducees, which, from

exegesis at any level can only be orthodox and effective if, in fact, it represents the "spoken Torah," which is not simply a collection of interpretations that have been appended to it by men, but which is really of supra-human origin. It is the divine revelation or word hidden in Scripture as the "spirit of the letter"; this spirit has been crystallized by the sages of Israel, in its esoteric aspect, in the teachings and the writings of the Kabbalah, and in exoteric mode in the teachings and writings of the Talmud and their rabbinical expansion.

Although the "spoken Torah," as an interpretation of the "written Torah," may appear to have been developed later, actually, as we have seen, both were revealed at the same time; at Sinai, Israel saw the spiritual contents of the letters that were written in heaven. The purely spiritual, luminous Word of God was His "spoken Torah" which immediately took shape in His "written Torah," and this written record was destined to be a permanent point of departure and an established criterion for any analysis and application of revealed Truth and Divine Will. Therefore, exegesis and the realization of the contents of the Torah are nothing more than the extraction and assimilation of the spirit, or the light, that was crystallized in the "letter." The two *Torot* are two aspects of the single Sinaitic revelation, which complement each other perfectly in the divine work of illumination and redemption of the Chosen People. As in the Kabbalah, the Talmud insists on this twofold unity of the revelation, but it envisages the spoken Torah in the first place under its aspect of exegesis, that is, as a Torah that appears to devolve from the written Torah. What does the scriptural text mean when it says: "I will give thee tables of stone, and a law, and commandments which I have written; that thou mayest teach them" (Exod. 14:12)?

The "tables of stone" are the Decalogue (which represents the synthesis of the whole Torah, written and spoken, together with the Prophets and the Hagiographs); the "law" is the Pentateuch (*Hamishah humshe Torah*, the "five fifths of the Torah" or five books of Moses); the "commandments" are the *Mishnah* (or repetition of the spoken revela-

the second century B.C.E., rejected all words of traditions that had not been chronicled in the written Torah. In opposition to the Pharisees, who cultivated the spoken Doctrine, they fiercely denied the orthodoxy of that Doctrine. Because their Judaism based itself exclusively on the written code of the Pentateuch centering on Temple ritual, the destruction of the Temple almost immediately brought about the extinction of the Sadducees' trend. Pharisaism, on the contrary, allowed Israel to adapt the religion to the fearful conditions the Jews now faced, by turning to traditional interpretation of the Scripture; without the spoken Torah, Judaism would no longer exist.

tion), from Moses to Esdras who transmitted it, with the Scripture, to the doctors of the "Great Synagogue," or *Soferim*, "Men who dealt in scriptural Science"; they repeated it to the *Tannaim* or Authorities of the doctrine, the last of whom, Yehudah the Saint, who died about 220 C.E., completed the compilation and final written version of the *Mishnah*; the phrase "which I have written" refers to the Prophets and the Hagiographs (which, in the treatise *Rosh hashanah*, 7a of the *Mishnah*, are together described by the term *Qabbalah* which, as we have seen, means "esoteric tradition"; in fact, the prophets and the hagiographers were the real masters in this tradition and confirmed, revived, and fortified Judaism "from within"); "that thou mayest teach them" refers to the *Gemarah* (the "complement" to or commentary on the *Mishnah* which represents the whole of the account of the *Amoraim*, the "orators" or "interpreters" of the spoken Doctrine which follows the *Tannaim*—third–fifth century C.E.); thus, it is the *Mishnah* and the *Gemarah* which combine to form the Talmud, the exoteric "study" of the Torah—*Talmud Torah*—in the strict sense of the word. We must add that the *Gemarah* of the Talmudic schools of the Jews exiled in Babylon and the *Gemarah* of the Palestine Jews, being based on one and the same *Mishnah*, finally resulted in the "Babylonian Talmud" and the "Palestinian" or "Jerusalem Talmud" respectively. The Talmud deals with both the "active" and the "contemplative" aspects of the religion: traditional activity is described by all the relevant texts in the *Halakhah*, the "Way" to be followed according to the Law, whereas the contemplative aspects are created in the *Haggadah*, the biblical and symbolical "Narrative"; this latter aims at a greater spiritual understanding of the Torah, in order to lead to the "Knowledge of the Holy One, blessed be He" which is, strictly speaking reserved to those who are initiated in the Kabbalah; thus, the *Haggadah* forms one of the links between exoterism and esoterism. Finally, the Talmud also takes in the numerous *Midrashim* or rabbinical "treatises" which appeared in great numbers up to the twelfth century C.E.; together with the *Mishnah* and the *Gemarah*, they constitute the Talmud in the broader sense of the word, but not the whole "spoken Torah" itself. The "spoken Torah" also comprises the esoteric commentary on the Scriptures; the *Qabbalah* or "Receiving" of pure and universal Truth, which in its turn is chronicled in a rich traditional literature concerning the "Mysteries of the Torah." The text (of the scriptures interpreted in this fashion) shows that "all this was given to Moses at Sinai."[28] Let us recall that they received not only "that which the Prophets were destined

---

[28] *Berakhot*, 5a.

to announce to the latter generations," but also that "even that which a distinguished disciple was destined to teach in the presence of his master, had already been said to Moses on Mount Sinai."

## The Kabbalah

Another text in the Talmud, part of which we quoted at the beginning of this article, alludes to the precedence of the *Qabbalah* (Kabbalah) in the simultaneous act of divine revelation and its reception by man; as we have seen, the Kabbalah or direct "reception" of the Divine "Mysteries of the Torah" on Sinai, took place first of all, being the direct entry of an entire people into the "inward" or esoteric field of religion, their spiritual union with God Himself, under the guidance of Moses: "Moses, [and with him the whole of Israel,] received (*qibbel = qabbalah*) the written [and spoken] Torah on the summit of Mount Sinai; he transmitted it [with all its basic interpretations, rules, and levels of sacred exegesis, both esoteric and exoteric] to Joshua; Joshua transmitted it to the Elders, the elders to the Prophets, and the Prophets transmitted it to the men of the Great Synagogue."[29] All this took place "from inward to outward"; from the "*qabbalah*" or direct "reception" of the only Real and True to the exoteric "study" of the Torah, *Talmud Torah*; and all this was made possible by the spoken tradition itself which was protected by revealed hermeneutic rules. It was essential for the spoken revelation made to Moses and Israel to contain in itself that rule which laid down the indisputable exegetical criteria since otherwise it could well have withered with the passing of time into even more deviated speculation and finally have succumbed to heterodoxy. These rules, or methods of exegesis, are a kind of unalterable framework which have supported the changeless teaching of the spoken doctrine down through the centuries; because of the various degrees of understanding and application, they extend from elementary exoterism to the highest realms of esoterism. The practice of exegetical methods can be reduced to four, and the initials of the words describing them form the key word *PaRDeS*, the "Paradise" of drawing near to God. They are: *Peshat*, "Simple" literal interpretation of the Scriptures; *Remez*, "Allusion" to the manifold meanings concealed (in the symbolism of the phrases, letters, and signs of the Torah); *Derash*, Homiletic "exposition" of doctrinal truths which embrace all possible interpretations of the revelation; and *Sod*, "Mystery," initiation into the "Mysteries of the Torah" (*Sitre Torah*), the esoteric teaching of the Kabbalah.

---

[29] *Pirkei Avot*, 1:1.

These basic categories of exegesis amount to four degrees of spiritual ascent of which the second and third form the passage between exoterism and esoterism. Indeed, the methods which correspond with these intermediate categories are used by both Talmudists and Kabbalists; but although the Talmud joins the Kabbalah in this respect—and prepared for it to a certain extent—it is centered on the "logic" of it, whereas the Kabbalah identifies itself with the "Holy Spirit" (*Ruah ha-Qodesh*) which surpasses human reason and unites man with Him who reveals Himself:

> Consider how Scripture proceeds where man is concerned: first it proceeds to man. . . . And when man approaches Scripture, it speaks to him through the curtain [the "letter"] which still separates it from him. . . . Then man slowly begins to understand: he is at the stage of syllogistic interpretations. Then Scripture speaks to man through a more transparent veil, the veil of enigmas and parables which, by unveiling their symbolism, lead him to the real and purely spiritual significance of the "letter." . . . And finally, when man has familiarized himself with Scripture [at the stage when he moves from the "letter" and its symbolism to the "inspired word"], the Scripture shows itself openly and reveals the [divine] Mysteries and the secret ways [which lead to the One], which it has kept hidden since the beginning of time [and the "sacred store" of which is the *Sod*, or the *Qabbalah*]. Only then can man come to a perfect knowledge of the Scriptures, and only then does he become "Master of the House" [the universal House of God], for all the Mysteries have been revealed to him, and not one of them remains hidden (*Zohar*, 2:99a–b).

Let us quote that other passage from the *Zohar* concerning the ascent from the "letter" or the "body" of the Torah up to its "soul," its "root," its divine essence:

> The foolish see only the clothing of a man; if it is beautiful, the wearer is also beautiful. But the clothing covers something even more precious, and that is the soul. The Torah also has a body, which is the commandments [objects of the *Halakhah*], . . . it also has raiment, and those are the narrations corresponding to the *Haggadah* which, from one point of view, is inferior to the *Halakhah*, and, from another, superior; . . . Fi-

nally, the Torah has a soul which was penetrated by those who were present near Mount Sinai, that is the fundamental root of all things, the real Torah [the real, revealing, and redeeming Presence of God, which is realized directly by the Kabbalah] (3:152a).

Although the two exoteric and esoteric domains may be very clearly distinguished in the ascent to the summit of the "inward Sinai," they are also intertwined, as we have seen, in order to lead man, by spiritualizing his body and his soul, to the encounter with "Him who descends upon the mountain" of the heart. In fact, after Moses, Joshua, the Elders and the Prophets, and the elite of the Great Synagogue, it was the greatest "men of scriptural science"[30] from among the *Tannaim*, *Amoraim*, and *Rabbanim* who were masters of both the Talmud and the Kabbalah, that is, of the whole spoken Tradition; they formed the main "links" in the "chain of Tradition" (*shalsheleth ha-Qabbalah*) which is outwardly Talmudic, but inwardly initiatic or Kabbalistic. This uninterrupted "chain" is destined to last until the final coming of the Messiah; exoterism and esoterism must fulfill each other through the centuries and millennia, like body and soul, in order to constitute the viable unity of the Tradition reflecting the "Higher Unity":

> For, even above [in the heavenly realms] there are clothing, body, soul, and also Soul of the soul. The heavens and their hosts are the clothing. The "Community of Israel" is the [mystical, heavenly, and spiritual] body that accepts the soul, which is named "Beauty of Israel" [the Revelation of the Supreme, His Eternal Torah, His luminous and beatific Descent]; and this Soul of the soul is the Ancient of Days [the Supreme Self]. All these [divine, spiritual, and heavenly] realities are linked [to one another and to the Holy Tradition which reflects them and manifests them on earth]: "Woe to the guilty who pretend that the Torah [the Divine Reality of the tradition, the luminous Presence of the Supreme] is nothing but a simple narrative. . ." (*Zohar*, 3:152a).

---

[30] Editor's note: Here, as elsewhere in the translations of Schaya's writings, we should remember that the French word *science*, though translated with its English cognate, also can mean "knowledge." A traditional linguistic relationship between "science" and "knowledge" continues to exist in many European and Semitic languages, although the terms in English are now generally quite distinct.

The Kabbalah is distinguished from the Talmud as is the soul from the body; in other words—symbolically—it is like the midmost organ of the body, the heart, which directly receives the "soul [of Scripture] revealed to those present at Mount Sinai"; and by receiving it today, just as at Mount Sinai, the Kabbalah identifies itself immediately with that soul which, as we have seen, is the light, the Real Presence of the "Supreme Soul." The Kabbalah animates, illuminates, and sanctifies the "body"—which is at the same time the letter of the Scripture, the whole Mosaic law, and the Chosen People itself—in order to unite it with the *Shekhinah* and, through that, with the Holy One, Blessed be He. In order to achieve that purpose, the Kabbalah uses, as we have seen, amongst others, the same methods as the Talmud, the methods of the *Halakhah* and the *Haggadah*, as well as the exegetic modes *Peshat*, *Remez*, and *Derash*; and in connection with the latter, it uses the sacred science of letters and numbers.[31] But even more, and by definition, the Kabbalah uses methods which are proper to it, such as the science of the *Sefirot* and the divine Names. These two fundamental sciences belong respectively to the two great Kabbalistic categories: the "theoretical" or contemplative Kabbalah (*Qabbalah yiunit*) and the "practical" or operative Kabbalah (*Qabbalah maʾasit* which, in this case, does not refer to its deviations into magic).

These two categories complement each other and interpenetrate. In fact, although the "way of the *Sefirot*" (*derekh ha-Sefirot*) is mainly contemplative and the "way of the Names" (*derekh ha-Shemot*) is operative, the latter sustains contemplation by the illuminative and unitive grace of the invocation of the Sacred Names, which correspond to the *Sefirot* or divine aspects; moreover, the contemplation of the *Sefirot* is operative in itself; like true contemplation of the Divine, it contains its own transforming graces, the greatest of which is to metamorphose the contemplating subject into the contemplated Object. However, these graces can also join with invocation to guide the Kabbalist who proceeds according to the initiatic rules and in particular with the required *kawwanah* (intention, attention, or concentration) to meeting and union with Him who reveals Himself.[32] In other Kabbalistic

---

[31] The three best known procedures of science of letters or numbers in Judaism are the *Gematria*, which makes use of the numerical values of the Hebrew letters; *Notarikon*, which uses the initial, middle, and final letters of the words; and *Temurah*, the method of permutations and combinations of letters.

[32] This unifying meeting can involve different modes of union; amongst others, it can renew the Sinaitic separation of the body from the soul which then ascends to the Supreme Essence. An illustration of this is given by the following narrative concerning

methods, such as the Vision of the "Chariot" (*Merkabah*) or the divine Throne, which is associated with the revelation to Ezekiel and which implies a spiritual ascent through the heavens or different super-terrestrial degrees of the cosmos, the invocation of the Sacred Names plays an important role in connection with contemplation. In all these methods there is, in fact, a spiritual progress, or ascent through these cosmic degrees or directly beyond them as far as to the sefirotic degrees, whose acme is *Keter Elyon*, the "Supreme Crown," identical with *Anokhi*, the Divine and Infinite "Self." This is also true of such methods as the spiritual realization of the "work of Genesis" (*Maaseh Bereshith*), the metaphysical object of which is the eternal "Ontogenesis," namely, the divine "Emanation" (*Atsilut*) of the *Sefirot* from the "Supreme Crown" into creation, "a descent" which is finally crystallized in that of the *Shekhinah*, or Divine Immanence, which the Kabbalist "receives directly" as a revelatory and real Presence so that he might be united with It and re-ascend, by Its grace, to the Supreme Principle.

## The Soul of Israel

However, the methods of the Kabbalah are far too numerous to be dealt with further here. Its contemplative and operative procedures are situated, as we have seen, together with those of exoterism, on manifold grades or degrees of exegesis and application of divine revelation; one stands before a veritable Jacob's ladder rising up from the earth towards the Infinite (*Ein Sof*), through all human, heavenly, and spiritual spheres. And it is on this same mystical ladder that the revelation of the Infinite comes down; it descends from the "degrees above," the hierarchy of the *Sefirot*, to manifest itself in the innumerable cosmic degrees which are made up by the reflections of those sefirotic or on-

Rabbi Moshe of Kobrin (who died in 1858 C.E., and was one of the spiritual successors of the famous Rabbi Israel ben Eliezer, who was called Baal Shem or Baal Shem Tov, the "Master of the Good [Divine] Name," founder of Polish Hasidism, 1700–1760): "When Rabbi Moshe was interrogated by a writer about the Kabbalah, or secret Doctrine, and the *kawwanot* or secret intentions aimed at a supra-terrestrial effect, he answered, 'Listen to me well: The word *qabbalah* is derived from *qabbel*, to "accept" or to "receive," and the word *kawwanah* comes from *kawwen*, to "orientate" or "direct toward." For, the ultimate significance of all the wisdom of the Kabbalah is to accept the yoke of the divine Will and the final significance of the practice of the *kawwanot* is the orientation of one's heart toward God. When someone says "The Lord is my God," which means that He is mine and I am His—how could his soul not leave his body?' As soon as he had spoken these words, he fell into a deep ecstatic trance" (excerpt translated from Martin Buber, *Erzählungen der Chasidim* [Zurich: Manesse-Verlag, Conzet & Huber, 1949], p. 368).

tological grades. And it is to spiritual degrees of receptivity, which are realized in created receptacles, that these grades correspond. It was in the image of the "ten degrees above," that all the souls of Israel (including those of past and later generations) were grouped at Sinai into a hierarchy of receptacles. This was accomplished in order to receive the divine revelation according to their respective degrees of receptivity. Every soul in Israel, even before it was brought into existence, has shared in or been identified with one of the *Sefirot*, one of the great Divine Archetypes in which all the other Archetypes are reflected and of which every soul is thus a "hidden vase," a predetermined mode of ontological receptivity. All inherent receptivity is reflected on the "face of the [cosmic] waters," the supreme degree of creation, which is also called *Arabot* or the "seventh heaven." It is here—in the dwelling called *Guf*, its prototypical "Body"—that the created soul awaits the divine command to descend into an earthly body, the body of a human being, of an Israelite. Before that descent, the soul enjoys the vision of God face to face, according to that soul's own degree of "receptivity."

Thus, the souls of Israel that were not incarnated at the moment of the Sinaitic revelation received the order to descend to the "Celestial Land"—the *Shekhinah*—which lay above the mountain, and to attend, together with the incarnated souls (which were temporarily detached from their bodies) the revelation of the ten *Sefirot*, which took the shape of the Ten Commandments that summarize the entire Torah. At that time, each soul received the sefirotic revelation directly, according to its own degree of receptivity which, as we have seen, is essentially linked with one of the *Sefirot* without, however, being separated from the others. Each *Sefirah* contains all the others in the light of its own infinite Quality or Perfection: it unites the soul through that Perfection, which is its eternal Archetype, with the indivisible Unity of all the *Sefirot*. Therefore it is this Divine Unity which is revealed to each soul, according to its own eternal degree of receptivity,

> separately, to the captains of the tribes, to the women, to the leaders of the people . . . as it is written [in Deut. 29:10–13, concerning the Renewal of the Covenant with Moab, which the Kabbalah, as we have seen, spiritually identifies with the Sinaitic event]: "Ye stand this day all of you before YHVH your God; your captains of your tribes, your elders, and your officers, with all the men of Israel, . . ." which indicates the five degrees on the right side [of the Divine Clemency, which corresponds to a powerful, or "solar," spiritual receptivity], whereas

the five degrees on the left side [Rigor, which refer to a lesser or "lunar" receptivity] are [according to the rest of the scriptural text] "your little ones, your wives, and the stranger that is in thy camp, from the hewer of thy wood unto the drawer of thy water [which indicates the possibility of the conversion of non-Jewish souls to Mosaicism and thus, of their assimilation into Israel]: in order to enter into the covenant of YHVH, your God, and into the oath of the covenant which YHVH your God concluded with you on this day, in order to establish you today as His people and to be your God Himself. . . ." These ten degrees [which obtain from the subdivision of Israel effected in the verse just quoted] correspond to the ten [sefirotic] degrees mentioned, through which Israel received the ten words [or commandments] and which are its eternal possession, the essence of all the commandments, the good [or Divine] part of Israel (*Zohar*, 2:82a).

These ten degrees of receptivity were, in their turn, subdivided into as many steps as there were souls present at the revelation; for each soul is, in its essence, a "unique" receptivity (*yehidah*) of the One (*Ehad*), even if it shares roots in a particular *Sefirah* with others. As we have seen, each soul at Sinai saw, in the light of the *Sefirah* from which it originated and according to its own participation in that *Sefirah*, all the other *Sefirot* at the same time as its own; it saw, in its own "unique" way, the sefirotic Infinity, the divine Unity in all Its aspects. And that is how there was erected the immense ladder of all the shades of interpretation and authentic application of the seventy fundamental aspects which each word of Divine Revelation presented. All this spiritual richness, the whole Torah, which is a boundless ocean of shining lights, is forever stored in each soul of Israel. But although, in the seventh heaven, the Jewish soul perpetually enjoys the beatific and unifying vision of Him who reveals Himself and, although this was bestowed here below on Sinai, this spontaneous vision came to an end after the renewal of original sin in the presence of the golden calf. The "eyes" of the soul have been veiled, and the soul has lapsed into imperfections and transgressions, as the history of Israel shows. That is why the Psalmist (119:18) wrote "Take off the veil from mine eyes. . . ," and that is why, in the name of all the prophets of Israel, he urged his people to realize the Divine Will and Truth as revealed in the Torah. "Take off the veil from mine eyes, that I may consider the wonders locked within the Torah." Only the Torah, written and spoken, only the final comprehension of its Divine Contents, can restore to Israel cognitive union with God.

But how is it possible that the soul which has its eternal ground in God, which dwells in constant union with Him in the seventh heaven, which remains, even here on earth, sacred in its "subtle pinnacle" hidden in the heart's depths, and which received the entire treasure of the Torah at Sinai, can voluntarily become estranged from its own divine essence and founder into sin? Here lies the mystery of man's free will: the mystery of man, who can choose to follow either of the two opposite paths which the Creator Himself has gifted to him: the path to the true and good, named *Yetser tob*, the "leaning towards the good," and the path to error and evil, *Yetser hara*, the "leaning towards evil." *Yetser tob* springs up from the divine light in man and attracts him towards his own luminous and absolute essence. *Yetser hara* is like the shadow of that light, an obscuration or an inner veil, which separates and estranges the soul from its divine essence or from the One, in order to lure it into "vanity" (*habel*), which is the illusion of the "other-than-the-One"; this is the illusion of the "I" and the "world," of the multitude of created things supported by the cosmic substance, the very objectivation and coagulation of the shadow or inward darkness.

In the beginning, this substance was still transparent, like a tenuous veil through which divine and beatific light illuminated creation; but because of sin, the fruit of the leaning towards evil, and because of attachment to the "other-than-the-One," and thus to multiform substance, the light was withdrawn, causing the darkness of this substance to appear. According to the Kabbalah, this entire process of negation reflects the principial "retreat" (*tsimtsum*) of the Divine light into its own Infinite Essence, whereby the actualization of primordial darkness, and of the finite and created within it, became possible. The darkness of the created substance, which in the beginning was illumined by the *fiat lux*, re-emerged to a certain extent, as we have seen, following upon original sin, and upon attachment to this substance shot through and through with every kind of illusion and becoming ever harder in proportion to the growth of attachment to it, until it became an opaque "encrustation" (*q'lipah*) enclosing the Divine light. The human soul perceives and pursues no more than the crowd of "sparks" that fell into the darkness of the "I" and the "world" when the light of the One was withdrawn. Divine and luminous as it was, the soul has become dark, dissipated, manifold; its substance is, as it were, an aggregate of different psychic layers, of various "souls" of diverse natures which come together to form a whole that is individual but not homogeneous, being deprived of its primordial spiritual unity.

Man possesses a "sacred soul," *neshamah*, which mounts up unceasingly to its supreme source and whose light it reveals because its nature is identical to the ascendant "inclination to the good" (*Yetser tob*); and he has a "vital" or animal soul, *nefesh*, which, on the contrary, goes down unceasingly into the darkness of the earthly body, which materialized with Adam's fall, when he lost his luminous body. Even so, the corporeal soul is not itself identical with the "inclination to evil" (*Yetser hara*), for God created the human body "in His image," the image of the infinite "Body" of the ten *Sefirot*, so that man, realizing his "deiformity" can return from his "fall-point" to his supreme starting point. And man realizes his deiformity not by attachment to his theomorphic, yet fallen, body, but by the submission and uniting of his body or corporeal soul to the spirit or to the sacred and spiritual soul filled with the true Presence of the *Sefirot*, with all the Divine Perfections capable of being manifested. This submission and union are the work of the reasoning soul, *ruah*, the discursive spirit of man, his mind: this is the specifically human soul, which is called upon to distinguish between the inclinations to good and to evil, between good and bad, true and false, real and unreal, spiritual and material, Divine and non-divine. The "reasoning soul" can turn either to what is above or to what is below; it can make the upper descend into the lower and raise the lower to the higher. *Ruah* can have the spiritual soul subdue the animal soul, or it can refrain from doing so; it can reveal or veil the light of *neshamah*, it can make the darkness of *nefesh* triumph, or not; it is the intermediary; the mediator or the separator between the upper and the lower soul; it identifies itself either with the inclination to good or with the opposite. Through the positive influence of *ruah*, the animal soul is subjected to the Divine Will, its bodily "shell" is itself integrated into the union of reason with *neshamah*, into the spiritual ascent of the being towards Truth; it loses the "weight" acquired through the fall of Adam and serves as a vehicle, a sacred "chariot" for the ascent of man towards God, as it was in Paradise and, later, on Mount Sinai during the great theophany.

In this paradisical state, the threefold soul is homogeneous and reveals two supplementary aspects of its inward and Divine unity. Its intermediary element is no longer *ruah*, reason, but *neshamah* which from then on serves as mediator between the individual soul with its two aspects, the mental (*ruah*) and the animal or corporeal (*nefesh*), and the supra-individual or universal soul of man; *neshamah* constitutes the universal, and even divine, center of the individual earthly soul, *ruah-nefesh*, and it is in this center, this spiritual heart, that man has received, and can continue to receive, Divine revelation directly— or receive the Sinaitic revelation if he is one of the children of Israel. Indeed, just as *nefesh* has two psychic layers which together represent man's individual and lower inferior soul where evil can reside, it also enfolds the two supreme, universal and divine aspects of the human soul; these are the two transcendent aspects of the eternally pure and sacred essence of man, whereas *neshamah* is the immanent aspect of it which is not, however, affected by the existential vicissitudes of the psychic-physical individuality of the human being. These two transcendent aspects are: *hayah*, the (eternally) "living soul," which dwells in the seventh heaven in perpetual union with Him who reveals Himself; and *yehidah*, the "unique soul" which has never come out from Him, but which constitutes the eternal archetype of the human being in the transcendent world of the *Sefirot*. Thus, *neshamah* radiates divine light into the individual sphere of man, illuminates his "mental soul" and nourishes his "vital soul" on the one hand; but ascends on the other—thanks to that enlightening and life-giving light, up through all the heavens as far as *Arabot*, the seventh heaven or the "surface of the waters," in order to integrate itself into *hayah*, united with Him who "rides on heaven, by His name *Yah*" (Ps. 68:4).[33] Thus the sacred soul, by means of union with the Divinity truly present in the supreme degree of creation, regains access to His Transcendence where, from eternity to eternity, *yehidah* is hidden, at one with *Yahid*, the "One and Only."

The man who wanders here on earth suffers no decrease in the purity of his sacred and universal soul, but he can tarnish his individual soul to the point that it remains cut off, as it were, from its Divine essence: it then suffers the consequences of its errors until it has eliminated the impurities of its vital "shell," *nefesh*, and restored the transparency of its mental "veil," *ruah*. God then "removes" this "veil," and the "eyes" of *neshamah*, which are *hayah* and *yehidah*, are "opened," so

---

[33] The word *HaYah* is composed of the initial of *hayim*, "life," or of *hokhmah*, "wisdom," and *YaH*, one of the essential Divine Names, the Name of the "Merciful Father." The two letters *Y* and *H* of the name *YāH* form the first—and "transcendent"—half of the Tetragram *YHVH*, and, from another point of view, the "synthesis" of it, combining the initial and the final letters. According to this Kabbalistic interpretation, the word *HaYaH* indicates the union of the immortal or eternally "living" and "knowing" soul with the "transcendent" which has made Itself immanent in the supreme degree of the cosmos in the form of the "Merciful Father."

that man, now illuminated and united with the One, "sees the miracles contained in the Torah." In this way, a child of Israel realizes on earth what he perpetually and eternally possesses above, where he is at one with Him who reveals Himself to all the souls on the surface of the waters, and who has revealed Himself in particular to Israel at the summit of Mount Sinai in assuming the form of the Torah.

But here again, the question arises of how it can be possible that the souls of Israel, as soon as God had "lifted the veil" and "showed them His miracles," His own Aspects, His truly present and entire Glory, and had thus joined them to Himself, could lapse into "the inclination to evil" through the adoration of the golden calf, which is a crude illusion of an "other-than-Him"?

Actually, what we have just stated concerning the constitution of the human soul refers only to the possibility of sin in general without touching upon the particular sin committed at Sinai almost immediately after the enlightenment of Israel and its union with God. We must revert, therefore, to the events of Sinai: there, Israel saw the spiritual reality of each word of the Decalogue; it saw the synthesis of the Torah and, in that synthesis, the essence of the revelation, God Himself. The Lord revealed Himself to His people in His first word: *Anokhi*: "I," which is His "I-ness" as well as the Divine "Self" of all beings. Each child of Israel embodied *Anokhi*, and thereby "penetrated into the Mystery of supreme Wisdom." Time and space were, for one instant, obliterated "in the eyes of all the people"; and yet—and this is one of the essential factors which lead to a better understanding of the drama of Israel—the cyclical conditions into which this event intervened were not reabsorbed thereby once and for all; they re-asserted themselves once more as soon as the great theophany faded. For one moment, paradise on earth and a dazzling spiritual ascent of an entire people towards God had become actual, but the time for perfect, final, and universal deliverance had not yet come. It had been no more than momentarily prefigured in the heart of an ethnic collectivity as yet imperfectly prepared to receive the supreme Gift. The human receptacles stood in different degrees of closeness to the Mountain of light; their outward remoteness corresponded to their inward distance from the Divine Presence. Although for one moment God's light obliterated that distance, He did not remove it. The cycle of humanity towards the end of time had to evolve in the direction of a general downfall, a spiritual downfall broadly involving all the people in the world, including Israel.

Indeed, if all evil had totally vanished at Mount Sinai, each Israelite could have followed Moses closely in his approach to God, and could have united with Him in a perfect, final way, as all the chosen will do, by the grace of the Merciful, at the final coming of the Messiah. But the Lord did not want his Sinaitic community to "break" all the spiritual "barriers" yet or to realize—with the "righteous of all nations"—Messianic Plenitude. That is why He said to Moses: "Go down, charge the people lest they break through unto YHVH to gaze, and many of them perish. And let the priests also, which come near to YHVH, sanctify themselves, lest YHVH break forth upon them." And: "Come up unto YHVH, thou, and Aaron, Nadab and Abihu, and seventy of the elders of Israel; and worship ye afar off. And Moses alone shall come near YHVH: but they shall not come nigh: neither shall the people go up with him" (Exod. 19:21–22, 24:1–2). Thus, within one and the same community of visionaries of God, a spiritual hierarchy was crystallized out. Union with God was actualized in an immense ladder of degrees which could then be scaled according to the measure of intensity of "thirst for the One" which each of them bore in his heart. Supreme union and final deliverance were accorded only to those who enjoyed an extremely heightened state of inward preparedness. For the others, union with the Divine was transitory, but each retained an indelible imprint of it in his heart such as to serve as a permanent support for spirituality and ultimate union with YHVH. All the souls of the former and later generations of Israel, present at Sinai, were impregnated in the same way. Each child of Israel saw God and would be able to see Him again and find Him again in his heart: that was and is the immense, and lasting, grace of the Sinaitic theophany.

The foregoing remarks permit us to come to a conclusion about the serious problem of Israel's having seen God and been united with Him, yet still remaining capable of worshiping an idol. Such a fall from the state of union can occur—right up to the ultimate and Messianic Redemption—when union is simply passive and bestowed upon man by pure grace, when man himself has not cooperated actively in the realization of union, as was the case with Adam and Eve in paradise and with most of the children of Israel at Sinai. In this event, the soul is open to the influence of the enshrouding and separative power of the dark "shells" of created substance. These subtle or psychic "shells" envelop, as we have seen, the spiritual light that dwells in creatures and emanates from their divine and uncreated essence. In order for man to be able to dominate this anti-spiritual and dualistic influence which separates and estranges him from his own Divine Self, he must devote all his intelligence, will, and faith to the *active* and *integral* purification of the dark outer layers of his soul. With the help of God he must strive to transform and re-integrate them completely into his own original immaculate substance, the "Primordial Ether" (*Avir Qadmon*), the "chariot" (*merkabah*) or transparent vehicle of the Spirit that is hidden in his heart; he must—with the help of God—aspire to triumph completely over his "inclination to evil" which leads to *habel*, vanity, illusion, unreality, by means of his "inclination to good" which attaches and unites him with *Emeth*, the "Truth," the One and Only Real. Finally, he will become part of—or, seen "from above," be made part of—the "One without second," which implies that he will be totally effaced and, at the same time, spiritually resurrected in Him. Then, and only then, will he be a perfect servant of God, delivered forever from the "I" and the "world." So long as he has not completely conquered the double illusion of an "other-than-the-One"—and thus is not yet true "Master of the cosmic house"—he risks falling away even from such paradisical and angelic purity as the Children of Israel obtained "without fee" at Sinai, after two days of specific preparations.[34] This preparation was sufficient for a passive union, but could by no means take the place of integral, spiritual realization; for most Israelite souls it could, however, be a point of departure, charged with a quite exceptional super-abundance of grace. On the other hand, there seems no reason to doubt that this same preparation coincided with the final phase of the active spiritualization of the elite, which probably started at the beginning of the ministry of Moses and Aaron, before the Exodus. This spiritualization was such as to lead, in an active and perfect way, to the Sinaitic union with God on the part of the chosen, preventing them and their followers from worshiping the golden calf.

### The Sin of the Golden Calf

According to the *Zohar* (2:191a–192b) the fabrication and worship of the golden calf were due to the initiative of the Egyptians who, recognizing the superiority of YHVH over Pharaoh, joined Israel at their exodus. But during the forty days and nights spent by Moses on Mount Sinai in the presence of his Lord, these Egyptians succumbed again to the influence of the "shells": they began to be impatient and to play a role analogous to that of the tempter who entered the Garden of Eden to beguile Eve, and then Adam, into evil. The Kabbalah considers these

---

[34] This is why, apart from purely contemplative reasons which induce them to teach the permanent invocation of God, the spiritual Masters—of whom we quote Rabbi Nahman of Bratislava (1772–1810)—generally insist on the need ceaselessly "to raise one's heart up to God," "to cry out to Him unceasingly with one's whole heart"; for man is in great danger in this world."

Egyptians as being "intruders" into the earthly paradise created at the foot of Mount Sinai. In the manner of Satan clouding the minds of the first men these "intruders," and especially the "magicians" amongst them, made so many Israelite souls cynical and impure that the brother of Moses feared that the Covenant with YHVH would be utterly revoked. It was because Aaron wanted to limit the loss of Israelite souls as far as possible, that he permitted the fabrication of the golden calf at the urgent request of the Egyptians and their followers. But he also had an altar constructed and dedicated to YHVH so that the pure could demonstrate their opposition to the impure, and the worship of the true God of Israel would annul, if possible, the fruits of idolatry. Without the intervention of Moses, who was prepared to give his life for his people, Israel would have been crushed by God's wrath despite Aaron's gesture; and it was only after the expiatory death of thousands of apostates that His wrath was fully appeased.

However, the first Tablet of the Torah, the first state of union between Israel and God, and the Sinaitic paradise were lost, and had it not been for another intervention by Moses, YHVH would not have accompanied this "stiff-necked people" to the Promised Land. The Lord had meanwhile warned Moses of the risk he would run by accepting the Egyptians into Israel's bosom, but he, in hopes of their genuine conversion when they saw the works of the living God, put their case favorably to YHVH. Finally, God allowed man to exercise his free will, as He had before when Adam and Eve in paradise fell victim to the "intruder" in spite of God's warning. Thus it was that original sin and man's fall came to be repeated at Sinai and the reinstatement of the paradisical state and union with the One assumed the aspect of a simple planting of the seed that would grow into universal Redemption, and only then, would evil disappear from the earth forever.

This seed had fallen on the soil of a collective soul, which would have to be tilled for thousands of years by legions of the pious, the just, and the prophets, in order to bear a spiritual harvest leading to final Deliverance. From the pure spirituality of the first Tablets, Israel moved on towards the exoterism of the second; but the esoterism of that first hour, the Kabbalah, the "reception" and realization of the "Mysteries of the Torah," was conserved by the elite. Despite all the failings of the Chosen People, the "chain of the Esoteric Tradition" (*shalshelet ha-Qabbalah*), the initiatic transmission of the sacred means that lead to the vision of the Divine and to union with Him, has remained intact since Moses and must necessarily endure until the final coming of the Messiah. The luminous traces of the original Tablets are hidden in the letters of the second Tablet, the Torah, and in the hidden light dwells the first state in *unio mystica*. In order to recover that state of beatific vision and sacred union of Sinai, Israel must return to the Torah and immerse itself in it until it penetrates its intimate reality. The history of Israel is an ineluctable coming-and-going between fidelity and faithlessness towards the Torah, between the worship of YHVH and that of the "golden calf" or other false gods. It is for this reason that the Eternal destroyed the two Temples of Jerusalem, exiled the people from the Holy Land, and withheld Himself from the inner eye of most of the Children of Israel. Even before the destruction of the second Temple, he forbade the invocation of His holy Name *YHVH*, that essential vestige of the first Tablet through which many a soul of Israel had achieved union with Him after His revelation at Sinai. In that Name God had placed all His Goodness, Grace, and Mercy. He had uttered it before Moses so that Moses could speak it out aloud before Israel and Israel could invoke It and thus be enlightened and delivered by the Infinite Goodness and True, Redeeming Presence contained in that most precious utterance of the Eternal:

> I will make all my goodness pass before thee, and I will pronounce the name of YHVH before thee; and will grant grace to whom I will grant grace, and will show mercy on whom I will show mercy (Exod. 33:19).

> And YHVH descended in the cloud, and stood with him there, and proclaimed the name of YHVH. And YHVH passed by before him, and proclaimed YHVH! YHVH! God, merciful and gracious, long-suffering and abundant in goodness and truth, keeping mercy for thousands, forgiving, forgiving iniquity and transgression and sin, and that will by no means clear the guilty; visiting the iniquity of the fathers upon the children, and upon the children's children, unto the third and fourth generation (Exod. 34:5–7).

With the loss of the invocation of the Name *YHVH*, Israel was subjected to the worst of all punishments and degradation: the loss of immediate union with God. In fact, the particular grace of this Name consists in the immediate and redeeming "descent" of the Transcendent—whose symbol is formed by the first two letters of *YHVH*. His descent is represented by the letter *V*, the ideogram of the Messiah, who operates on earth through the letter *H*, which is the symbol of the real and revealing Presence, the *Shekhinah*. It is this redeeming descent that procures union with the Divine and which is represented by the last two letters of the Tetragram—its "immanent half"—which was taken away from the Jewish people. Only a few rare initiates of the "Kabbalistic chain" who were qualified for direct union could continue secretly to invoke the Holy Name, the Divine Content of which must be permanently actualized here on earth "from generation to generation" (see Exod. 3:15). However, God left the "first [transcendent] half" of His Name—that is, *YH*, pronounced *YaH*, to all Israel. This is the Name of His Merciful Transcendence which, together with certain Names of His Immanence, such as *Elohenu* (Our God) and *Adonai* (My Lord) continues to manifest His Grace within the withdrawal of His Grace: this manifestation is weakened and "indirect," and is thus appropriate to the limited receptivity of the generations of the "last days," who are no longer capable of assimilating and supporting a direct descent of the Divine.

Another disgrace of the most terrible kind, and not unconnected with what has just been recounted, was inflicted upon Israel with the destruction twice of the Temple, the House of the "final *H*" of *YHVH*, His *Shekinah*, His Presence as It was tangibly manifested to the people. Priestly service, sacrifices offered for the reconciliation and union of Israel with YHVH, no longer exist. The saving presence of the *Shekhinah* no longer radiates from the divine "Center of the world"; it was exiled with the people wandering through the earth. His Light is, as it were, dispersed in countless sparks that have fallen into the darkness of a world nearing its end, and Israel can do no more than search for those sparks, collect them and raise them to their Divine Source, in order to rise up once more and, from the depth of continuous suffering, ascend to YHVH. This great spiritual effort is possible, in spite of the loss of the Sanctuary and of the Name *YHVH*, for three fundamental reasons declared by Tradition: in the first place, "the *Shekhinah* has accompanied Israel in its exile," so that God has not abandoned His people, but is close to each of the children of Israel that love Him; secondly, He has allowed the Israelites to replace the sacrifices by prayers and invocations—such as the invocation of His Name *YaH*; thirdly, the Torah still exists and it perpetuates the Tablets of Testimony formerly kept in the Ark of the Covenant, the Holy of Holies of the first Temple. For the children of Israel, who transcribed the Torah onto countless scrolls and carried it to the four corners of the earth, it represents the Dwelling of the *Shekhinah* itself, the Sacred House of the True Presence in Synagogues all over the world. Ritual readings, observation, intellectual study, and spiritual realization of the Torah—including the ensemble of canonical prayers, invocation of the Divine Names, contemplation of the Qualities (*Middot*) of God or the *Sefirot*, as well as other revealed modes of union with the One—are the means by which the Eternal Light can be actualized, the "sparks" raised up to their Supreme Source, and Israel united with the *Shekhinah* and, thereby with the Holy One, Blessed be He.

### The Inextinguishable Light of Sinai

Thus it is that God, after revealing Himself at Sinai in His redeeming Light, in the form of His Word, the Torah, has remained with His people through all the vicissitudes of history. After coming down from His glorious Throne to the summit of Mount Sinai and raising Israel from the foot of the mountain up to Himself in heavenly union, He descended again, clothed in the Torah, so that Israel too could descend and conclude the Covenant of Sinai on earth with Him. It was a Covenant of Love, sealed with the divine "kiss" which the children of Israel were given when the Voice of God

> spoke to each of them and asked: "Will you accept Me with My commandments [the Torah]? . . ." The Israelites answered: "Yes!" Then the [divine] voice [of the Torah] . . . kissed each Israelite on the mouth, as is written (Song of Solomon 1:2): "Let Him give me kisses from His Mouth. . ." (*Zohar*, 2:146a–b).

And although His unfaithful people have broken the Covenant many times, the Lord in His Mercy renews it whenever one of the children of Israel comes back to the Torah, in which God is truly present. To return to the Torah is to return to YHVH and seal the Covenant of Love again. This return to God through the mediation of the Torah is liturgically symbolized in the way the Israelites approach the Sacred Book to recite it or greet it during the procession in the synagogue where it is carried by the officiant: on these occasions, they kiss the scroll of the Torah in remembrance of the kiss of the Covenant and the union with God at Sinai; and they know that they must embrace it with their whole being and their whole life—which comes forth from the very Essence of the Torah—if they wish the Supreme Spirit and their own spirit to "unite until they are one," as it was on Sinai.

This holy union is possible today as it was in earlier times, not only because each soul is divine in its essence and because, coming from God, it sees Him and is united with Him before descending to earth, but also because the souls of the Israelites, including those of present generations, "were present at Mount Sinai and saw God face to face," being at one with Him before they returned to earth. Union is possible now as it was in the past, because each Israelite soul that has come down into this world "sees God again" at the moment of circumcision (girls participate in a passive way in the grace of this Abrahamic rite reserved to newborn males).

This "Abrahamic Covenant," which is renewed on the eighth day after the birth of a male child by circumcision, is the opening move on earth in the direction of the Divine Mysteries. According to tradition, the immortal prophet Elijah is invisibly present at this rite and bestows his spiritual influence on the child. This Abrahamic Covenant—described in Genesis 17:9–14—realizes the "union" of the sacred soul (*neshamah*) with the body animated by the vital soul (*nefesh*) which envelops the mental soul (*ruah*). At the moment when the body of the child is "marked with the sacred sign," he "sees God" and the real Presence, the *Shekhinah*, settles in his heart.[35] This "sight of God" is, in fact, no more than a transitory and passive "contact" with the Divine, but it suffices to place the *Shekhinah* into the soul; and the "Sinaitic Covenant," renewed by the male child at the age of thirteen by his formal admission to the ritual recitation of the Torah—which enables him to participate fully in the "Sacred Community of Israel"—opens up to him the possibility of realizing this first passive "vision" of God actively, and then of being united forever with the Presence which dwells both in his heart and in the revealed Book.[36]

---

[35] See *Zohar*, 1:94a.

[36] Here again, girls benefit by passive participation in the grace that is bestowed upon male children. The mystery of female participation in the graces granted to the male is explained in Judaism by the biblical revelation according to which man was created "male and female," that is, androgynous. Eve came from a "rib" of the androgynous Adam, who was then divided into man and woman. This is why each woman has a male sister soul, the graces of which she shares, either before marriage, in the absence of the male, or through a spouse who is only a "symbol" of the real sister soul. In marriage this participation can blossom on all human levels, its highest point being the union of two sister souls: "they will become one flesh," one soul, one spirit: they will be one in the image of the One. "On the day that God created man, in the likeness of God [who Himself possesses the two "masculine" or "paternal" and "feminine" or "maternal" aspects] made He him. Male and female created He them [or manifested them—His two aspects—in the form of an androgynous human being], and blessed them, and called their name Adam. . ." (Gen. 5:1–2); ". . . and God said unto them, Be fruitful and multiply and replenish the earth. . ." (Gen. 1:28). After procreation, male and female souls, united in heaven, descend separately to earth where they seek each other out. If these "sister souls" do not find each other in this world, the law of partici-

The active and unitive realization of revealed Truth begins with ritual admission to the Torah. This admission normally implies the assimilation of the letter of the Scripture, followed by the assimilation of its traditional exegesis and, of course, obedience to the commandments, all of which is intended to integrate the psychic and physical elements of man into the *Shekhinah*. The realization of the Truth is furthered by progressively more profound interpretation and application of the Revelation; and this spiritual intensification leads the elite, beginning with exoterism or the Talmud, up to initiation into the "Mysteries of the Torah," which can raise man up to the Sinaitic vision and supreme union.

We have seen to what extent "union" was given to the whole of Israel at Mount Sinai during the great theophany, and how this was crystallized in the first Tablets of the Torah. We saw them broken after the worship of the golden calf. Except for its elite, Israel was relegated from the domain of the "Mysteries," or esoterism, to that of the "Law," or exoterism. The law and its esoteric essence was concretized in the second Tablet of the Torah, which no longer communicates the Mysteries directly but hides them under the veil of the commandments and sacred history, to be unveiled by the assimilation and realization of the spoken doctrine in the two aspects of Talmud and Kabbalah.

Instead of being able to contemplate God through the transparency of the first Tablets of "heavenly sapphire," the Jew is required to strive humanly and spiritually to "break" the opaque stone of the second Tablets—at the same time as the "stone" in his heart—and to free the sparks of the Hidden Light.

In this task, each Child of Israel is, in virtuality, a visionary of God, a "part [or portion] of YHVH" Himself, a spark of the Supreme Sun, destined to flame in love and knowledge of his own Divine essence, until he becomes the "Great Light," the Infinite Light which radiates without cease from the eternal Sinai.

---

pation has a spiritual role; each feminine element possesses a masculine complement, and all Jewish souls are united in spirit, through their common *corpus mysticum*, the "sacred Community" that is realized on earth in the ethnic unity of Israel, which in itself is nothing but the *Shekhinah*, the real Presence of the One amongst His people. In celibacy—which is an exception in Israel—the "sister soul" can be found spiritually in union with the One.

# CHAPTER 5

# Torah and Kabbalah[1]

## I

All the light that God has given to Israel is hidden in the Torah (law, doctrine, or direction); the Torah is the crystallization and mysterious permanence of the Sinaitic revelation. On Sinai, the real presence of *Hokhmah*, divine "wisdom," appeared before the "Chosen People": "Israel penetrated the mystery of *Hokhmah*," says the *Zohar*,[2] and "on Sinai the Israelites saw the glory [or real presence] of their [divine] King face to face."

Now the descent or revelation of the first Tables of the Torah must be distinguished from the second. The *Zohar* teaches that the first Tables emanated from the Tree of Life, but that Israel, by worshipping the golden calf, "was judged unworthy of benefiting from them." Therefore, Moses, following the divine command, gave the people other Tables, "which came from the side of the Tree of Good and Evil." The law of the second Tables is in fact made up of positive commandments and negative precepts: "this is permitted, this is forbidden"; life flows from what is permitted, death from what is forbidden. The first Tables, says the Kabbalah, were the light and doctrine of the Messiah, the outpouring of universal deliverance, the source of eternal life on earth. The second Tables represented the indirect or "fragmented" manifestation of this light; *Hokhmah*, pure and redemptive wisdom, was no longer immediately accessible, but was hidden behind the "curtains" of *Binah*, the cosmic "intelligence" of God.

---

[1] Editor's note: This article comes from the first chapter of Leo Schaya's book *The Universal Meaning of the Kabbalah* (Hillsdale: Sophia Perennis, 2005).

[2] The *Sefer ha-Zohar*, "Book of Splendor," is composed of several treatises chiefly in the form of Kabbalistic commentaries on the Torah. Written in a rather distorted form of Aramaic, it claims to be the teaching of Rabbi Simeon ben Yohai (second century C.E.) but is generally accepted as the work of the Spanish Kabbalist Moses de Leon (thirteenth century C.E.); it is the most widely known and influential work in all the esoteric literature of Judaism. Regarded by many Jewish mystics as a collection of inspired texts, this book was often called the "Holy *Zohar*," and venerated equally with the Torah and its canonical commentary, the Talmud. (The quotations from the *Zohar* are, with a few exceptions, taken from the English translation by H. Sperling and M. Simon [London: The Soncino Press, 1949].)

The manifestation of the "uncreated Torah" had changed, but not its essence, *Hokhmah*. The real presence of divine wisdom dwells in the second manifestation as in the first, with the difference that in the second case man is prevented by *Binah* "from advancing his hand, taking from the Tree of Life, eating from it and living eternally." In order to gain access to *Hokhmah*, he must "cultivate the soil" of his soul by discriminating between good and evil and by practicing the divine law; and he must seek with great zeal the truth hidden behind the letters of the Scriptures.

Spiritual penetration of the Written Doctrine (*Torah Shebikhtav*) is facilitated by the Oral Doctrine (*Torah Sheba'al Peh*), the second being the explanation of the first. The two doctrines represent the two inseparable—and "simultaneous"—aspects of the Mosaic revelation. The Written Torah, or static "letter," serves as the unchanging point of departure for spiritual contemplation of revealed truth; such contemplation could not be effective without the traditional interpretation of the "letter engraved in stone"; the interpretation, the Oral Doctrine, is "like a hammer which shatters the stone," thus freeing from it the spiritual "sparks" of *Hokhmah* which dwells within it.

The simultaneous revelation of the Written and of the Oral Torah is based on the Scriptural verse (Exod. 20:18): "And all the people perceived the thunderings and the lightnings and the voice of the horn and the mountain smoking." The *Zohar* comments on this verse by saying that the divine words were imprinted on the darkness of the cloud that enveloped the real presence of God, so that Israel at the same time heard them, as Oral Doctrine, and saw them, as Written Doctrine; and the *Zohar* points out that every word was divided into seventy sounds—revealing the seventy fundamental interpretations of the Scriptures—and that these sounds appeared to the eyes of Israel as so many sparkling lights; and, finally, that the precepts of the Decalogue were the synthesis of all the commandments and that at the moment of their revelation Israel penetrated into all the mysteries enclosed in the Scriptures.

## II

The Oral Torah is the transmission, from generation to generation, of the mysteries and "interpretations" contained in the Written Torah as "sounds"—inspired words—or "sparkling lights"—spiritual visions. It follows that the saying in *Pirkei Avot* (1:1): "Moses received the Torah on Sinai and transmitted it to Joshua, Joshua to the elders, the elders to the prophets, and the prophets to the men of the Great Synagogue" refers both to the Written and to the Oral Torah.

When the Holy One, blessed be He, revealed Himself on Sinai in order to give the Torah to Israel, He delivered it to Moses in this order: the Scriptures [the written Torah]; the *Mishnah*, the Talmud, the *Haggadah* [which, taken together, designate the Oral Torah] (*Exodus Rabba*, 47:1).[3]

Every orthodox oral teaching, even presented as the personal expression of a teacher, goes back to the "sounds" and "lights" of Sinai. "Even what an outstanding disciple was destined to teach in the presence of his master had already been said to Moses on Sinai" (*P. Peah*, 17a).

Now the *Haggadah*, or the Haggadic *Midrashim*, form the link between Talmudic or public instruction and the secret teaching of the Kabbalah, the "reception"[4] of pure wisdom, intended for the spiritual elect of Israel. The *Haggadah* leads from the "service of God" to the "knowledge of the Holy One, blessed be He." "Do you desire to know the One who spoke and brought the world into being? Study the *Haggadah*, for by that you will arrive at the knowledge of the Holy One, blessed be He, and hold fast to His paths" (*Sifre Deuteron.*, 49:85a).

The Oral Doctrine interprets the Scriptures by four fundamental methods of exegesis that lead to the Kabbalah, to the sphere of *sod*, "mystery," or, as the Talmud calls it, *Pardes*, the "Paradise" of divine knowledge. The four consonants of the word *Pardes* (*PRDS*) themselves designate these four methods, namely: P = *Peshat*, the "simple" interpretation of the Scriptures, approaching it by all the ways available

---

[3] The Written Torah, in the strictest sense, consists of the Pentateuch (*Hamishah Humshei Torah*, the "five-fifths of the Doctrine," or five books of Moses) and, in the widest sense, also the Prophets (*Nebiim*) and the Writings (*Ketubim*). The Oral Torah includes, on the one hand, the Talmud, the public "Study" or exoteric commentary on the Scriptures (which consists, in the strictest sense, of the *Mishnah* or "Repetition" of the oral teaching, and the *Gemarah*, "Complement" or commentary on the *Mishnah*; and, in the widest sense, also of the *Midrashim*, rabbinical "Explanations," and the *Haggadah*, traditional "Narration"—historical and symbolic—which includes the non-lawgiving parts of the *Gemarah* and *Midrashim*); on the other hand, the Oral Torah comprises the Kabbalah, esoteric commentary on the Scriptures and initiation into the "Mysteries of the Torah."

[4] The word *qabbalah* (*kabbalah*), derived from *qabbel*, "to receive," "to welcome," or "to accept," has come to mean secret tradition.

to elementary reasoning; *R* = *Remez*, "allusion" to the many meanings hidden in every phrase, every letter, sign, and point of the Torah; *D* = *Derash*, the "homiletic exposition" of doctrinal truths, including all possible interpretations of the Torah; *S* = *Sod*, "mystery," initiation into *Hokhmah*, the divine wisdom concealed in the Scriptures and called, insofar as it is a teaching, *Hokhmath Hakabbalah*, the esoteric "wisdom of the tradition."[5]

This fourth method, which teaches the "mysteries of the Torah" (*Sithre Torah*), consists essentially of the spiritual exegesis and application of the first chapter of Genesis (*Maaseh Bereshith*, the "Work of the Beginning") and of the first chapter of Ezekiel's prophecies, containing the vision of the divine throne as a celestial "chariot" (*Maaseh Merkabah*, the "Work of the Chariot"). But besides these fundamental teachings concerning the emanation from the universal principle and reintegration into it, all of the Scriptures can serve as a point of departure for the exegetical method of *sod*. The ten *Sefirot*, "numerations" or determinations of the divine aspects, play the part in this method of supports for contemplation, whereas the divine names represent the operative means of uniting the Kabbalist—who invokes them according to initiatic rules—with the "light of Sinai," the real presence of God.

## III

As we have just seen, the Kabbalah is the doctrinal essence of the Torah, the repository in the heart of Judaism of the "mysteries hidden since the beginning of time." God has revealed these mysteries in many traditional or religious forms; but this diversity is only the expression of the infinite "richness" of the one truth and in no way affects its transcendent and immutable unity. The Kabbalah is therefore nothing but the Jewish branch of that universal "tree" of deifying wisdom which is discovered at the base of all orthodox ways leading to pure and integral knowledge. This knowledge of divine truth was given to the patriarchs of Israel and to their chosen disciples and was finally crystallized in the Sinaitic revelation. Moses transmitted it to Joshua, Joshua to the elders, the elders to the prophets, the prophets to the men of the Great

---

[5] The Kabbalistic method makes use for exegesis among other things, of the science of "letters" and "numbers." The three most highly developed procedures in this science are: *Gematria*, the science of the numerical value of letters; *Notarikon*, the science of the first and last letters of words; and *Temurah* the science of the permutation and combination of letters.

Synagogue, and they in turn communicated it to the members of the "initiatic chain" (*shalsheleth ha-Qabbalah*). This "chain" seems to have remained intact up to our day; it is destined, in fact, to link the wisdom of Adam with that of the Messiah. After the return of the people from Babylon, when prophecy in Israel had come to an end, it was Ezra who, in a definitive way, bequeathed the Torah with its laws and mysteries to the Jewish world. His spiritual legacy was guarded by the "men of the Great Synagogue," the *Sofrim* ("men of letters") and their disciples, the members of the "traditional chain"; the latter transmitted it to the *Tannaim* (first to third century C.E.), who were doctrinal authorities such as the great Kabbalistic masters, Akiba and Simeon ben Yohai. After the death of the last of the *Tannaim*, who was Judah the Holy (the editor of the written *Mishnah*), the oral doctrine was taught by the *Amoraim* (third to fifth century C.E.), those doctors of the *Torah* "who were no longer authorities in themselves" but repeated and commented on the traditions of the *Tannaim*; their supplementary teachings on the Torah were collected in the *Gemarah*, the "complement," or commentary on the *Mishnah*. The Rabbis or spiritual "masters" carried on the exoteric and esoteric teaching of the *Amoraim* by "expositions" (*Midrashim*) and initiation into the mysteries. At the time of the dispersion of the Jewish people throughout the world, the secret "chain of the tradition," while still connected with the Holy Land, travelled through the Near East and down to the Yemen; it went through Egypt to North Africa and across most of Europe. The teaching of the mysteries of the Torah and the practice of Kabbalistic methods were known through the entire Middle Ages and right down to modern times. The most important collections of the esoteric doctrine of Judaism are the *Sefer Yetzirah*, the "Book of Formation," the teaching in which is believed to derive from Abraham, and the *Sefer ha-Zohar*, the "Book of Splendor," on which the present exposition of the mysteries of Israel is chiefly based. These collections and other authoritative mystical treatises which have been preserved down to our day make it possible to discover the Kabbalah, the true "reception" of divine wisdom, behind the letters of sacred Scripture.

*Translated by Nancy Pearson*

# CHAPTER 6

# Creation, the Image of God[1]

*Lift up your eyes on high and see*
*who hath created these?*
Isaiah 40:26

## I

The principal aim of tradition in regard to the forms and laws of the cosmos is to connect all things with their first and divine cause and thus show man their true meaning, the sense of his own existence being likewise revealed to him thereby. Now, in the sight of the "One without a second," the whole of existence has no being of its own: it is the expression of the one reality, that is to say the totality of its aspects, manifestable and manifested, in the midst of its very infinity. Things are no more than symbolic "veils" of their divine essence or, in a more immediate sense, of its ontological aspects; these aspects are the eternal archetypes of all that is created.

If one understands creation in this way, it is revealed as a multitude of more or less perfect images of God or of His qualities, as a hierarchy of more or less pure truths leading toward the only truth; for if God is the first origin and highest prototype of creation, He is also its final end as Proverbs 16:4 testifies: "YHVH has made everything for his own purpose."

The only reality cannot do otherwise than work for itself and in itself. But in its pure selfness it does not act or wish for any; in it nothing whatsoever is determined, there is no distinction between subject and object, cause and effect, a god and a creation. In this non-duality, God rests in Himself, nameless and without any knowable aspect; it is only on this side of the supreme and supra-intelligible essence that His knowledge "makes its appearance," which is to say His intelligent and intelligible being, including His causal and efficient will. His being, His knowledge, His will, and His action are indivisible aspects of His ontological unity; this unity is not affected by any of His attributes nor by any of His manifestations: the One is what He is, knows Himself,

---

[1] Editor's note: This article comes from the third chapter of Leo Schaya's book *The Universal Meaning of the Kabbalah*.

through Himself, and works in Himself for Himself without becoming other than Himself.

His work is the manifestation of all the aspects of His being in the midst of His being itself. In sefirotic language it is said that *Keter*, the supreme principle, sees itself through *Hokhmah*, the "wisdom" or first irradiation, in the mirror of *Binah*, the "intelligence" or infinite receptivity. In this supreme mirror God contemplates His seven lordly aspects: *Hesed*, His "grace"; *Din*, His "judgment"; *Tif'eret*, His "beauty"; *Netsah*, His "victory"; *Hod*, His "glory"; *Yesod*, the cosmic "foundation" or His eternal act; and *Malkhut*, His "kingdom," or immanence. The irradiations of His aspects come together in the last *Sefirah*, *Malkhut*, as in a lower mirror, and there form the multiple picture of what in reality is only one; this image of the infinite and indivisible aspects of the One is the Creation.

All created things emanate from God's being and from His knowledge; they are essentially His ontological and intelligible possibilities, the "sparks" of His light, the "ideas" that spring from His "wisdom" or "thought" like so many spiritual and existential "rays."

> When God designed to create the universe, his thought compassed all worlds at once, and by means of this thought were they all created, as it says, "In wisdom hast thou made them all" (Ps. 104:24). By this thought [*Mahshabah*]—which is his wisdom [*Hokhmah*]—were this world and the world above created. . . . All were created in one moment [the eternal moment of divine action]. And he made this [terrestrial] world corresponding to the world above [the celestial and spiritual worlds which are themselves "pictures" of the infinite world of the *Sefirot* or supreme archetypes], and everything which is above has its counterpart here below . . . and yet all constitute a unity [because of the causal sequence of all things and their essential identity with the only reality] (*Zohar, Shemot*, 20a).

The knowledge of God is the *alpha* and *omega* of the work of creation. The world is born from the knowledge that God has of Himself; and by the knowledge that the world has of God, it is reabsorbed into Him. God made everything for this knowledge that unites to Him; all other knowledge is only an ephemeral reflection of it. When the world sees God—through man—it sees its supreme archetype, its own uncreated fullness, and is effaced in its essence, in the infinite. This cognitive and deifying act is the ultimate fulfillment of the creative work; it is for that—for Himself—that God created the world.

The knowledge of God does not depend on any science, but all human knowledge depends on it and derives from it. Receptivity alone, face to face with God, is enough, in principle, to obtain the influx of His light in which the spirit can see Him. A science, even a revealed science such as cosmology, is only a possible, not an obligatory way of searching for knowledge of God; it is a way which makes it possible to receive the truth through His symbolic "veils," that is through the worlds, on whatever scale. To see the eternal cause in cosmic effects raises a man above the illusions of the phenomenal world and brings him closer to reality. Baal-Shem[2] said:

> At times, man has to learn that there are an indefinite number of firmaments and spheres beyond, and that he himself is located in an insignificant spot on this small earth. But the entire universe is as nothing in the face of God, the Infinite, who brought about the "contraction" and made "room" in himself so that the worlds could be created in it. But although man may understand this with his mind, he is not able to ascend toward the higher worlds; and this is what is meant by: "The Lord appeared to me from afar"—he contemplates God from afar. But if he serves God with all his strength, he actualizes a great power in himself and rises in spirit, and suddenly pierces all the firmaments, and ascends beyond the angels, beyond the celestial "wheels," beyond the Serafim and the "thrones": and that is the perfect "service."

## II

When Baal-Shem says that "God, the infinite, brings about a 'contraction' and makes 'room' in himself where the worlds can be created," he is alluding to the Kabbalistic doctrine of *tsimtsum*. The term *tsimtsum* can be translated by "contraction," "restriction," "retreat," or "concen-

[2] Israel ben Eliezer, called Baal Shem (Master of the Divine Name), 1700–1760, was the greatest Jewish saint of the last centuries. He founded Polish and Ukrainian Hasidism; this term comes from the word *hasid*, the "devout" in regard to God. His movement developed toward the middle of the eighteenth century in Poland and spread into all the Slav countries; in the last (nineteenth) century it included nearly four million adepts.

tration"; it had been used in Jewish esoterism since Isaac Luria (1534–1572) to describe the divine mystery on which creation depends. "The Holy One, blessed be he, withdrew his powerful light from one part of himself, and left a void to serve as 'a place' for cosmic expansion"; it concerns "that part of the divine essence in which the light was weakened to allow the existence of souls, angels, and the material worlds."

Through this symbolic language, the Kabbalah then tries to express the mysterious genesis of the finite in the midst of the infinite. In reality, God, the absolute One, has no "parts," but an infinity of possibilities, of which only the creatural possibilities have the illusory appearance of separate forms; in themselves, these forms are integrated, as eternal archetypes, in the all possibility of the One. As for that "part from which the light has been withdrawn" to make room for the "place" of the cosmos, it is nothing other than the receptivity of God that actualizes itself in the midst of His unlimited fullness; this receptivity has a transcendent aspect and an immanent aspect: "above," it is identified with *Binah*, the "supreme mother," which is eternally filled with the infinite and luminous emanation of the "father," *Hokhmah*; "below," it is *Malkhut*, the "lower mother," or cosmic receptivity of God. The latter absorbs both the influx from the *Sefirot* of mercy which are luminous and overflowing, and the influx from the *Sefirot* of rigor which are "dark" or "empty"; that is why, in contrast to *Binah*, which is always revealed as filled with the infinite, *Malkhut*, or divine immanence, can take on the appearance of a dark void in the midst of its radiant fullness. Indeed, *Binah* is said to be "without all rigor, although rigor emanates from it"; while *Malkhut* receives the emanations of rigor together with those of grace, to produce and dominate the cosmos and hold it in equilibrium through the interpenetrating of the two simultaneously opposite and complementary influxes.

Now, the rigor which emanates from *Binah* is *Din*, "judgment" or universal discernment, the principle of concentration, distinction, and limitation; it produces *tsimtsum*, divine "contraction," in the heart of *Malkhut*, the plastic cause. Through the effect of *tsimtsum*, the divine fullness withdraws to a certain extent from the "lower mother," and awakens creative receptivity in her; the latter, when actualized, takes on the aspect of the void or "place of the world," ready to receive cosmic manifestation. Then, all created possibilities spring up from the existential seed which is left behind by divine fullness on its withdrawal—as a luminous "residue" (*reshimu*) in the midst of immanent emptiness. Thus, thanks to the divine "contraction" and to the void it brings about in the *Shekhinah*, the expansion of the world takes place;

and everything living in the immanence of God is a small world created in the image of the macrocosm: it is a void to which life is given by a luminous "residue" of the only reality, by a central and divine "spark" that projects onto it the reflection of some eternal archetype.

The Kabbalah expresses the same cosmogonical process in other symbolic terms as the *pargod* or cosmic "curtain." The *Idra Rabba Kadisha* (the "great and holy assembly," included in the *Zohar*) says of the "Ancient of Ancients" that "he draws a curtain down before him" through which His kingdom begins to take shape. This image and that of the *tsimtsum* not only point to the same truth but from one point of view also complement each other. Thus it can be said that God appears to "withdraw" Himself into Himself to the extent that He draws down a "curtain" before Him. The "curtain" hangs before Him like a darkness; and this darkness in reality is nothing other than His cosmic receptivity, which allows His reality to appear through it as a light. But His infinite light appears through the dark veil only in a "weakened," fragmented, and limited way, which is the mode of existence of the finite.

God is hidden in everything He creates, somewhat in the way that light is contained in the innumerable reflections that produce a mirage. To go further in this symbolism, it could be said that the desert where the mirage is produced represents the "void" or the "place" of the world made by *tsimtsum*, and the imperceptible screen on which appear the vanishing forms that lead the pilgrim astray represents the "*pargod*," which is the "curtain" or "mirror" of the *Shekhinah*. In fact, in the face of the "One without a second," creation—the apparition of a "second"—as well as the creative causes themselves, come to appear as existential illusions. That is why the Kabbalah brings in a third idea, in addition to those of *tsimtsum* and *pargod*, to define the nature of creation, namely, *habel*, "vanity," derived from Ecclesiastes 1:2: "Vanity of vanities (*habel habalim*), all is vanity!" The *Zohar* (*Shemot*, 10b) teaches on this subject:

> King Solomon, in his book (Ecclesiastes), treated of seven "vanities" [*habalim*, lit. breaths] upon which the world stands, namely the seven [sefirotic] pillars [of universal construction] which sustain the world in [causal] correspondence with [their first created effects] the seven firmaments, which are called respectively *Vilon, Rakiya, Shehakim, Zebul, Ma'on, Makhon, Arabot*. It was concerning them that Solomon said: "Vanity of vanities" says the *Koheleth*, "all is vanity" (Eccl. 1:1).

As there are seven firmaments, with others [existential planes such as the seven earths and seven hells] cleaving to them and issuing from them, so there are seven *habalim* and others emanating from these [and filling all creation], and Solomon in his wisdom referred to them all [as well as to their causes and archetypes, the seven *Sefirot* of construction].

The Kabbalah does not say that the seven cosmological *Sefirot* are illusions in themselves, for they represent the creative aspects of one and the same reality; nevertheless, insofar as they project the mirage of an existential multitude in the midst of its undifferentiated unity, they manifest as so many principles of illusion or causal "vanities."

But if they are considered outside of their relation with creation, they are integrated into absolute unity. Insofar as the One is looking at Himself alone, He does not go out of His supreme trifold-unity, *Keter-Hokhmah-Binah*; but when He wishes to contemplate the creative possibilities in Himself, He opens His "seven eyes" or *Sefirot* of "construction," projecting all the cosmic "vanities" through their gaze. "Vanity," according to Ecclesiastes, is to be found "under the sun"—a symbol of the *Sefirah Tif'eret*, which synthesizes the six active *Sefirot* of "construction"—and "is made upon the earth"; now the "earth" is one of the synonyms of *Malkhut*, the receptive and substantial *Sefirah* of cosmic "construction": there alone, in the divine immanence, the mirage of creation is produced, maintained, and effaced.

That is why "the beginning of Genesis," says the *Tikkune Zohar*,

is concerned only with the *Elohim* [principle of immanence] designating the *Shekhinah* [and not with the transcendental principle, YHVH]. Everything created, from the *hayoth* and the *serafim* [higher angels] down to the smallest worm on the earth, lives in *Elohim* and through *Elohim*. The creation is the work of the *Shekhinah* who takes care of it as a mother cares for her children.

The entire creation is an illusory projection of the transcendental aspects of God into the "mirror" of His immanence. The *Zohar* notes, in fact, that the verb *baro*, "to create," implies the idea of "creating an illusion." But although the creation is by nature illusory, it contains something of reality; for every reflection of reality, even remote, broken up, and transient, necessarily possesses something of its cause. Even if the creation is taken as being pure illusion, that something which is real and which constitutes its essence still cannot be excluded. Illusion itself is not just a real nothingness, for there cannot be any such thing. By its very existence it would no longer be nothing; illusion is a "mixture" of the real and the ephemeral or—in Kabbalistic terminology—of "light" and "darkness."

Creation is made from the "dark void" that God established in the midst of His luminous fullness and which He then filled with His existential reflections. This "dark void" is the "mirror" or plane of cosmic reflection, inherent in the receptivity of the *Shekhinah*. Indeed, receptivity is both emptiness and darkness; but while the nature of the void is transparency or translucence, that of darkness is opacity or contraction. Thus, when the creative influx of the *Sefirot* fills the receptivity of the "lower mother," its emptiness or translucence transmits the divine radiation in all the directions of the cosmos, while its darkness contracts, condenses, and becomes substance-enveloping light. In its first and celestial condensation, substance is still subtle and resplendent with the radiation that only lightly veils it; but it becomes opaque and gross in its corporeal and terrestrial solidification, which hides the light from above, just as thick clouds mask the sun.

The "vanity" of things consists in this darkness which fleetingly takes on the appearance of substance; however, substance becomes a mirror of truth when the forms it assumes are recognized as the symbolic expressions of the eternal archetypes, which are none other than the divine aspects.

## III

The ten fundamental aspects of God, or *Sefirot*, are manifested at first on the macrocosmic level in the form of ten heavens. The three supreme *Sefirot*, *Keter-Hokhmah-Binah*, are revealed in the three "heavens of heavens," the triple immanent principle: that is, *Shekhinah-Metatron-Avir*. *Shekhinah* is the immanence of *Keter*, the presence of divine reality in the midst of the cosmos. *Metatron*, the manifestation of *Hokhmah* and the active aspect of the *Shekhinah*, is the principial form from which all created forms emanate; *Avir*, the ether, is a manifestation of *Binah*;[3] it is the passive aspect of *Shekhinah*, its cosmic re-

---

[3] Sometimes *Avir* is identified, by metaphysical transposition, with the supreme principle, *Keter*; it is the substantial indistinction of the ether which, in this case, serves as a "symbol" of the indeterminateness of the absolute essence.

ceptivity, which gives birth to every created substance, whether subtle or corporeal. The triple immanent principle, *Shekhinah-Metatron-Avir*, in its undifferentiated unity, constitutes the spiritual and prototypical "world of creation," *Olam ha-Beriyah*.

The seven *Sefirot* of cosmic construction, *Hesed-Din-Tif'eret-Netsah-Hod-Yesod-Malkhut*, which emanate from the supreme trifold-unity, are the causes and archetypes of the seven created heavens; the latter issue from the three "heavens of heavens," as the constituent degrees of the "world of formation," *Olam ha-Yetzirah*. In this world all creatures undergo their first and subtle formation; it is situated beyond space and time, in the indefinite expansion and duration of the supra-terrestrial cosmos. *Olam ha-Yetzirah* is imperceptible to the senses and serves as a dwelling place for souls (before or after they pass through the earth), for angels, and for spirits.

The seven degrees of the "lower Eden" or earthly Paradise, inhabited by angels and blessed souls, are situated between the seven subtle heavens and the "seven earths" which issue from them, and they are further manifestations of the *Sefirot* of construction; in this intermediary world there also exist darkened inversions of the heavens, namely the seven hells or abodes of the demons and of the damned.

The corporeal universe that includes the "seven earths" is called the "world of fact," *Olam ha-Asiyah*; it is conditioned by time, space, the material elements and, from the microcosmic point of view, by sensory perception. The seven earths represent different states of our universe; they are described as "seven countries," hierarchically "constructed and all populated"; one of them, the "higher earth," is our own, which the six others resemble without attaining its perfection; in the same way their inhabitants possess only an incomplete or unbalanced kind of human form. On the other hand, the seven *Sefirot* of construction—which are also called the "seven days of [principial] creation"—are manifested in time in the following septenaries: the seven days of the week; the seven years forming a "sabbatical" cycle; the seven times seven years between one "Jubilee" and another; the seven thousand years representing a great cycle of existence; and the "seven times seven thousand years" ending at the fiftieth millennium, on the "great Jubilee," when the world is reintegrated into the divine principle.[4] Finally, the seven *Sefirot* of construction determine the six

[4] When the Kabbalah says that the total duration of the world is fifty thousand years, this figure should be taken as a symbolic expression of the law which constitutes its eternal foundation. This law resides in the mystery of the seven *Sefirot* of construction,

directions of space and their spiritual center, called the "Holy of Holies."

Man is the most perfect image of universal reality in the whole of creation; he is the "incarnated" recapitulation of all the cosmic degrees and of their divine archetypes. Indeed, through his spiritual faculties, psychic virtues, and corporeal forms, he represents the most evident symbol of the ten *Sefirot*, and his integral personality embraces all the worlds: his pure and uncreated being is identified with the sefirotic "world of emanation" (*Olam ha-Atsilut*); his spirit, with the prototypical "world of creation" (*Olam ha-Beriyah*); his soul with the subtle "world of formation" (*Olam ha-Yetzirah*); and his body, with the sensory "world of fact" (*Olam ha-Asiyah*). The law of man, the Decalogue, is a manifestation of the ten *Sefirot*, as is the "sacred community" of Israel, which is complete only when ten Jewish men come together.

The human being is the principal "point of intersection" of the sefirotic rays in the midst of the cosmos; through him, the divine riches are revealed in all their spiritual radiance and by the explicit symbolism of thought, word, forms, and corporeal gestures. Of all beings, man alone—in his perfect state—is the one being whom God causes to participate fully in His infinite knowledge; and through man's intermediary God brings everything back to Himself.


## IV


If creation is the image of God, cosmogony operates—just like a reflected projection—by the law of inversion or, more precisely, by inverse analogy. This law derives from the principle of divine "contraction," *tsimtsum*; by the effect of this "contraction," the infinite, *Ein Sof*, appears as *nekuda*, the causal "point" or supreme "center" of the finite, and the limits of the finite are extended, taking on the appearance of unlimited existence. The "contraction" or first inversion is reflected in the midst of existence itself, with the actualization of a multitude of "central points," each surrounded by an expanse, which serves both as "veil" and "mirror" for its contents. All these "centers" are connected among themselves and with the "supreme Center," by the "middle pil-

each one of which recapitulates, in its way, the whole. Thus one is faced with a unity of "seven times seven" or forty-nine sefirotic degrees, which are manifested through as many cyclical phases, its total duration being that of the indefinite existence of the cosmos; these forty-nine degrees issue from *Binah* and return to it. *Binah*, as their "end," is the "fiftieth" degree, or the supreme and prototypical "Jubilee."

lar" or universal axis, which is none other than the creative, regulating, and redemptive "ray" of the divine principle. The "spheres of activity," which surround their respective centers, are all the worlds, great and small, together making up the cosmic expanse; whether they appear as worlds properly so called, as beings, or as things, each of these spheres constitutes, therefore, the "envelope" or "shell" of such and such a "kernel" or existential point of departure, hierarchically included in the "middle pillar." Finally, every "point" representing the center, the immediate principle or prototype of such a world, itself functions as the "field of action" of a higher center, and so on up to the supreme Center, which is its own "sphere of activity" embracing all the others.

Thus we are confronted by an indefinite series of existential states, formed by as many "inversions" or exteriorizations of their respective points of departure. We have just seen that all these "points" are coordinated, in accordance with the law of causality, in the universal aids, which is the "descent" of the "supreme point" across the center or "heart" of everything; thus, each thing, in spite of its dependence on what is hierarchically above it, contains in its innermost depth the "center of centers," the real presence of God. Every created thing is in its own way a synthesis of the whole of creation, whether in a conscious, developed, or seminal mode and it includes in its essence the principle itself. The principle or universal and divine center is not comparable, therefore, to a point or geometric axis, localized in any one place:[5] it is the omnipresent medium.

Terrestrial man, "last born" of the creation, is the "lower point" where cosmogony stops in its creative inversions and returns toward the "supreme point." When this "inversion of inversions" starts to work in man, it is said that he is seized by *teshubah*, "conversion," "repentance," or the "return" to God; indeed, when man "performs *teshubah*," with all his heart, all his soul, and all his might, he ends by being absorbed into his pure and divine "self" and by integrating—within himself—the whole of existence in the cause. This is given to man by the mystery of his inner and universal person which embraces everything from the terrestrial "world of fact" to the very principle of the "world of emanation"; that is why the voluntary "return" of man to God involves the "return" of all the worlds. "Great is *teshubah*, for it heals the world.

---

[5] It should be made clear that if the divine immanent center is not "localized" in any one place—because it penetrates all—it nevertheless reveals itself by preference in a sanctified place or being; the latter thereby represents the living expression of the universal center.

Great is *teshubah*, for it reaches the throne of glory. Great is *teshubah*, for it brings about redemption" (Talmud, *Yoma*, 86a).

By his absorption in God, man actualizes universal deliverance in himself and thereby "hastens" cosmic redemption. The latter occurs when the entire multitude of subtle and corporeal manifestations has been exhausted in the midst of the two created worlds. At that moment the "grand Jubilee" takes place, the total and final deliverance;[6] it is the ultimate phase of *tsimtsum*, the "inversion of inversions," which is not only the "contraction" of the corporeal universe, but of the entire cosmic expanse: the "withdrawal" of the whole creation into its uncreated center and principle. Then, every immanent spiritual light regains its transcendent brightness, and every terrestrial and celestial substance is reabsorbed in the "higher ether" (*Avir ilaah*), which is eternally integrated into the infinite essence. Such is the return of the cosmic "image" to divine reality.

*Translated by Nancy Pearson*

---

[6] The definitive reintegration of the cosmos into the principle, which is to be accomplished at the end of "seven times seven millennia" or great cycles of existence, is prefigured by transitory restorations of the paradisal state, which take place every "seventh millennium" or "great Sabbath" of creation. One of these "moments of rest" or transient absorptions of the created into the divine immanence was the cycle of the *Fiat Lux*, the other, that of the adamic *Eden*; according to tradition, we are now at the dawn of a new cosmic Sabbath, the "Reign of the Messiah."

# CHAPTER 7

# The Great Name of God[1]

*For from the rising of the sun, even unto the going down of the same,*
*my name is great among the nations, and in every place*
*offerings are presented unto my name.*
Malachi 1:11–12

## I

The Judaic confession of divine unity, the scriptural formula of which—
the *Shema*—combines several names of God, represents for the Jew
one of the most important "means of union"; another central or direct
means of attaining union with God lies in the invocation of a single
one of His names.

The Tetragrammaton *YHVH*—the "lost word"—was above all others the "saving" name in the tradition of Israel; it is known as *Shem
ha-Meforash*, the "explicit name," the one, that is, of which every consonant reveals and symbolizes one of the four aspects or fundamental
degrees of divine All-Reality. It is also called the "complete name" and
the "synthesis of syntheses," because it includes all the other divine
names, each of which, by itself, expresses only one or another particular aspect of the universal Principle; it is also called the "unique name"
because it is for the "unique people," and more especially because of its
incomparable spiritual efficacy, in that it gives the possibility of direct
actualization of the divine Presence (*Shekhinah*). It was exactly on account of the direct outpouring of divine grace brought about by the
invocation of the name *YHVH* that the traditional authority in Israel
found it necessary, even before the destruction of the second Temple,
to forbid the spiritually fallen people to invoke, or even merely to
pronounce the Tetragrammaton. In his *Guide for the Perplexed*, Maimonides says on this subject:

> A priestly blessing has been prescribed for us, in which the
> name of the Eternal [*YHVH*] is pronounced as written [not in
> the form of a substituted name] and that name is the "explicit

---

[1] Editor's note: This article comes from the eighth chapter of Leo Schaya's book *The
Universal Meaning of the Kabbalah*.

name." It was not generally known how the name had to be pronounced, nor how it was proper to vocalize the separate letters, nor whether any of the letters which could be doubled should in fact be doubled. Men who had received special instruction transmitted this one to another [that is, the manner of pronouncing this name] and taught it to none but their chosen disciples, once a week. . . . There was also a name composed of twelve letters, which was holy to a lesser degree than the name of four letters; in my opinion it is most probable that this was not a single name but one composed of two or three names which, joined together, had twelve letters [representing their synthesis].[2] This was the name which was substituted for the name of four letters wherever the latter occurred in the reading [of the Torah], just as today we use the name beginning with the consonants *Alef, Daleth* [*ADoNaY*, "My Lord"]. Doubtless this twelve-letter name had originally a more special meaning than that conveyed by the name *Adonai*; it was not at all forbidden to teach it and no mystery was made of it in the case of any well-instructed person; on the contrary, it was taught to anyone who wished to learn it. This was not so in respect to the Tetragrammaton; for those who knew it taught it only to their sons and disciples, once a week. However, as soon as undisciplined men, having learnt the twelve-letter name, began thereafter to profess erroneous beliefs—as always happens when an imperfect man is confronted by a thing which differs from his preconceived notion of it—they began to hide this name also and no longer taught it except to the most devout men of the priestly caste, for use when blessing the people in the sanctuary; it was indeed on account of the corruption of men that the pronunciation of the *Shem ha-Meforash* had already been abandoned, even in the sanctuary: "After the death of Simeon the Just," so say the Doctors, "his brother priests ceased to bless by the Name [*YHVH*] but blessed by the name of twelve letters." They also say: "At first it was transmitted to every man [in Israel], but after heedless men increased in number, it was no longer transmitted save to men of the priestly caste and the latter allowed [the sound] of it to be absorbed [during the priestly blessing] by the [liturgical] melodies intoned by their fellow-priests."

---

[2] Like the eight-letter name: *YAHDVNHY*, which is the synthesis of the two names *YHVH* and *ADONAY* (My Lord).

Even after the destruction of the second Temple, however, invocation of the "explicit name" appears to have continued as the sacred prerogative of a few initiates who were unknown to the outside world and who served as the spiritual poles of the esoteric "chain of Tradition" (*shalsheleth ha-Qabbalah*). The function of this chain is the initiatic transmission—uninterrupted through the ages—of the "mysteries of the Torah," which include, among others, the mystery of the invocation of the holy names; except for the extremely restricted "elect" who retain the high function of guarding and secretly invoking the "complete name,"[3] no one may know its exact pronunciation. Although today Hebrew scholars render the name *YHVH* by "Jehovah" on the strength of the Masoretic vocalization given in the Bibles and prayer books, or by "*Yahveh*," in an attempt to imagine some way to pronounce it, these introductions of vowels into the Tetragrammaton certainly do not correspond to the authentic pronunciation, and that is why it is written here only in the form of the four consonants which are its known basis.

The prevailing ignorance as regards the pronunciation of the "explicit name" is certainly not the result of mere "forgetfulness" nor of a purely human decision arrived at some two thousand years ago. The suppression of the teaching and pronunciation of this name—by decree of the traditional authority—is so categorical and so radical in its consequences that it can be affirmed that God Himself has withdrawn this name from the mass of the people of Israel. However, such intervention "from above" expresses not only the rigor, but also the mercy of God, who foresaw that the human recipients of "the last days," no longer possessing the requisite theomorphism, would be shattered by the weight of His lightning descent.

The "complete name," therefore, cannot be the medium for deifying invocation in our age, which in the prophecies is called the "end of time"; this being so, we must consider its fragmentary substitutes without particular reference to the "twelve-letter name," the ritual use of which lasted only a short time. As we have seen, it had to be replaced by the name *Adonai*, which has been pronounced, ever since the destruction of the Temple, every time the Tetragrammaton occurs in the reading of the Torah and the daily prayers. It should be noted that the substitution of the name *Adonai* was decreed only in respect to

---

[3] According to the word of God addressed to Moses: "Thou shalt say unto the children of Israel: 'YHVH, the God of your fathers, the God of Abraham, the God of Isaac, and the God of Jacob hath sent me to you. This is my name for ever, and this is my memorial [*zikhri*, the invocation of God] unto all generations'" (Exod. 3:15).

the exoteric ritual, whether performed in the synagogue or in private, the aim of which is the salvation of the soul in a restricted sense, that is, within the confines of the ego; it does not have in view the invocation which is intended to raise man's being to the highest "place" (*hamakom*) which embraces all that is. The restriction does not apply to the "two-letter name," YH (ה׳), which is pronounced "Yah" (ה׳) and which is nothing other than the first half of the "name of four letters," YHVH (יהוה), from the very fact that it is directly substituted for the *Shem ha-Meforash*; this name must have the same esoteric potentialities as the latter, without, however, involving the danger of a too sudden actualization of the divine.[4] This even appears obvious, firstly because the "name of two letters" has the same transcendent significance as the Tetragrammaton, which includes it and further, in a more general way, because every divine name not referring to a particular quality to the exclusion of other qualities, refers to the being or essence of God.

## II

In order fully to grasp the spiritual significance of the name *Yah*, we have to return once more to the metaphysical basis of the name *YHVH*, of which it forms an integral part. Now comprehension of the foundation of the holy names, as they were revealed to the Jewish people, is connected with the comprehension of the ten *Sefirot* which themselves represent the "contemplative names" of God. Each *Sefirah*, although synthetically invoked through one of the letters of *YHVH*, has besides an "appellative name" of its own.[5] As we have already pointed out, *Ehyeh*, "Being," is the name proper to *Keter*, while *Yah* refers to *Hokhmah*, the first and undifferentiated emanation of Being; *Yehovih*—*YHVH* vocalized as *Elohim*, "Gods," is the name of *Binah*, for through it the All-Reality, YHVH, begins to be revealed in distinct emanations or

---

[4] In his commentary on the *Sefer Yetsirah* written in 931 C.E., Gaon Saadya de Fayyum says: "When it is said: '*YaH* has two letters, *YHVH* has four letters,' what is meant is that *YaH* is one half of the name *YHVH*. Now, the half was said everywhere and at all times, but the whole was only said in the Sanctuary in a particular period and at the moment of the blessing of Israel." And the Talmud (*Erubin*, 18b) states: "Since the destruction of the Sanctuary, the world need only use two letters" [as a means of invocation, that is, the two first letters of *YHVH*, forming the name *YaH*].

[5] In certain Kabbalistic schools, the proper names of the *Sefirot* themselves were used as "appellative names."

"Gods"; *El*, "God," or *Elohai*, "my God," signifies the personal God, or the *Sefirah Hesed*, divine "grace"; *Elohim*, "Gods" (the One in distinctive or separative manifestation), is the name of *Din*, "Judgment" or universal Discrimination; *YHVH* designates *Tif'eret*, "Beauty," or *Da'ath*, "Omniscience," the whole consciousness of God, uniting His transcendent aspects (the ideogram of which is *YH*) with His immanent aspects (symbolized by *VH*);[6] *YHVH Tsebaoth*, "YHVH of the Hosts," designates the principle of the affirmative cosmic powers, *Netsah*, divine "Victory"; *Elohim Tsebaoth*, "Gods of the Hosts," is the appellative name of the principle of the negative cosmic powers, *Hod*, divine "Glory"; *El Hai*, the "living God," or *Shaddai*, the "All-Powerful," is a synonym of *Yesod*, cosmic "Foundation," the eternal, creative, and redemptive act of the *Sefirot*; and *Adonai*, "my Lord," signifies the immediate and "maternal" Cause of the cosmos, *Malkhut*, the "Kingdom" of God.

Before explaining in a more precise way the spiritual content of the names *YHVH* and *Yah* by means of their sefirotic synonyms, we should consider for a moment the outer forms of these names, which have a special and very great significance, particularly from the operative point of view. In their form, which is abstract and non-comparative, these two names are indeed different from a name such as *Adonai*; their content on the plane of ideas is not to be found, as in *Adonai*, in a direct analogy with some notion derived from the created and, more particularly, from human qualities and activities, but above all in the symbolism of the consonants and of their vocalization and punctuation (so far as these are known). One knows that the letters of the Hebrew alphabet and the way to pronounce them in order to form one word or another are a part of the mystery of sacred language, in which every consonant and every vowel, as well as every punctuation mark, indicates the eternal archetypes or divine aspects. The "science of letters," which, thanks to the fact that every Hebrew consonant represents a definite number, is linked with the "science of numbers," gives cognitive and operative access to these mysteries; but what is important for us here is simply to show the origin of the sacred "ideography" or "ideophony" which creates names such as *YHVH* and *Yah* and is to be distinguished from the formation of names by analogy or comparison. Whereas comparison in regard to God has chiefly to do with His existential aspects—His relationships with the cosmos—

---

[6] Besides being applied particularly to *Tif'eret*, the Tetragrammaton is the "universal name" *par excellence*, the name which includes all names, all *Sefirot*.

the abstract and ideophonic names refer to His essential and integral aspects, as for instance, *Yah* to transcendence, and *YHVH* to His All-Reality. Ideophony makes it possible to synthesize the most diverse attributes in one short and harmonious name, as in the Tetragrammaton, and also to express the highest ontological realities, bordering on the ineffable, as in the case of *Yah*; thus he who practices invocation is given the possibility, on the one hand, of directly integrating all the apparent antinomies of the divine into the unity of the one Reality, and on the other hand, of going beyond every comparison or cosmic "image" of the divine, that is, of becoming absorbed in that which is without form, without limit, without any definition whatsoever. We do not mean to say that comparative names like *Adonai* are lacking in sacred ideophony; yet their operative significance lies primarily in their literal and analogical meaning and only secondarily in their ideographic and numerical meaning, whereas the abstract names are *a priori* beyond literal and comparative meaning, from which they are liberated like "kernels" from the "nutshell," in such a way that they cannot be perfectly understood discursively (even if their implied meaning of "to be" is known, as it happens for *YHVH* and *Yah*) without the help of the sefirotic symbolism of their letters.

Thus the letter *yod* (*Y* = י), in *YHVH* and *Yah*, is revealed on the discursive level as the sacred ideogram of the undifferentiated unity of the ten *Sefirot*—for the *yod* has the numerical value of ten—and in particular of the unity of the two supreme *Sefirot*: *Keter*, the "Crown," and *Hokhmah*, "Wisdom." The fine upper point or "crown" of the י designates *Keter*; it is the supreme "Root," the root of Being (*Ehyeh*) in the midst of Beyond-Being (*Ayin*), itself "symbolized" by empty space, the absence of any symbol. From this infinitesimal point, lost in the supra-intelligible, springs the first cognitive and active emanation, *Hokhmah*—the "Father"—shown by the thick, horizontal stroke of the י and ending in a fine descending line which symbolizes being as it turns toward its manifestation.

The second letter of *YHVH* and *YaH*, the *he* (*H* = ה), is called the supreme "Mother," synonym of *Binah*, the onto-cosmological "intelligence" of God, or His receptivity, which is the passive cause. This is the second emanation of *Keter*, the third *Sefirah*, which, together with the first two, constitutes the name *YaH*, the "transcendent half" of *YHVH*.

According to the *Zohar*, the union of the *yod* (the "Father" or active Principle, *Hokhmah*) with the *he* (the "Mother" or passive cause, *Binah*) produces the *vav* (*V* = ו), called the "Son." The letter *vav* has the numerical value of six, and in fact represents the metaphysical synthesis of "the six active *Sefirot* of cosmic construction": *Hesed, Din, Tif'eret, Netsah, Hod,* and *Yesod.* The *vav,* or "Son," is also called *Da'ath,* universal "Knowledge," Omniscience or Consciousness of all God's ontological emanations and cosmic manifestations, which "transmits the [sefirotic] heritage to the daughter."

The "Daughter" is the last *he* of the name *YHVH,* the symbol of the *Sefirah Malkhut,* "Kingdom"; this is the last of the seven *Sefirot* of cosmic "construction," namely, their passive aspect; in other words, it is the receptive cosmological principle, the uncreated and creative substance, fed by the "Son" or active mediator, from which it receives all the sefirotic emanations and projects them onto the cosmic plane.

This is how the divine "family" is constituted, identical with the "complete name": the "Father" (*Y*), the "Mother" (*H*), the "Son" (*V*) and the "Daughter" (*H*), the last being inseparable from the *vav* or universal Spirit, which would not be able to manifest its dazzling irradiation on the cosmic plane, without the covering (which is simultaneously protective and generative) of "pure and imperceptible Substance."

As we have just seen, there is a parallelism between the two first and the two last letters of the Tetragrammaton, its "transcendent half," *YH,* being reflected in its "immanent half," *VH.* The *yod,* or active ontological Principle, manifests in creation through *vav,* the active cosmological Principle, which, from the ideographic point of view, appears in fact as the prolongation downward, or a "descent" (ו) of the "supreme point" (י). Similarly, the two *he* of the *Shem ha-Meforash* express the one maternal and receptive Principle, seen first in its ontological aspect and then in its cosmic function. *Binah,* therefore, is called the "upper *he,*" or the "supreme Mother," and *Malkhut* is called the "lower *he,*" the "lower Mother" or the "Daughter." Let it be added that the letter *he* has the numerical value of five, so that the two *he* together, *Binah* and *Malkhut,* make the number ten; they are the two divine "coverings" which, in the passive mode, contain the entire group of ten sefirotic enumerations.

Finally, and still in relation to the same symbolism, the four letters of the name *YHVH* signify in particular the archetypes of the "four worlds" or fundamental degrees of divine All-Reality. The *yod* (*Keter-Hokhmah*) represents the archetype of *Olam ha-Atsilut,* the ontological "World of Emanation," which is nothing other than the infinite level of the ten *Sefirot.* The first *he* (*Binah*) symbolizes the archetype of *Olam ha-Beriyah,* the ideal "World of Creation," a purely spiritual level on which dwells the divine Immanence (*Shekhinah*). The *vav* (the unity of the six active *Sefirot* of cosmic "construction") is the archetype of *Olam ha-Yetzirah*, the subtle, celestial, and psychic "World of Formation," the cosmic level on which dwell angels, souls, and genii, on various planes. The final *he* (*Malkhut*), is the archetype of *Olam ha-Asiyah*, the sensory "World of Fact," the corporeal universe.

# III

Since the "complete name" was withdrawn from the Jewish people, they have used above all the following three names, which together replace the unity of the "four letters"; firstly the name *YaH* which integrates the two first letters—the "transcendental half " of *YHVH*; secondly the name *Elohim*, "Gods,"[7] which includes the six active causes of cosmic construction and represents divine immanence as first revealed in the subtle, celestial, and psychic world, symbolized by the *vav*; thirdly, the name *Adonai*—an exoteric replacement for the name *YHVH*—designates *Malkhut*, the final *he*, representing divine immanence as manifested particularly in the corporeal world.

But the name which concerns us here is *Yah*, the transcendental nature of which leads, in principle, to the state of *Yobel* (Jubilee), final "deliverance" (in the same sense as the Hindus understand the word *moksha*). This name seems to represent not only the "means of grace" *par excellence* of the final cycle of Jewish history, but also that of its beginning. In fact, it can be deduced from Scripture that *Yah* was the divine name used particularly by Jacob and his people, whereas *YHVH* was the "name of Israel" so long as Israel represented the "portion of YHVH." In the Psalms (135:3–4) it is said: "Praise *Yah*, for He is good! YHVH, sing praises to His name, for it is pleasant! For *Yah* has chosen Jacob unto Himself, and Israel for His costly possession," the possession, that is, of YHVH, according to Deuteronomy (32:9), "For the portion of YHVH is His people." And Isaiah (44:5) explicitly distinguishes between the "name of Jacob" and the "name of Israel": "One shall call himself by the name of Jacob (*Yah*) and another shall subscribe with his hand, unto YHVH and surname himself by the name of Israel." This distinction can be explained in relation to the history of Israel, all the phases of which are contained in three fundamental cycles: the first, or "patriarchal" cycle, from Shem to Jacob's victorious struggle at Pen-

---

[7] *Elohim*, in His exclusive relationship with the Chosen People, is called *Elohenu*, "our God."

iel with the divine manifestation; the second, or "Israelite," cycle, from Peniel, where Jacob and his people received the name of Israel, to the destruction of the second Temple; and the third, or "final," cycle, from the collapse of the priestly service and theocracy to the advent of the Messiah. Now Shem was the "seed" of the Jewish race; Abraham was the "father of many peoples" and Isaac the "sacrifice of oneself to God," while Jacob gave birth to the twelve tribes and the "mystical body" of Israel; so the latter is considered above all others as the patriarch of Israel and the people of God are called "Jacob" until the struggle at Peniel.

"Jacob was chosen to belong to *Yah*," that is, to be raised up in spirit to divine transcendence. But at Peniel there was a fundamental change in the mystical destiny of Jacob and his people, for it was said to him (Gen. 32:28): "Thy name shall be called no more Jacob, but Israel [he who struggles with God], for thou hast striven with God and with men and hast prevailed." In the language of the Kabbalah this means that after having "wrestled with God until victory"—absorption in the transcendence of *Yah*—Jacob prevailed also at Peniel over the divine manifestation called "man," that is, over the "descent" of God into humanity. This revelatory and redemptive "descent" is symbolized, in sacred ideography, by the *vav* (ו). According to the *Zohar* (*Terumah*, 127a): "When the *vav* emerges mysteriously self-contained from the *yod-he* (*YaH*), then Israel attains to his costly possession," its *corpus mysticum*, which is identical with the *Sefirah Malkhut*, represented by the last *he* of the Tetragrammaton. Thus, thanks to the sacred struggle of its patriarch, the people entered into possession of the reality hidden in the last two letters of the *Shem ha-Meforash*—the spiritual (*V*) and substantial (*H*) fullness of the divine immanence—and itself became, in its mystical body, the "final *he*," the "portion of *YHVH*."

It appears, therefore, that during the "Jacobite" phase the people were not yet the "possession of YHVH," just as YHVH—the "complete name" or actualized unity of divine transcendence (*YH*) and divine immanence (*VH*)—was not yet the "possession of Israel." The people of "Jacob" was centered on the transcendent aspect of God: *Yah*. In that cyclical moment and in that environment, spiritual realization must not necessarily have required initiation into the sacred sciences (symbolized by the *vav*), any more than it needed the priestly service in the sanctuary (represented by the last *he* of the Tetragrammaton). It was only when YHVH established the roots of the earthly center of His presence in the midst of Jacob's family—which thereby became "Israel," or the Chosen People—that the *vav* or "mysteries of the faith" had to be communicated to it through the intermediary of its patriarch. These mysteries, transmitted from generation to generation to the "children of Israel," were lost at the time of their servitude in Egypt, but were reborn and permanently crystallized in the revelation on Sinai; and the "final *he*" of *YHVH*, the pure and imperceptible substance of the *Shekhinah*, called the "Community of Israel," entered into the Holy Land and took up its abode in the Temple of Jerusalem, where the High Priest blessed all the people by the *Shem ha-Meforash*.

By the grace of the "complete name," the Chosen People long ago actualized the "kingdom of God" in the Holy Land, but on account of their sins the first Temple was destroyed and Israel had to suffer exile in Babylon:

> During the whole seventy years of exile [says the *Zohar, Shemot*, 9b], Israel had no divine light to guide her and, truly, that was the essence of the exile. When, however, Babylon's power was taken away from her and Israel returned to the Holy Land, a light did shine for her, but it was not as bright as before [when Israel received the emanation of the "complete name," which was broken up by the sins which also caused the destruction of the first Temple], being only the emanation of the "lower *he*" [the *Shekhinah*, or "mystical body" of Israel, identical with that of the second Temple], since Israel did not return to purity to be a "peculiar people" as before. Therefore the emanation of the supernal *yod* did not descend to illumine in the same measure as before, but only a little. Hence Israel was involved in many wars until "the darkness covered the earth" and the "lower *he*" was darkened and fell to the ground [so that Israel was forbidden to invoke the "complete name"] and the upper source was removed as before [as at the time of the destruction of the first Temple], and the second Temple was destroyed and all its twelve tribes went into exile in the kingdom of Edom.[8] The *he* also went into exile there.

[8] This is the name of ancient Idumea, situated between the Dead Sea and the Gulf of Elath. Now, according to the Kabbalah, Edom symbolizes sometimes the imperfect or unbalanced state of creation preceding its present state—the latter being an ordered manifestation of the *Fiat Lux*—and sometimes the idolatrous world of antiquity and, by extension, every materialistic, profane, or atheistic civilization, such as our own. The Bible (Gen. 36) identifies Edom with Esau, who sold his birthright—implying the right of the first-born, the major patriarchal blessing—for "a mess of pottage." Therefore, in the Jewish tradition, Esau or Edom is opposed to Jacob or Israel, as the animal and materialistic tendency of man is opposed to his spiritual and theomorphic tendency.

The *Shekhinah* was "decentralized," dispersed with Israel all over the world. It continued to radiate only through weak "reflections" wherever there was a community of orthodox Jews; nevertheless, its sacred "embers" have continued to flare up with an increased light and, sporadically, its true "grandeur" has been recaptured amidst the elect; these are the *Mekubalim*, or initiated Kabbalists, who—with certain exceptions, such as the "false Messiahs"—formed the "pillars" of the exiled people; but they appear to have become a negligible minority in the era of the triumph of "Edomite" civilization, this modern world of ours which has even been transplanted to the Holy Land itself.

According to the *Zohar*, David, through the holy spirit, foresaw the end of the last exile of Israel—identifying it with the very "end of days" in accordance with the prophecies—and revealed it in Psalm 102:19:[9] "This shall be written for the future [or the last] generation and a people which shall be created [in the time of the "end"] shall praise *Yah!*" The same prophecy is hidden in the verse from Malachi (3:23):

> Behold, I will send you Elijah [my God is *Yah*] the prophet [whose very name reveals which divine name was to be invoked during his pre-Messianic ministry and who represents, not only the type of the eternal master of masters, but also the type of all prophetic activity preceding and directly preparing the universal redemptive act of God's anointed], before the coming of the great and terrible day of YHVH.

Finally, the *Zohar* shows the exact reason why the name *Yah*—as in the time of Jacob—represents the means above all others of salvation in the period from the destruction of the Temple to the advent of the Messiah; and this reason becomes fully apparent in our day, when even the believing Jews can no longer live in freedom from the materialistic and profane organization of the modern world and so are unable any longer perfectly to carry out the Mosaic law, which presupposes as its "sphere of activity" either a theocracy or a closed traditional world.[10]

---

[9] This Psalm is called the "prayer of the unhappy man" whose "days vanish into smoke" and "are like a shadow at its decline." These phrases refer to the end of time.

[10] That the name *Yah* applies to the present time is made clear not only in the saying from the Talmud (*Erubin*, 18b) which we have quoted, but also in the following formulation, amongst others, which was used in the school founded by the great master Isaac Luria (1534–1572) and which shows that a spiritual method was based upon it as modern times approached: "For the sake of union of the Holy One, be He blessed, with his *Shekhinah*, in fear and in love, that the name *Yah*, be blessed, may be unified

Now, the *Zohar* (*Terumah*, 165b) says, referring to the name *Yah*:

> All is included in this name: those that are above [epitomized in
> the *yod*, the ideogram of pure transcendence, *Keter-Hokhmah*]
> and those that are below [hidden, in its principial and undif-
> ferentiated state, in the "upper *he*," *Binah*, the archetype of im-
> manence]. In it the six hundred and thirteen commandments
> of the Torah, which are the essence of the supernal and terres-
> trial mysteries, are included.

When this name is invoked sincerely, then it is as though one were
carrying out all the commandments of the Jewish religion. This name
compassionately forgives and compensates for the inadequacy of man
in relation to the divine will; that is why the psalmist and "prophet of
*Yah*" cried out: "In my anguish I called upon *Yah*; *Yah* heard my prayer
and set me in a large place" (Ps. 118:5).

> I shall not die, I shall live and declare the works of *Yah*. *Yah* has
> chastened me sorely, but he has not given me over to death.
> Open the gates of righteousness before me; I will enter into
> them, praising *Yah*! (Ps. 118:17–19).

God can and will save Zion, not by his rigor, but by his compassion,
when "time shall have come to its end":

> Thou wilt arise and have compassion upon Zion; for it is time
> to be gracious unto her, for the appointed time is come! (Ps.
> 102:13).[11]

---

in complete unification." It should be remembered that the phrase "to unify the name"
has the meaning, from the point of view of method: to invoke the divine name.

[11] "For He hath looked down from the height of his sanctuary; from heaven did YHVH
behold the earth to hear the groaning of the prisoner [of the civilization of "Edom"] and
to loose those that are appointed to death [represented by the anti-spiritual life of the
modern world]" (Ps. 102:19–20). "YHVH is full of compassion and gracious, slow to
anger and plenteous in mercy. He will not always contend, neither will he keep his anger
forever. He hath not dealt with us after our sins, nor requited us according to our iniqui-
ties, for as the heaven is high above the earth, so great is his mercy toward them that
hear him. As far as the east is from the west, so far hath he removed us from our transgressions. Like a father hath compassion upon his children [and *Yah* is precisely the
name of the divine "father," *Hokhmah*] so hath YHVH compassion upon them that fear
him. For he knoweth our frame; He remembereth that we are dust [and can in no way
change the cyclical conditions in which we are born and have to live]" (Ps. 103:8–14).

## IV

The name *Yah* does not have the "descending" efficacy of the *Shem ha-Meforash*; it lacks the direct influx of the *vav* or "living God," the spiritual brilliance of which cannot be borne without the presence of the "final *he*," represented at the same time by the Temple and its priestly service, the transmission and practice of the sacred sciences, the functioning of theocratic institutions, and the conformity of an entire people to the divine will. Yet the reasons for the substitution of the name *Yah* for that of *YHVH* are not only restrictive, for, since they are connected, from the cyclical point of view, with the "end of time," this end ceases also to be of a purely negative character; on the contrary, according to the prophets, it precedes a positive renewal, namely, the creation of "a new Heaven and a new earth"—more perfect than those now existing—as well as the creation of a new Jerusalem, whose "places shall be sacred to YHVH and will never be laid waste nor destroyed." By the very fact that it is the name to be invoked by the "last generation," *Yah* is also the name for the return to the "beginning," to the perfect original of all things. It is different from the Tetragrammaton, the efficacy of which is above all "descending," revelatory, and existential, for the name *Yah* is in fact the name of "ascent" and of redemption; it is exactly the name of the "beginning" and of the "end" of every ontological emanation and cosmic manifestation of God, while the name *YHVH* is the whole emanation, and the whole manifestation.

The "upper [or transcendent] *YHVH*" manifests through the "lower [or immanent][12] *YHVH*"; in the same way, the "upper [or ontological] *Yah*" manifests through the "lower *Yah*" or cosmic principle, which retains its transcendent nature everywhere, even "below." Therefore, if the "lower *YHVH*" represents divine immanence, the "lower *Yah*" then represents "transcendent immanence." The *yod* which, in its pure transcendence "on high" is the unity of *Keter* and *Hokhmah*, signifies "below," in the metacosmic center of the cosmos, the unity of the *Shekhinah* and its active aspect, *Metatron*, the cosmic intellect, the inner regulator of creation, while the following *he* represents its passive aspect *Avir*, "ether," the quintessence—the *he* having in fact the

---

[12] These two aspects of YHVH are revealed to Moses in the Scriptures (Exod. 34:6) when God shows him His attributes (*Middot*) beginning with the twice repeated: "YHVH YHVH El rahum wehanun. . ." (*YHVH YHVH*, God merciful and compassionate. . .).

numerical value of five—of the four subtle and the four coarse elements; it is, as we have already seen, the undifferentiated principle of all subtle, celestial, or psychic substance and of all coarse or corporeal matter. If the *Shekhinah*, insofar as it dwells in the prototypical and spiritual world (*Olam ha-Beriyah*), is the "transcendent immanence" of *Keter*, then *Metatron* is that of *Hokhmah* and *Avir* that of *Binah*; now just as the three highest *Sefirot* cannot be separated one from another, since they represent the one infinite and indivisible principle, *Yah*, so also *Metratron* and *Avir* must not be separated from the *Shekhinah*, of which they are respectively the active or regulating aspect and the receptive or generative aspect. These three immanent principles, undifferentiated, compose the "lower *Yah*," also called the "heaven of heavens," the inseparable unity of the tenth, ninth, and eighth heaven being "the one who rides in *Arabot*,"[13] (the seventh heaven): *Yah* is his name (Ps. 68:4). The "heaven of heavens," identical with the prototypical "World of Creation" (*Olam ha-Beriyah*) is the intermediary plane between the sefirotic "meta-cosmos" and the created cosmos which begins in the seventh heaven, *Arabot*, the "surface of the lower waters." The "lower *Yah*" is therefore "transcendent immanence," the mediator between pure transcendence and immanence in that it penetrates that which is created and is called by the last two letters of the "lower *YHVH*."[14]

When YHVH comes down from the highest "place" to the center of this world, He brings the secrets of all the divine and cosmic de-

---

[13] It should be remembered that the word *Arabot* for the seventh heaven, translated sometimes as "clouds," sometimes by "plains," "desert," or "heaven," is derived from the root *A-R-B*, which means something mixed. In fact, *avir*, the undifferentiated ether, that "pure and imperceptible air" of the eighth heaven, is manifested in *Arabot* in its first differentiation, in subtle substance or "water" which reflects the uncreated light or spiritual "fire" descending from the *Shekhinah* or descending from its universal irradiation, *Metatron*. Now the "surface of the waters" shines so brightly in the light of the divine "fire" that it seems to be utterly fused or "mixed" in it. This "mixture" or more precisely this "immanence" of the spirit in the subtle substance, which endures as long as the cosmos subsists, produces the whole of the seven "heavens," *Shamayim*, this word being composed of *esh*, spiritual "fire" and of *mayim*, substantial "waters."

[14] The *vav* of the "lower *YHVH*"—having the numerical value of six—symbolizes the *Shekhinah* which penetrates the first six of the seven heavens constituting the subtle "World of Formation" (*Olam ha-Yetzirah*). The "final *he*" of the "lower *YHVH*"—having the numerical value of five—represents *avir*, the quintessence, in that it has descended into the lowest heaven, there to dwell as the ether or undifferentiated principle of the four elements constituting *Olam ha-Asiyah*, the sensory or corporeal "World of Fact"; thus the "final *he*," dwelling in the lowest heaven, is the immediate and omnipresent center of our world.

grees, the "mysteries of the Torah" with their various graces; thus His "four letters" form what is pre-eminently the revealing Name, while *Yah* is enthroned on the "surface of the waters," where the "heavens and the earth" begin and end, that is to say the whole of the world "created in one single instant"; there it is that all creatures emerge from God and return to Him, in a single "cry of joy" which is nothing other than the "primordial sound." The name *Yah* is the revealed utterance of this inarticulate and universal "cry" or "sound" which manifests and reabsorbs the entire cosmos; it is the name of creative and redemptive joy. Thus the Psalmist (68:4) cries out: "Make way for Him who rides in *Arabot*: *Yah* is His name. Rejoice before Him!"

> What the verse tells us [comments the *Zohar, Terumah,* 165b], is that the Ancient of Ancients [the supreme Principle] rideth in the *Arabot* [that He is really present] in the sphere of *Yah,* which is the primordial mystery emanating from Him, namely the ineffable name *Yah,* which is not identical with Him [the Absolute], but is a kind of veil emanating from Him. This veil is His name, it is His chariot, and even that is not manifested [in the cosmos, but is enthroned on the "surface of the waters"]. It is His "great Name.". . . For when all is well with this name, then harmony is complete, and all worlds rejoice in unison.

*Yah,* in its immanent aspect, is the immediate cause of the cosmos, the cause that transcends all its effects: it remains hidden in the proto-typical world, as uncreated and infinite Light. But its irradiation pierces through its envelope, the ether, with a "sound" which is that of the revelatory, creative, and redemptive "word"; this is the "voice" of the Creator, the "primordial sound" which produces the two lower worlds, the world of subtle "formation" and the sensory world of "fact." It is the "inner voice" which sounds in the innermost depths of all things, so that it is said that

> the heavens declare the glory of God, and the firmament showeth His handiwork. Day unto day uttereth speech and night unto night revealeth knowledge. There is no speech, no language where the sound is not heard: their voice resounds through all the earth and their words go out to the end of the world. . . (Ps. 19:2–5).

## V

The "inner" (divine) voice is in truth the very light of God, an infinite light which, by refraction in the ether, has been transformed into revelatory, creative, and redemptive "sound." That is the universal "name" of God, inwardly His light, outwardly His voice, emitted spontaneously and in innumerable modes—articulate or inarticulate—by "everything that has a soul." This is why the Psalmist calls, not only to men, but to everything he sees as animated by the universal Name, to invoke that Name for the glory of the "Named" and the salvation of the world; he even goes so far as to exhort the "heavens of heavens" to join in the invocation, because it is from there, from *Yah* itself, that the voice in effect descends and resounds on the "surface of the waters"—where the created heavens begin—and is thence transmitted throughout the whole of existence, even to the earthly "abysses."

> Praise *Yah*! Praise *YHVH* from the height of the heavens! Praise Him in the heights! Praise ye Him, all His angels! All His hosts, praise ye Him! Praise ye Him, sun and moon! Praise Him, all ye stars of light! Praise Him, ye heavens of heavens and the waters that are above the heavens! . . . Praise *YHVH* from below on the earth, ye sea-monsters and all ye deeps; fire and hail; snow and vapors; stormy wind fulfilling His word; mountains and all hills; fruitful trees and all cedars; beasts and all cattle; creeping things and winged fowl! Kings of the earth and all peoples; princes and all judges of the earth; both young men and maidens, old men and children; let them praise the name of *YHVH*! For His name alone is exalted; His glory is above the earth and heaven. . . (Ps. 148:1–13).

For the prophet-king, the synonym of this universal praise is either the call to the "Great Name," *Yah*, or the call to the "Complete Name," *YHVH*;[15] this is why his exhortation begins with the words: "Praise *Yah*! Praise *YHVH*! . . ." This universal invocation is made up of the indefinite multitude of modes in which the divine voice chooses to speak through His "organs" which are His creatures; however, where

---

[15] The name *Yah* is the direct and synthetic articulation of the "primordial sound," whereas the name *YHVH* is the indirect and "explicit" articulation of the same; every holy name moreover represents a more or less explicit utterance of the divine voice, but to a lesser degree than the name *YHVH*.

all worlds, all beings, all things emerge directly from their first and divine unity, that is, from *Yah* "who rides on *Arabot*," there is only one mode of invocation, a single sound, a single cry, which expresses the joy of myriads of creatures in union with the One, the Unique. For where all beings issue from God is the place where all return to Him without delay; here, on the "surface of the waters," in the seventh heaven, *Arabot*, all that becomes separated from the Lord is separated only in order to be reunited with Him. In effect, His creative act and His redemptive act are experienced there as one and the same thing: thanks to separation from Him, union with Him takes place.

Beings emerge like so many "sparks" from the irradiation of the *Shekhinah*, that is to say of *Metatron*, the divine "sun" which contains them all insofar as they are immanent and unseparated archetypes. On leaving this luminous world, where all is one with God, the sparks become enveloped in the differentiated manifestation of *Avir*, that is, in the subtle "waters" of the seventh heaven, over the surface of which the "wind of *Elohim*" breathes and produces innumerable "waves." This wind is the cosmic spirit, *Metatron*, which sets *Avir*, the universal substance, in motion in order for it to produce subtle "waves," that is, souls each one of which is animated, illuminated, and inhabited by a spiritual "spark," a "living being." Each "wave" appearing on the "surface of the waters," whether issuing from God or returning from the depths of the cosmic "ocean," bursts into a single cry of joy and expands over the whole extent of the existential sea, the whole of *Arabot*.

Over this hovers the eighth heaven, *Avir*, the undifferentiated and translucid ether, which is wholly penetrated by the spiritual sun, *Metatron*, so that the whole firmament itself appears like a sun, illuminating the "surface of the waters" from one end to the other. As we have said, each "wave" produced on this surface instantly expands in the supreme invocation and becomes the whole of the indefinite expanse, the immense "mirror," which is so filled with divine light that it mingles—in essential "fusion" and not in qualitative "confusion"—with the "radiant Face" of *Yah* inclined toward it. Thus each being is simultaneously united with the whole of existence and with the infinite Source of existence.

But if it is said that this integral union takes place at the instant when the created being issues from uncreated Being, one may wonder how the being then descends to the lower heavens and down to this earth in the form of a separate individual or separate "world." This descent takes place as follows: The "fine upper point" of the created being, which is its spiritual or divine "spark," remains in the seventh heaven in constant fusion with the infinite Light of God, whilst its extension downwards—inwardly a spiritual vibration, outwardly a subtle "wave"—begins to expand on the "surface of the waters" and descend into the midst of the cosmic "ocean," there to follow its predestined path. The created being is similar in this way to a letter of the Hebrew alphabet, which, starting from its upper point, opens out first in the form of a horizontal stroke and is prolonged in one fashion or another in the direction of its lower limit. Just as letters, when pronounced, return to their origin—the silent world of the uncreated and creative Word—so do animate beings or subtle "waves," having issued with the "primordial sound" from the divine silence and having vibrated through the heavens as far as here below, then return from their terrestrial end-point toward their celestial point of departure, from which they have never been separated and which is itself in permanent union with God.

We have seen that all created beings without exception issue through the same invocation—the "primordial sound"—from their divine origin and return to it through this same "cry for joy." This simultaneously creative and redemptive sound is heard when the vibration of the divine Light falls on the first subtle and cosmic expanse of the ether, on the "surface of the waters." Each of the waves formed therein truly "bursts" with joy and is nothing but an exclamation of gladness which expands over the whole of *Arabot*; each being there is just a "voice" vibrating with bliss, joined with all the other "cries" in the one "voice of YHVH" which "resounds over the waters" (Ps. 29:3). This "voice," this first and universal sound, expressed simultaneously by the Creator and by all His creatures, is symbolized in sacred ideophony by the vowel *a*; this issues from the *y(od)*—from the unity of *Shekhinah-Metatron*—and spreads out indefinitely to the confines of the existential "ocean," through the *h(e)* or *Avir*, that "very pure and imperceptible air" coming from the mouth of God. Such is the genesis of the divine great name, *Yah*, of which it is said (Ps. 150:6): "Let everything that hath breath praise *Yah*! Halaluyah! [praised be *Yah*]."[16]

---

[16] In Revelation 19:6–7 there is also an allusion to the invocation of *Yah* by the "waters" of the cosmic ocean; St. John speaks of their "voice" which says *Hallelujah*! and of the redemptive joy which goes with the invocation: "And I heard as it were the voice of a great multitude and as the voice of many waters, and as the voice of mighty thunderings, saying: Hallelujah: for the Lord God omnipotent reigneth!"

    Let us remember that "Hallelujah" represents not only a form of invocation of "*Yah*" in Judaism, but also became, by way of the Psalms, a praise of God in the Christian tradition.

God, by invoking His creative and redemptive Name, causes everything that exists to issue from Him and to return into Him; by invoking His name with Him, every being is born from Him, lives by Him, and is united with Him.

*Translated by Nancy Pearson*

## CHAPTER 8

# The Worldview of the Kabbalah[1]

The Jewish doctrine called the Kabbalah had a strong influence on Friedrich Christoph Oetinger,[2] as has been the case with other Christian thinkers. That is why Dr. Schäfer suggested that I should talk to you about the worldview of the Kabbalah—not about how Oetinger's ideas relate to it, which will be left to other speakers, but about the Kabbalah as such. The fact that a Jewish worldview can have an influence on staunch Christians is not astonishing in itself, since Christianity is, historically speaking, based upon Jewish monotheism and messianism; I say "historically speaking" because the message of the Gospels as such is a direct, independent, and universal revelation. It is "universal" in contrast to the monotheism of Moses since the latter in its far-reaching form as a detailed law limits itself to the people of Israel, while Christianity—and Islam after it, though in a different way—has divested monotheism of this racial framework and made it accessible to all mankind. Christianity, in addition, has unveiled and universalized the innermost essence, the deepest hidden truth and doctrine of Judaism, as the following medieval saying confirms: *Quod Moyses velat, Christi doctrina revelat* ("What Moses veils, the teaching of Christ reveals").

In their Jewish form, the doctrine and truth veiled by Moses and unveiled by Christ are the Kabbalah. In their Christian form, they are the Gospels. The Kabbalah reveals the secrets of infinite All-Reality, which is the basis of all created existence and which is immanent in it; the infinite All-Reality both embraces and redeems creation. The Kabbalah shows how the divine All-Reality determines[3] itself within the

---

[1] Editor's note: This paper was read by Leo Schaya at a symposium on Friedrich Christoph Oetinger held in Stuttgart and Marbach, Germany, September 29 through October 2, 1982. Other notable speakers at the symposium were Antoine Faivre and Roland Pietsch. This is the first publication of this paper in English.

[2] Editor's note: Friedrich Christoph Oetinger (1702–1782) was a German author and translator whose numerous works dealt with theosophy (he was often called a "kabbalist"), Lutheran theology, and philosophy.

[3] Editor's note: This verb, to "determine," is used metaphysically to describe how something that is by definition uncreated, limitless, and eternal in its supra-worldly essence can assume lower forms of existence, including material manifestation. The author uses the noun "determination" in a similar way. For example, through a se-

transcendent being of man as the prototype and savior of all creation. This uncreated, transcendent, divine Man is, spiritually, All-Creation itself. Due to his immanent unity with the highest Reality, he unites all that is created, all the fallen sparks of God, with God, thus redeeming everything in Him. Under this aspect of savior, the *Adam ilaah* ("Transcendent Man") or *Adam Qadmon* ("Primordial Man") becomes the "Anointed" of God, the *Mashiach* (Messiah); in Greek, this is *Christós*. In this descent from the highest threefold-Unity, *Keter-Hokhmah-Binah*, "Crown-Wisdom-Understanding," the Kabbalah also calls Transcendent or Primordial Man *Bar* or *Ben*, the "Son." These are, in short, some of the most essential aspects of the Kabbalah, of the secret teachings of the "Old Covenant," and of "Messianism" and "Christianity" (i.e. the "New Covenant"), as delineated by the prophets.

These few elementary facts alone show how deeply the Christian doctrine, despite its independent revelation and message, is connected to Jewish doctrine; this connection is also confirmed by the unity of the Bible, which as sacred scripture includes the Old and the New Testament. Above all, the cosmogony, anthropology, and ethics stemming from the tradition of Moses, and, in the realm of liturgy, the Psalms, link the two religions. The Gospel often presents itself as an inner interpretation of the Hebrew Bible, as a spiritualized revelation of the old scriptural words; the Kabbalah had already been that, though as a secret oral tradition. The Gospel testifies to this tradition reserved for the spiritual elite and to the other oral teaching meant for the mass of the people when, for example, the Apostles say to Christ, "Why speakest thou unto them in parables? He answered and said unto them, Because it is given unto you to know the mysteries of the kingdom of heaven, but to them it is not given" (Matt. 13:10–11). Only by the spreading of the Gospels through the Apostles was it given to all to hear the secret interpretation of the words of Christ. This corresponds to the mission of the Messiah, of which the Kabbalah in its most famous and most voluminous literary expression, the *Sefer ha-Zohar* (the "Book of Splendor") says the following: "The Holy One, blessed be He, does not wish that the mysteries should be revealed to the world; but when the days of the Messiah come nearer, even children will discover the secrets of wisdom. . . . At such time our mysteries will be revealed to everyone" (1:118a).

ries of progressive "determinations," God enters the world of created forms. In many metaphysical and cosmological traditions, including that of the Kabbalah, a hierarchy of "determinations" or manifestations proceeds from the unseen realm of Beyond-Being through various progressions and intermediary stages "down" to our material and perceptible world.

Even though Christian doctrine springs forth from an independent revelation of the divine Mysteries, the above-mentioned inner bond between it and Jewish esoteric teaching still exists. Thus, through the Kabbalah, it can happen that certain Christian thinkers will rediscover this inner bond during times when Christian doctrine is no longer transmitted in its original, purely spiritual, and all-embracing essence; ideally, they may be able to experience and realize this essence anew. They are not, as they are often called, "Christian Kabbalists," but simply Christians who have rediscovered the real spiritual scope of their own religion, thanks to the Jewish inner doctrine. Only an orthodox Jew who is initiated and guided by a master of the Kabbalah is a Kabbalist, owing to the fact that the Kabbalah is the heart of the Jewish-mystical body, to which only the children of Israel belong. In the same way, only Christians are members of the mystical body of Christ, which also includes diverse means of grace for the realization of the Divine.

This is how we should regard those Christian thinkers who have studied the Kabbalah, some of whom are familiar to us through their writings. The thirteenth century Spanish mystic Raimundus Lullus (c. 1232–1315) is sometimes considered to be one of them, and he seems to have been influenced by the writings of the Kabbalist Ibn Gabirol and by the Neoplatonists; he was also an alchemist. However, from a purely Kabbalistic point of view, he cannot be considered as one of this group. It is not the same for Giovanni Pico, the Count of Mirandola, born in 1463, whom Johannes Reuchlin (1455–1522) in his book *De Arte Cabbalistica* calls the Christian discoverer of the Kabbalah. Reuchlin himself further developed this discovery in his book *De Verbo mirifico* and influenced, among others, his contemporary Heinrich Cornelius (1486–1535), who was called "Agrippa," and who himself left some Kabbalistic works. Around the same time, in Italy, two figures were engaged in the study of the Kabbalah: the Franciscan Francesco Zorzi (or Giorgi), who was called "Venetus" (c. 1460–1540), author of *De Harmonia mundi*, which was added to the *Index*;[4] the other Italian figure was Hieronymus Cardanus (1501–1576). In the Germanic regions, there was Theophrastus Paracelsus (1493–1541); in Holland, Jan Baptist van Helmont (c. 1577–1644). In England, there was Robert Fludd (1574–1637). Again referring to the German region, there was Jacob Boehme (1575–1624); later, there were researchers of the Kabbalah such as Baron Knorr von Rosenroth (1636–1689), who

---

[4] Editor's note: The "Index of 1559" was a list of prohibited books, compiled by order of Pope Paul IV.

translated some parts of the *Sefer ha-Zohar* and who was a teacher of the philosopher Leibniz (1646–1716). Some other names could be mentioned, but I think what has been said suffices to draw a picture of friends of the Kabbalah who have come to light since the Renaissance. Such an outstanding mind as Oetinger's must certainly figure among that number, along with some others of the eighteenth century.

But I would like to add a word about Boehme, even though Dr. Pietsch will give a detailed account of this extraordinary religious phenomenon. For me, Boehme seems to be a special case among the Christian "Kabbalists." Regardless of whether or not he read Paracelsus, or if he met a renowned Jewish personality, he undoubtedly received his knowledge, which reminds one of the Kabbalah, by direct inspiration from above. His worldview may be similar to that of the Kabbalah, but it seems to me that the origin of this worldview is altogether independent of it. It is as a Christian, no doubt, that Boehme refers at times to terms taken from the Old Testament. Boehme appears to me to be the living proof of this innermost link, one purely on the level of essence, between the Old and the New Testaments; however, this does not make the Christian revelation dependent upon the Judaic one. That is why it can be said that someone like Oetinger was, on the one hand, influenced by the Kabbalah and, on the other, by Boehme, among others.

As far as my actual subject, the worldview of the Kabbalah, is concerned, the time reserved for me will not be enough to deal with it comprehensively, of course. Therefore, I would like to point out that there are some recent books of Jewish literature, in German, which explain the major terms and the history of the Kabbalah extremely well. I am thinking here, above all, of the works of the recently deceased researcher of the Kabbalah Gershom Scholem; but also of Ernst Müller, and also Martin Buber, who focuses in particular on eastern Jewish Hasidism, the movement of the Hasidim (i.e. of the "pious") which emerged in the eighteenth century and which introduced the Kabbalah into the general religious life of the people. I will also take the liberty of mentioning what I myself have written in German about the Kabbalah, namely my book titled *Ursprung und Ziel des Menschen im Lichte der Kabbala*,[5] and my chapter about the Kabbalah in the collection of essays *Wissende, Verschwiegene, Eingeweihte* published by Herder (1981).

Incidentally, it is inevitable that I will repeat several things which I have already published since I will be dealing with basic, immutable,

---

[5] Editor's note: Published in English as *The Universal Meaning of the Kabbalah*.

and thus eternal truths. This will, however, not prevent me from speaking to you about some observations which I have not yet treated in my works—or not treated in sufficient depth—and especially about those observations which have been maturing in me recently. The Kabbalah is like a fountain of youth in which one is spiritually reborn again and again on one's inner path towards the infinite. It is not a cold or purely objective body of knowledge which stands impassably between the human subject and his goal of knowledge; it ultimately reveals itself like a whirlpool in a boundless sea which draws one in to the depths of the divine Essence. It is a way of experiencing God which I have been allowed to witness from the time of my childhood, since my parents and ancestors were all fervent Hasidim.

So, the Kabbalah is not only concerned with knowledge but with the inner experience as well: with faith, with intuition, and ultimately with the purely spiritual assimilation of the Truth. Similarly, the Hebrew word *qabbalah* [from which our term Kabbalah comes], meaning "acceptance," "assimilation," and "reception," is derived from *qibbel*, which includes the derivatives *qewal*, *qawal*, and *qabbal*, which mean: "in the face of," "face-to-face," and "in the presence of." It points to the direct spiritual reception of the pure Truth and Reality by someone who has immersed himself in the presence of God. In Judaism the prototype of this person is Moses, who first experienced the divine Presence by himself at the burning bush, and later, while surrounded by the people of Israel, again at Mount Sinai, where he not only received the basic teachings of the Torah (i.e. of the Jewish "doctrine" or the "law"), but above all a new self-revelation of God, as the Ten Commandments commence with the words: "I am the Eternal One."[6]

Before they were finally integrated into the letters of the Bible, Moses, as well as the whole people, saw the light and heard the words of this theophany directly at Mount Sinai. "All the Israelites saw the Glory [or the real Presence] of their Lord face to face on Mount Sinai," says the *Sefer ha-Zohar* (2:82b). The Bible (Exod. 20:18) does not say: "And the people as a whole *heard* the thunder," but that they "*saw* the thunderings, and the lightnings, and the noise of the trumpet, and the mountain smoking," and through these phenomena they encountered the real Presence of God. Each person assimilated the Presence of God

---

[6] Editor's note: The Hebrew word is *Anokhi*, and the reference is to the first two verses of Exodus 20. They introduce and lead up to the Ten Commandments. See Schaya's essay "The Sinaitic Theophany According to the Jewish Tradition" in the present volume, which deals extensively with this esoteric interpretation of those two verses.

to the extent that his spirit was receptive to it, which explains how numerous but still correct interpretations of the revelation could arise: from purely metaphysical interpretations to those fixed on the holy word or on the letters of the Decalogue. This is the origin of the *Torah Shebaʿal Peh*, the "oral teachings" of Israel, which finally crystallized in four major stages of interpretation, while the Lord imprinted the ten foundations of His revelation onto the Tablets of the Law, which is the origin of the *Torah Shebikhtav* or the "written teachings," the rich divine extension of which was captured word-by-word by Moses. These written teachings, as found in the Bible, were henceforth to become the secure foundation for all interpretations. These interpretations comprise the oral teachings, whose four fundamental stages, as mentioned above, are referred to by the Hebrew word *PaRDeS*, the "Paradise" of gnosis.

The four consonants of the word *PaRDeS* are the initial letters of the names of these four stages: *P* signifies the lowest stage, which is called *Peshat*, i.e. the "simple" but exact linguistic notion of the revealed words of God; *R* is *Remez*, the "allusion" or symbolism of these words; *D*, or *Derash*, is the public "exposition" of the scriptural interpretations and which derive not only from the two preceding stages but also from all logical conclusions that are in conformity with the Torah; and *S*, or *Sod*, is the "secret," the secret initiation into the *Hokhmah*, the revealed "Wisdom" of God, which in relation to its doctrinal transmission and spiritual reception is called *Hokhmat ha-Qabbalah*, the "Wisdom of the Kabbalah," the Jewish inner teaching or esoterism. The word *qabbalah*, i.e. "reception," has indeed become a synonym for this secret lore; but those Kabbalists or esoterists who are on this fourth and highest stage also base their interpretation of Holy Scripture on the three lower levels on which the Talmudists or exoterists move. The higher shall not exclude, but include, the lower. That is why the Kabbalists employ all of these levels of interpretation, thus serving the exoteric or the outer teaching as well. Because of this, they are often not only masters of the Kabbalah but also of the Talmud, the exoteric "study" of the Torah, and thus are the spokesmen of the oral tradition as a whole.

Moses is the exemplar here as well, since not only does the tradition of the Bible originate with him, but its fundamental esoteric and exoteric interpretation does too. This is expressed by the Talmud as follows: "Even what an outstanding disciple was destined to teach in the presence of his master had already been said to Moses on Sinai" (*P. Peah*, 17a). And in the Talmudic "Sayings of the Fathers" (1:1) it says: "*Moshe qibbel Torah mi-Sinai. . . ,*" "Moses received the Torah on Sinai and transmitted it to Joshua, Joshua to the elders, the elders to the prophets, and the prophets to the men of the Great Synagogue." This chain of transmission, which is said to continue uninterrupted until the end of time, is called, under its esoteric aspect, *Shalshelet ha-Qabbalah*, the "Chain of the Kabbalah." The Talmud itself points to this aspect when, in the sentence quoted above, it uses the word *qibbel* for Moses' reception of the Torah, from which the term *qabbalah* is derived.

But, as has been mentioned, not only Moses but all the people of Israel received the Torah at Mount Sinai in a direct and, at the same time, tangible and spiritual, outer and inner (or Kabbalistic) way. In addition, the *Zohar* (2:82a, 83b) recalls the following passage (Deut. 29: 14–15): "Neither with you only do I make this covenant and this oath; But with him that standeth here with us this day before the Eternal, our God, and also with him that is not here with us this day." From this it can be concluded, according to the commentary in the *Zohar*, that "the souls of all the past, present, and future generations of Israel— whether incarnate or not—were present there . . . and each [soul] . . . received the Words [and the presence of God] according to his degree [of spiritual receptiveness]." Thus, in its own way each soul of Israel has seen God at Mount Sinai—each soul, those of Jews today and the future, too. This is one of the most important teachings of the Kabbalah, coinciding with its conception that each soul, through its heavenly primordial birthing from God, has received the direct self-revelation of Him. This double teaching implies that every Jew who is faithful to the Law and who immerses himself completely in the Holy Scriptures (which are nothing other than the crystallized Sinaitic theophany)— that everyone—can experience inwardly the self-revelation of God once more. But, beyond being faithful to the Law, immersing oneself completely in the revealed Holy Scriptures means piercing through the exoteric or Talmudic interpretation of the Torah (i.e. through its shell) and reaching down through the depths to its kernel, its vital divine Origin. This must be done not only with one's thoughts but with one's whole being, and it is accomplished through the assistance of the Kabbalah's teachings and methods of realization.

Whoever reaches the kernel discovers this Origin in his own heart and realizes that it is in fact a Non-Origin, an infinite and absolute Essence, our own uncreated and eternal Being; it is what the Kabbalah calls *Ein Sof*, the "Infinite," or *Ayin*, the divine "Nothingness," Non-Being or Beyond-Being:[7] it is the pure, highest Truth and Reality. The perfect Kabbalist is he who has rediscovered this boundless Kingdom

---

[7] Editor's note: See note 7 on p. 13 above for more on the use of this term.

of God in himself. He "rediscovers" it because his created soul has arisen from it and because the innermost, uncreated Essence of his soul is eternally one with this infinite Realm. This divine Essence of man is the *Adam ilaah*, "Transcendent Man," or *Adam Qadmon*, "Primordial Man," whose primordial, uncreated, and infinite "body" reveals the ten fundamental aspects of God. These are the ten keys of universal knowledge in the Kabbalah, ten spiritual keys which in summary "enumerate" the innumerable aspects of the divine All-Reality, and which are therefore called *Sefirot* or "enumerations."[8]

The head of *Adam Qadmon* is crowned with the highest of the ten *Sefirot*, *Keter Elyon*, the "Supreme Crown," or Reality, which in any case is *Ayin*, God's absolute Beyond-Being, and *Ehyeh* or *Havayah*, His "creative Being." The right part of the head of this Universal Man is the second *Sefirah*, called *Hokhmah*, the non-dualistic and unifying "Wisdom" of God, the infinite self-knowledge of His one pure Being; the left part of the head is the third *Sefirah*, *Binah*, the discerning, universal "Intelligence" of God, which manifests itself through seven other creative *Sefirot*. The three highest *Sefirot* which are mentioned above are also called the "threefold brain" of Primordial Man, wherein the "Supreme Crown" is the "hidden brain," "wisdom" is the "right brain," and "understanding (or reason)" is the "left brain." This is the supreme threefold-unity, a pre-figuration of the Christian Trinity, while the following seven creative *Sefirot* still reverberate in the "seven spirits" of the Apocalypse (4:5) and in the "seven gifts" of the Holy Spirit. The six active *Sefirot* of those seven—which are also called the seven divine "Primordial Days"—are the two arms, the heart or the torso, the two thighs, and the procreative organ of Primordial Man, while the seventh or the last *Sefirah* (or the tenth, if one includes the three highest *Sefirot*) is the divine receptiveness, the female birth-giving aspect of Primordial Man; this can even be represented by his feet, which extend downwards so far as to reach into All-Creation.

In other words, this lowest aspect is the direct, divine source of creation, as well as the immanence of God therein—His all-present,

---

[8] Editor's note: See Figure 1, "The Tree of the *Sefirot*," at the end of this chapter. It may be helpful in visualizing the downward progression of these "enumerations." The interrelatedness of the *Sefirot* is also illustrated in the tree. Although the analogy used here is a "tree," it is quite easy to visualize the various aspects of the uncreated "body" of Primordial Man using the same figure. The reader may be able to imagine superimposing the schema of this archetypal "body" directly over his own, as if one were stepping into a suit of clothes; thus, the right side of the figure corresponds to the right side of the archetypal "body." This "tree," of course, proceeds downward from its crown.

all-encompassing Immanence which is, however, also transcendent at the same time, like the six other transcendent "*Sefirot* of cosmic construction."

The first of them is *Hesed*, the "grace," or *Gedullah*, the "greatness" of God, the right arm of the *Adam Qadmon*, which makes finite existence possible. The second is *Din*, the "judgment," or *Gevurah*, the "power" of God, which orders and rules existence; it is the divine Rigor or the left arm of Primordial Man. This is followed by a *Sefirah* radiating from the center, which, in its infinite love, harmonizes the rigor of God with His grace, and at times even makes the former disappear completely in the latter: This is *Tif'eret*, the "beauty," or *Rahamim*, the "mercy" of God, the heart or the torso of Transcendental Man—also called the "Son," who includes in himself all six of the active seven *Sefirot* of cosmic construction. The next *Sefirah* originating from Him is his right thigh, the grace of God flowing down into existence, *Netsah*, the "victory" of His unity amidst all duality of creation; while His left thigh, the rigorous primordial power, *Hod*, which denies all duality and separation, is the divine "Majesty." There is then a *Sefirah* located at the center, namely at the lower center of the transcendent primordial body, where it combines the latter two opposite *Sefirot*, as well as all the others mentioned before, in the one creative act of God: It is the sixth *Sefirah* of cosmic construction, *Yesod*, the procreating "foundation" of God's creation, or the procreative organ of *Adam Qadmon*.

Below this is, as mentioned above, the seventh or tenth (i.e. the final) *Sefirot*, which receives the "holy semen" from the divine procreative Organ, fashioning itself into actual creation. This is God's immanence, *Malkhut*—His "Kingdom," also called *ha-Maqom*, the divine "Location" of creation. In fact, as I have said, the Immanence of God is both transcendent and infinite, so that it not only resides in all things but also transcends them and includes them. Thus, creation exists within God's All-Presence, whereas the archetype of creation rests eternally in the divine Transcendence. Furthermore, we have just seen that this archetype is epitomized in the prototype of divine Primordial Man, who is our own innermost essence. That is why the Kabbalist—who realizes his true essence—knows All-Reality within himself; thus, he "knows" the totality of creation as well as God's immanence and His transcendence that are encompassed by All-Reality. He sees God both in and above the world; and he sees the world both in God's All-Presence and in the world's own archetypal divine Essence. He sees all things connected and united in the infinite One, who is at the same time above and below. The Kabbalist sees these things in the One, apart from whom nothing exists; and he sees, as said earlier, the One in all (in all possible worlds), whose fundamental essence is Him, the one and only God.

This is what the great thirteenth century Kabbalist master Moses de Leon (1240–1305) has expressed as follows in his *Book of the Pomegranate*:

> Each thing is connected with another down to the lowest link of the chain; and the true Being of God is both above and below, in the heavens as on earth: There is nothing apart from Him. That is what our sages teach when they say: "When God gave the Torah to the Israelites He opened up the Seven Heavens for them, and they saw that in reality there is nothing therein but His Magnificence. He opened up the Seven Earths for them, and they saw therein nothing but His Magnificence. He opened the Seven Abysses for them and they saw therein nothing but His Magnificence." Contemplate this and you will understand that God's Being is linked to all of these worlds, and that all forms of existence are in turn connected with each other as they originate in God's Existence and Being.

This universal connection of all created forms of existence (i.e. the connection affirmed by Moses de Leon of all things through God's immanent Being as well as His transcendent Being and Beyond-Being) is not part of some doctrine of emanation which maintains that every created or finite thing flows without discontinuity or interruption from the Infinite. It is also not a question of an immanentist pantheism, wherein God is reduced to the world in such a way that God is the world and the world is God. When a master of the Kabbalah says that there is nothing but God, this means the following: God is infinite and there is nothing outside of the Infinite—not even nothingness, since if it was, it would possess some kind of independent being, and whatever has being cannot be "nothing." In the depth of all that is finite there is—within it, outside of it, and above it—only the infinite and the eternal All-Reality of God. This is what the Israelites realized at Mount Sinai and what every Jew can realize anew. The eternal Origin, the uncreated Essence of all that is finite, is none other than the transcendent Essence of the Infinite; and from Its Immanence in creation, from Its Being which is here and now, all created existence is directly derived. Thus, there is something in the Infinite which can adopt the aspect of something besides Him, and this is the eternal possibility of the finite.

The finite is existentially different from the Infinite but in its innermost depth, beyond its createdness, it is nothing other than the Infinite; it is created to realize this, to testify to this, and to return thereunto.

That the created is different from the uncreated stems from an eternal primordial determination and from a natural discontinuity. This discontinuity places the Infinite between Itself and the finite, but at the same time the finite remains in its deepest essence one with the Infinite and is the Infinite itself. This is due to the fact that the Infinite as such cannot allow any discontinuity in its one, pure All-Reality. The Infinite is the uninterrupted continuity that penetrates and connects all discontinuity; It connects all that is interrupted and separated and finally reunites each thing with that thing's own, inner infinity. Where the finite has completely reached its own limits, it is again its own, infinite, divine Being. The sea has innumerable waves, and its water—its substance—is in each wave; but a wave is not the sea, so long as it has not dissolved back into it. That is why the Kabbalah strictly delineates within its doctrine of unity that which is Divine, Uncreated, and Infinite, from that which is finite or created; consequently, it also emphasizes the gulf between the Real and the illusory, between the True and the false, and between Good and evil. These distinctions are related to the above-mentioned and necessary—but still relative—primordial discontinuity, without which there would not be any creation at all; this discontinuity is the dark abyss mentioned in the Bible between the Creator and the shining cosmos which arises from His *fiat lux*. It is from this same primordial darkness that creatures endowed with free will and the capacity for discernment extract the negating power of their own conscious, psychic, and spiritual separation (and distance) from the divine Reality and Truth, from the only Good there is. This is evil, and this is not the primordial discontinuity or darkness as such, which necessarily lies between the Infinite and the finite; in itself, however, the primordial discontinuity is also the cosmic receptivity to the radiance of God or of the Sovereign Good Itself. That is why the Kabbalist does not treat his own inner darkness as something bad but rather uses it as a positive quality, as his own pure spiritual receptivity for God; he knows that God's Light here-below shines into the darkness and that the darkness is not dark in God Himself. It is God's self-receptivity, eternally and infinitely full of His Light; because, as the Psalms say, even "darkness hideth not from thee; but the night shineth as the day: the darkness and the light are both alike to thee" (139:12).

But to return to the onto-cosmology of the Kabbalah, it not only distinguishes between a single divine Level and creation—or between the uncreated Metacosm and a single created world—but it encapsulates the countless stages of All-Reality into four major worlds. The highest of these is *Olam ha-Atsilut*, the "World of the Emanation" of God or of His ten *Sefirot*. This transcendent emanation flows, symbolically speaking, towards the future creation as God's *Shekhinah* or creative "Immanence," which contains *Olam ha-Beriyah*, the "World of Creation"—not the created universe, but its uncreated divine Image that descends from on high. The *Shekhinah* or *Malkhut* is God's receptivity, in which His creative act occurs. It is the lowest of the ten *Sefirot*, which is also called the "lower Mother" since it receives all the archetypes of creation like rays of God's Being from the nine higher *Sefirot* and it manifests them through a natural, but—as was said—relative discontinuity in the form of creatures, and this within its very All-Presence.

The "divine Mother" does not push her child out of herself but gives birth to it in herself; and this child, creation, consists of *Olam ha-Yetzirah*, the seven-layered celestial "World of Formation" for all things, and of *Olam ha-Asiyah*, the likewise seven-layered "World of Actualization"[9] of God on the earthly plane. Hell is regarded as nothing but a dark inversion, a shadow-like extension of heaven: it is heaven's "drop-off" in the double sense of the word;[10] it is a seven-layered abyss filled with "dark fire," and it is not added as a special fifth world to the four worlds of All-Reality. As far as that discontinuity is concerned, the one that exists between the two upper and lower worlds, the Kabbalah calls it, among other things, *Tsimtsum*, "contraction," i.e. the inward contraction of the Infinite; it is in this way, so to speak, that the Infinite separates its uncreated "Upper Waters" from the created "lower waters." The term *Tsimtsum* refers to a merely relative interruption, since an absolute discontinuity—caused simply by nothingness—would limit or split the continuity of divine Eternity. That is why for Kabbalists the notion of "creation from nothing" (*creatio ex nihilo*) is just a symbolic way to express how God's causal Being determines Itself; in respect to the creative act, It "sheds the skin," so to speak, of its "Nothingness" or its non-causal, absolute Being, without, however, actually separating Itself from It. This self-determination of the creative Cause is at the same time the primordial Determination of all created

---

[9] Editor's note: This term is also translated as the "World of Events," the "World of Action," or the "World of Fact."

[10] Editor's note: The author used the German term Ab-fall to indicate both a rupture in, or a breaking away from, the heavenly realm, as well as refuse or rubbish.

things *in divinis*, which in turn has actual creation as a consequence. Thus the so-called "creation from nothing" (*Beriyah yesh me-Ayin*) is nothing other than this self-determination of creative Being and the initial determination that proceeds from it; it also includes the bringing about of created existence from within the undetermined, unconditional, divine "Nothingness" or Beyond-Being. This supreme "Nothingness" (which in truth is the "Nothingness of all Nothingness") has, so to speak, its shadow in that contraction or relative discontinuity that exists between the Creator and creation—but without affecting the hidden continuity between the two. The Kabbalah describes all this in the *Tikkunei ha-Zohar* (19) as follows:

> If you consider that the Holy One, blessed be He, is infinite and that He fills all, one understands easily that any idea of a creation would have been impossible without the *Tsimtsum* [the "contraction"]. How is one to pour water into a vessel which has already been filled to the brink with it? That is why the Holy One, blessed be He, has contracted the holy light of His being; not that He has diminished Himself thereby—may God protect us from such a view! Since He is All-Reality, He can neither increase nor decrease Himself; but since His light is of such purity and brightness that it outshines everything, even the highest angels. . . , the Holy One, blessed be He, so as to make possible the existence of the heavenly and earthly worlds, has withdrawn His overpowering light [symbolically speaking] from a part of Himself, like a man who constricts one of his appendages in order to stop the connection of the blood above and below that constriction. Thus, the tradition relating to the Four Worlds divides them into the World of "Emanation" [*in divinis*], the World of [archetypal] "Creation," the World of [celestial] "Formation," and the World of [earthly] "Action." The first two worlds or stages are filled with the holy Light of God; everything therein is God, and God is everything. The two other stages or worlds form that aspect of the divine Being where His light was weakened in order to make possible the existence of the souls, the angels, and the corporeal worlds. This is the aspect of God which our holy masters call by the name of *Shekhinah* [the divine "Immanence" or "Indwelling"]. That is why at the beginning of Genesis there is only mention of [God as] *Elohim*, who signifies the *Shekhinah*, since all that has been created, . . . down to the

lowliest earthworm, lives in *Elohim* and through *Elohim* [who is at the same time the creative and universal indwelling of God]. . . . Creation is the work of *Shekhinah* [or "Indwelling"], and It takes care of it as a mother does her children.

There is so much that I could say about the worldview of the Kabbalah but I shall have to limit myself to what the time given to me allows. I would like to finish with a reflection on those Kabbalists who attain to the highest spiritual goal. Their lives of orthodoxy are filled with the invocation of God's Name, with contemplation upon and attainment of knowledge of the ten *Sefirot* (i.e. fundamental aspects of God) which, taken together, comprise each individual's own archetype and being. Thanks to all of this, these Kabbalists inwardly raise themselves up to the highest stage of All-Reality, to the highest *Sefirah*, *Keter Elyon*, the "Supreme Crown," the supreme darkness of the divine "Nothingness." They reach as far as the *histaklut el ha-Ayin*, the "contemplation of Nothingness," of complete nothingness, which requires not only the temporary annihilation of human thinking, but for *bittul ha-yesh* or "cessation of existence" to occur in the mind. It is a spiritual death, which basically allows one to return immediately to the still living body, from the supreme "Nothingness," or Beyond-Being, back to being. Following this immersion—which is no longer simply an intellectual one—in the knowing All-Being, there is an inner renewal and the great enlightenment of one's temporarily annihilated human existence.

As has been mentioned, the so-called "contemplation of Nothingness" transcends all intellectual activity; it is no longer "intellection" and even less a mental consideration or meditation: It is our entering into the eternal identity of our pure, highest Self with the Nameless and Inexpressible, which eludes all knowledge. Thus, here it is no longer a question of the oneness between a knower and something known, but of the entry or re-entry into our own divine Nothingness. It is the Nothingness that is greater than all that is: it is the unconditioned Real, the supreme Light; it is the supra-knowable Essence of all knowledge, wherein all affirmation and also all negation, every distinction between being and Non-Being, is transcended. The human being is here no longer a human being and indeed can no longer even be detected. He has been reconverted into his own, supra-human and nameless Essence, into the divine Supra-Essence, which rests in Itself without any expression, revelation, or existential manifestation. Of it the *Zohar* (1:254b) says: "The supreme Wellspring does not gush forth onto the world, so long as man is hidden in the [divine] Nothingness." I would like to add that once a man's being emerges from this, his highest Nothingness, it is itself the primordial source of all light and grace: the one, pure, radiating Being; the infinite beatific Self-consciousness of the One; the divine, all-encompassing Self-knowledge. Man's divine Being beholds Itself as the one, pure, primordial Source of all existence, and It beholds existence as Its own spiritual Universal "Body"; and from within Its supra-human Universal Body It beholds how Its own first human body forms itself, how Its celestial Form becomes the earthly-paradisical body. This earthly body stands inside the spherical All-Body; and at its center, in the heart of the body here-below, lies hidden the root of his All-Being, the supra-human Universal Man. The fully realized Kabbalist is this Universal Man, in whose heart-center the earthly body reveals itself first as a "column made of intangible ether" filled with Light (see *Sefer Yetzirah*, 2:6). It is the body of "man made in the image of God," the Primordial Man in Eden; he is resurrected in his supernatural beauty, his heavenly perfection; he is a pure holy container of God amidst a motionless sea of Light, which is his spiritual All-Body itself. Filled with, and submerged in, the universal Light, his earthly body radiates light as from a sun, rays of grace from the All-Body. Its Light totally fills his "emptiness": There is nothing but Light in him and around him.

His being has emerged like the dawn from the supreme Darkness of his supreme Nothingness and has enlightened everything with its overflowing brightness. His divine Spirit, his heavenly Soul, and his earthly body—all is Light within Light. No thoughts flow to his mind yet, which is like a bowl that is pure and open to the Infinite and which is thus filled with Its celestial brilliance. There is no desire yet in his heart, only the infinite love of God which breaks forth overwhelmingly from this its earthly source of grace to sanctify everything. This man's existence is still one with his pure, highest Being and all his activity still rests in his pure Self-knowledge and All-knowledge.

This "Nothingness," which is more than all that exists, is the inexpressible Supreme Beatitude; Being, which is both itself and everything that exists, is infinitely beatific Self-affirmation: To be conscious of one's own universal plenitude of Being is to recognize oneself as the Light that fills all. Whoever *is* the Light Itself, is the clarification of all knowledge. He does not think and act unless the self-determination of his pure Being, the divine Will hidden in him, should move his reason and resolve. Then the mortal man, who has recovered his inner immortality with the help of God, thinks and acts in the light of God

Himself. In all things he sees the Light of God, the divine primal Fountain of all light and life—as happened to the singer of the Psalms, who exclaimed: ". . . with Thee is the fountain of life: in thy light shall we see light" (Ps. 36:9).

But only the Kabbalist who affirms and follows the revealed truth and the will of God, who has been initiated and is guided by a true master, and who has chosen the path that in principle can lead him through all levels of the Spirit up to the highest (the path on which he has been liberated from the illusion of the ego and has been enlightened and fulfilled by the divine Self), may return from the "Nothing of Nothingness" to everything that exists, and from everything that exists back to the All-High, Only-True, and pure Real, to the one, transcendent Essence of all religion. Because, says Malachi (2:10), "Have we not all one father? Hath not one God created us?"

This unity is also manifested in the fundamental aspects of the spiritual cycle of man. Does not, for example, the aforementioned incarnation of man, which descended from the divine Nothingness or Beyond-Being, testify to the mystery of incarnation, which is reflected, among other possibilities, in Oetinger's sentence: "Corporeality is the end of the works of God"? But does not the return of the corporeal to God also show that the end of God's works is, at the same time, God—that His workings are like a cycle from Him to Him? It is, in any case, a spiritual-corporeal and a corporeal-spiritual realization of the Divine. Thus, one encounters the Old and New Testament realism of Oetinger, who bridges the gap between non-corporeal idealism and godless materialism. In doing so, his total *theologia emblematica* and *philosophia sacra* corresponds to the two lower and upper stages of the fourfold scriptural interpretation of Israel; and his understanding of the *cognitio centralis* reflects the unified all-encompassing sefirotic vision that is central to the Kabbalah, which leads to the highest self-knowledge and to All-Knowledge, to the supra-light-bearing, supra-existential Essence of man and of all creation—to that Him whom, St. John says, "no-one has ever seen."

*Translated by Gerhard Giesse*

## Figure 1: The Tree of the *Sefirot*

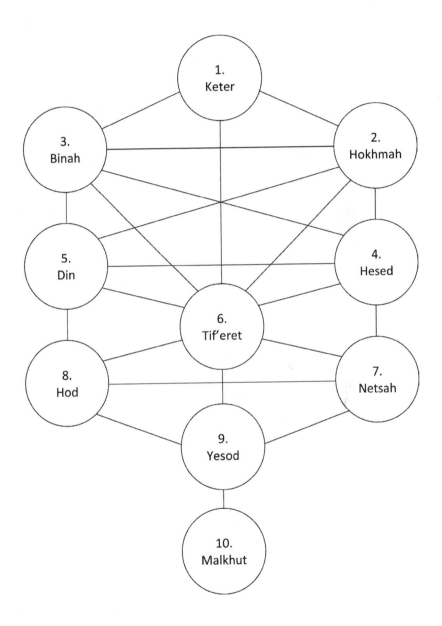

# CHAPTER 9

# Contemplation and Action in Judaism and Islam[1]

### Definition of Contemplation and of Action

Before considering contemplation and action in their specifically Judaic and Islamic modes, it may be useful to define them generally in the light of what Judaism and Islam have deeply in common and of what they share, each in its own fashion, with universal spirituality. We shall take the Latin etymology of the words "contemplation" and "action" as the point of departure since we shall use these terms throughout our exposition, and the etymological analysis will serve at the same time as a bridge between the Western terminology and that of the two Semitic traditions we are going to consider. So let us first recall that the word *contemplatio* is composed of *cum* and of *templum* and that *templum* denotes in general a consecrated place, but signified in particular the square imaginarily traced in the sky by the rod of the augur, the Roman priest whose function it was to interpret the omens read in the flight of birds, amongst other things, within this celestial field of observation.

But contemplation of the sky has not been restricted to the soothsayer looking for signs: men of all peoples and all times have raised their eyes towards the celestial vault, their gaze transfixed and ravished by the myriads of marvels there revealed to them. And men everywhere have been transported from this natural *contemplatio caeli* to spiritual *contemplatio Dei*, as in the case of the prophet Isaiah, who cried out: "Lift up your eyes on high and behold who has created these [things]" (Is. 40:26). In this verse from the Scriptures, apparently so simple, the word "who" (Heb.: *mī*) signifies, according to the esoteric exegesis of the Kabbalah, the supreme and supra-intelligible Essence; "to create" (*bara*) is a synonym of "cause to emanate"; and "these" (*eleh*) are all the intelligible aspects of the divine Being, the eternal archetypes of all things.

But *contemplatio Dei* does not follow naturally from contemplation of the heavenly phenomena alone. Thus Cicero, in *De Re Publica* (6:15) expanded the idea of *templum*, hence of *contemplatio*, to the

---

[1] Editor's note: This essay first appeared as a chapter in *Traditional Modes of Contemplation and Action: A Colloquium held at Rothko Chapel, Houston Texas*, edited by Yusuf Ibish and Peter Lamborn Wilson (Tehran: Imperial Iranian Academy of Philosophy, 1977).

magnitude of omnipresent Divinity, of "God, who has for his domain (*templum*) all that you behold" (*Deus, cujus hoc templum est omne quod conspicis*). And the Object of contemplation, at once supreme and universal, revealed itself in the Koran: "To whatever side you turn, there is the Face of *Allāh*" (2:109). Then the Prophet passed on to his Companions, and through them to all the faithful, in the definition of spiritual "virtue" (*al-ihsān*), the almost unconditional principle of contemplation. This contemplation does not start solely from apparent things but also from those that we do not see; it is dormant within our mind itself, before the mind reveals to us the light of its divine Object: "Virtue (*ihsān*) consists in your worshipping (or serving) *Allāh* as though you were seeing Him, and if you do not see Him, He sees you." This, finally, is the contemplation of Him whom man would not be able to see by himself, but who sees man and sees Himself through man by making the supra-human spirit of man participate in His own Vision; the Omnipresent One contemplates Itself in man through the "eye of the heart," until the earthly contemplator is able to say, with al-Husayn ibn Mansūr al-Hallāj: "I saw my Lord with the eye of my heart and said to Him: 'Who art Thou?' He said: 'Thou!'" Spiritual contemplation has as its object divine Reality, which is likewise the pure Essence of man: it leads to knowledge of the only Truth, the only Reality, which is also the true knowledge of self, of our divine Self. Muhammad said: "Who knows himself knows his Lord."

Contemplation can be the outer action of a sensory gaze attentively fixed on a given physical object. It can also be an inner fixation of the mind on an object which is imagined or remembered, or seen in a dream or in a prophetic vision; and it may be the essentially supra-mental or non-discursive concentration on an idea or abstract truth, on the Infinite, the Absolute, God, or on the reality itself of such an idea, on its direct or purely spiritual revelation. Furthermore, contemplation may be outwardly sustained by a physical symbol and, at the same time, inwardly supported by a meditation such as to deepen the truth or reality of the symbolic object by reflection; and finally, contemplation may pass from these two concomitant and peripheral activities to the very heart of its own action, namely to a direct and purely spiritual vision of the essence of the object or symbol. But passage from outer- to innermost contemplation by way of meditation of an eminently discursive nature may also be bypassed by the simultaneity or the complete coincidence of the sensory perception and the supra-sensory spiritual knowledge of an object. The object perceived will be the revelation, at once formal and supra-formal, of its own divine essence: its form will be "transparent" to the point of unveiling immediately its spiritual content, and so the "eyes" of the body and of the soul will participate directly in the contemplation of the "eye of the heart," which is the "eye of God" in man. The contemplative will thus see his object with the "eye that sees all": he will see God, the Omnipresent, in the object and he will see Him in the sensory mode and in the spiritual mode at the same time; as the prophet Muhammad promised believers: "You will see the Lord with your eyes." This promise was already fulfilled on Mount Sinai where the elect of Israel "saw God, and did eat and drink" (Exod. 24:11) and will be fulfilled again at the end of time, when "they will see with their eyes the return of YHVH[2] to Zion" (Is. 52:8).

In the sense in which we are using the term, contemplation is, on the physical plane, distinct from any kind of search through the senses that has no noble motive or object related to a spiritual source; and it is distinct on the psychic plane from that kind of reflection that has nothing to do with Truth or divine Reality. Spiritual meditation, though it may serve as an entry to pure contemplation, is distinct from this contemplation since its function remains discursive, i.e., attached to the indirect and dual knowledge of the mind. When meditation reaches its aim, it arrives—to quote the Kabbalah—at the "end of thought," at the entrance to pure contemplation, which is a supra-mental or non-discursive concentration of the spirit on the supra-formal and universal essence of the cognitive object, seen until then under the veil of its form, whether bodily or intellectual. Stripped of this form, the spirit of the object meditated upon is directly open to the spirit that contemplates it, and they become totally united. And in this union, the contemplator knows that his spirit and the spirit of all things are not two, but eternally and infinitely one: the "Spirit of Spirits," the One without a second.

But let us return again to meditation, which occupies an important place in the *via contemplativa* for, in the broadest sense, it already begins with the study of the revealed doctrine. Right away, this inclines the mind to God-centered reflection. In this state, the mind is no longer absorbed in its perception of the interplay between inner and outer phenomena; such perception does not reveal to the mind the ultimate causes or purposes of those phenomena. But in studying the revealed doctrine, the person is no longer absorbed in conjectures of purely

---

[2] Following the Jewish custom, we write this divine Name without vowels. It has been forbidden to pronounce it for more than two thousand years.

human reasoning, but is seeking to understand, with the help of traditional teaching, the reality of things. His sense of reality and of truth deepens, thanks to the gradual steps of traditional exegesis. This starts with the accurate assimilation of the literal meaning of the Holy Scriptures and ends with the spiritual knowledge of the divine Mysteries. Indeed, the revealed doctrine, with the sacred exegesis, teaches a man all he needs in order to realize the All. It enables him to know what the world is and what the human being is and—in some measure—what God is. It enables him to see how visible things reflect the invisible Reality, which is at once transcendent and immanent. He becomes capable of connecting these things in his thinking, and he comes to understand how they interact with their divine Source, which is our own Essence. Starting from there, a man can, in principle and on the microcosmic scale, integrate the multitude in the One. Thought, itself multiple and symbolically coextensive with All-Reality, instead of being dispersed and lost in a multitude of phenomena that it would have been unable to interpret correctly without the aid of sacred doctrine, discriminates between the illusory aspects and their profound reality; it brings all things back to their real and divine causes, even to the "Cause of Causes." This is the domain to which meditation belongs, the mental integration of the multiple in the One.[3]

Because every transcendental Cause, every eternal Archetype of a thing is an Aspect or a Quality or a Name of God, it also offers a direct access to the One. Having conformed his actions and his qualities to those of the One and having mentally brought all things back to Him, it is then sufficient for a person to meditate on one truth, one Aspect, one Quality, and one Name of God for his thought to fulfill the whole of the work assigned to him: to bring the thinking being back, step by step, with all its content, to the end of all thought, which coincides with the birth of one's being in the Spirit, which contemplates, in the depths of the heart, the supreme Principle of all things. This gradual raising

---

[3] Such is at least the scheme of the mental integration of the many in the One encountered in most traditional methods, whatever their particular modes of regarding and approaching the Absolute. As for these modes, they vary even within the boundaries of one tradition. The assimilation of the doctrine is achieved in different ways: more or less analytically; in the most elaborate sapiential forms as well as in the form of extremely simple teaching; by a teaching addressed above all to the "brain" or aimed directly at the "heart." In an extreme case, it may be that a single revealed word, a single truth, converts a man, awakens him to the Spirit. But here one must not forget that this one word of truth is heard normally in a traditional ambience saturated with doctrine, criteria, and landmarks given by a revelation and informing the whole of the life of a sacred community.

of thought towards absorption in the Spirit is symbolized, amongst other things, by the pyramid, whose volume diminishes and is "concentrated" progressively with the approach to the apex, where it finally vanishes in the "highest Point," without extension, infinite.

In other words, the broadly extended base of the pyramid of reflection or theocentric meditation represents the study of the revealed doctrine, whose richness reflects the incommensurable plenitude of the aspects of the divine All-Reality. On such a basis, the mental and spiritual integration of the multiple in the One begins; this integration becomes concentration or pure contemplation inasmuch as the thought unceasingly relates all things to their divine archetypes and, by way of consequence, to the "Archetype of Archetypes," to the Unique Essence of all that is. Arriving at the "highest Point," the thought can no longer reflect, meditate, expand as such, and is of necessity effaced in its pure inner light, which is the supra-human Spirit, the divine ontological cognitive Essence of man. This is the Essence of all things revealing Itself in highest contemplation, in uninterrupted intuition; this is the direct seeing of Him who alone sees and who alone is seen. Thanks to meditation—beginning from the study of the teaching and leading to pure contemplation as its end—a man thus realizes, on the mental plane, the microcosmic reflection of the divine and universal integration of all things in the One. In that way, he participates really in God's unitive work; he fulfills his function of mediator between creation and Creator. This cosmic or objective aspect of meditation is, by definition, inseparable from its subjective aspect relating to the individual himself, who, by meditating, integrates himself with all things in the One: it is only through his own union with God that the one who meditates is able to unite all with Him. If he is dominated by things, if his mind is attached to their ephemeral nature, lost in their multiplicity, he is unable to make their real synthesis, to realize their union in the One, for he is unable to make the union in himself: he remains distracted, dispersed, lost in the multiple.

This is why true meditation depends on discrimination between the only Truth, the only Reality, and the multitude of illusions: it demands that the mind, the entire being of a man withdraw from, be detached from, the unreal side of things, and that he reflect with all serenity on their real nature, their causal linkage, their relationship with the first Cause and their essential identity with It. And a man becomes the better able to detach himself from unreality by meditating sufficiently on the profound reasons for this detachment, on the illusory nature of things; he is the better able to attach himself to the only Truth and only

Reality by meditating deeply on the divine Aspects, Names, Qualities, Perfections, and seeking to assimilate them "with all his heart, with all his soul, and with all his strength": then the divine objects of meditation cease to be merely thoughts and become the virtues, the spiritual qualities proper to the man who meditates.

After having studied the sacred doctrine, after having reflected on it, meditated on the connections and the essential unity of man, the world, and God, the one who meditates—normally under the direction of a spiritual master—then reduces the host of objects of meditation to a few fundamental themes that summarize them, or even to one universal theme, one sacred formula, one divine Name, that embraces all the aspects of Reality. He concentrates all his thought upon this theme, this truth, this access to the One, and his concentration has to be such that meditation "flows in an uninterrupted fashion, like oil into a jar." Every distraction, everything that is opposed in the man to the truth he is meditating, must be eliminated with the help of this truth itself, and, if need be, of a supplementary "means of union" used at the same time as meditation, such as the invocation of a divine Name or the repetition of a revealed formula, identified in either case with the Truth or Reality meditated. This combination of meditation and invocation or repetition of a divine Name or revealed formula has its sufficient reason in the Real Presence of God, who dwells both in the heart, or spirit, of the man who meditates, and in the Word issued from the divine Mouth so that it might be voiced by man here below.

But neither meditation nor invocation should be considered as acting automatically, like the formulas in the practice of magic. We have seen that these spiritual exercises demand not only a knowledge of the sacred doctrine, but unflagging discrimination as well, between the True and the false, the Real and the unreal, and, *ipso facto*, attachment to the One. This attachment is itself not only correlative to detachment from the illusory multitude but also to realization of the One in the multiple, of His Perfections in the soul, of the virtues and right, godlike attitudes of man. Thus not only must a man try to assimilate the truths upon which he meditates, he must also apply them in daily life. The *via contemplativa* and the *via activa* have to be inseparably united; contemplation itself is nothing other than the first and innermost of all activities and all activities have to be determined by it. If a man acts against the truths he is meditating or contemplating, this contradiction will reappear in his meditation or contemplation in the form of an obstacle to the actualization of the real Presence, to spiritual union with the One. If, on the contrary, his way of acting and behaving in outer life is in harmony with the content of his meditation or contemplation, it will prove to be a strong support for his inner activity, a "throne of union": thought crystallizes into virtue and right attitude; truth through thought becomes flesh; the spiritualized flesh is not opposed to thought but sustains it and becomes one with it in contemplation of the only Truth and the only Reality; the being in which body and soul are united contemplates Him until it becomes one with the One Being.

In this contemplative union, the individual and formal unity of body and soul must disappear and be transmuted into the infinite, universal, supraformal Unity of God or of the divine Self in man. All that has form, whether body or soul, all feelings, thoughts, reflections, meditation—all that must cease. Meditation has played its part positively in the return to mind of the Truth which man, in essence, *is*; man had seen this Truth, therefore, before his birth here below and it is deep within him. This role of meditation implies the negation of every negation of the Truth, the elimination of all that is opposed to the inner Light, to pure Reality, to our own Self. Having played this part, meditation ends by denying itself insofar as it is in turn a screen which veils the Reality. Thought is transmuted into "being" through meditation, and now the individual, formal, human being remains to be transformed into divine, universal, supra-human Being, which comes about through pure, non-discursive, supra-mental contemplation. After the final negation of all that is not the "One without a second," effected during meditation, there is the eternal, direct, and total affirmation of the One. . . . This is the contemplation that is proper to It, wherein the one contemplating and the one contemplated are, at last, only one. Any state of pure contemplation is a participation in this supreme state of *contemplatio Dei*; and the participation that comes about every time the individual being is effectively absorbed in its own universal center, in its heart where God dwells, can become total, complete identification, full union, the final and highest spiritual state, pure Being. A state of contemplation—a state of grace, light, and union—can therefore be at first a passing result of spiritual efforts, and this passing result can be repeated and intensified before it is definitively acquired. Actually, if one considers contemplation in its broadest sense, i.e., as the *via contemplativa*, it represents the entire way of effort or spiritual exercise in the direction of the spiritual state properly so-called: contemplation is the entire path from natural perception to divine inner vision, from meditation to suspension of thought in pure concentration of the mind. It is the entire process of passing from the cognitive act to real union with the essence of the object contemplated, from all action to pure Being, and, by that very fact, it is the transition from all movement and all form to the immovable, supra-formal Reality of the Infinite. This contemplation is the bridge between the multiple and the One. It realizes profound continuity in the midst of discontinuity, the very One in all multiplicity, the One contemplating Himself in the multiple.

In fact, contemplation of the One is the unitive Act of the One Himself: His beatific Act of Being, Knowledge, and Union. In contemplating the One, man actualizes in himself His Being, His Knowledge, His Unity: man fully comes to realize being through Being, he knows all that is knowable through Him who alone knows; he is unified within himself and united to the One through the One. Perfect contemplation is the act wholly in conformity and essentially identical with Being; it is the act by which man realizes his being, and in his being, pure and supreme Being. It consists in "eating from the Tree of Life and living eternally" after bodily death. And this applies to every act that, as in contemplation, is truly in conformity with the divine Being, His Reality, and His Will. But of all these acts—whether of prayer, meditation, invocation of a divine Name, repetition of a revealed formula, visualization of a sacred symbol, or love of one's neighbor, any of which can easily be a direct support of contemplation—it is always contemplation itself (or, from another angle, the contemplative "effort," i.e., pure, non-discursive concentration of the mind) that effects in the most immediate way the transition from act to Being.

Spiritual contemplation, although a human act, is not done by man alone; in the image of its divine Object, it assumes both an outer and an inner aspect. It is in itself its own object: the Reality, Being, Knowledge, and Beatitude of the One. Just as the divine Being is outwardly revealed by its creative and redemptive Act, so is our contemplation extrinsically an act, but an act through which we participate directly in God's Act, whereas the essence of our contemplation is one with His Essence. Seen from the outside or from below, contemplation is passing from act to Being, from spiritual activity to spiritual Essence; seen from within, or from above, it is Being, Essence itself, or again: the movement from Being to act, or that of the supreme Light to Its own receptivity, which, in the heart of the Cosmos, becomes Its contemplative receptacle, the creature, man.

In defining contemplation in this way, from the earthly point of view as the passing from act to Being, and from the ontological point of view as the passage from Being to act, we have not used the philosophical vocabulary inherited from Aristotle. In this vocabulary, the term *actus* itself designates what really is, so that pure Act is thus pure Being without any restriction due to some or another virtuality of being. *Actus* then is equivalent to God Himself, for all one can conceive of true being is possessed by God and He has no need to acquire it by passing from potency to act. God, pure Being, is pure Act and, as such, the Prime Mover, the motionless Mover. In other words, God moves all things by His very Being, which is pure Act, the first Act, the supreme Act. And according to the Stagirite, this supreme Act is not only divine Being but also divine Thought; since it is divine Being, pure Act, the Thought in this sense could only have a divine object, namely Itself. It is therefore not comparable with human thought, as the great Master of Kabbalah, Moses Cordovero (1522–1570), so clearly pointed out in *Pardes Rimonim*:

> The Creator's Knowledge is not like that of creatures, for in the latter, knowledge is distinct from the subject of knowledge and has to do with objects that are likewise distinguished from the subject. This is what is referred to by the three terms: thought, what thinks, and what is thought. On the contrary, the Creator is Himself at once Knowledge, Knower, and Known. Indeed, His manner of knowing does not consist of applying His Thought to things as it were outside of Him; but it is by knowing Himself and of Himself that He knows and sees all that is. Nothing exists but that which is united with Him and found by Him in His own Essence.

Divine "Thought," *Mahshabah*, according to the Kabbalah, is none other than the infinite "Wisdom" of the One, *Hokhmah*, His first ontological Emanation, His intelligent Being which is also His intelligent Act and His Knowledge or Contemplation of Himself, which determines and produces all things; such is also the teaching of Hermes Trismegistus, inscribed on the Emerald Tablet: "All things come from the One and from the Contemplation of the One."

And so the Aristotelian terminology, from which our own differed somewhat at first sight, finally corroborates what we have said about the true nature of contemplation, namely that it is the Act, the very Being of the One, or His Act of Being, of Knowing and—seen from below—of supreme Union. It follows, besides, from this that if we speak of contemplation and action, we have to keep well in mind that these are not opposite terms, since contemplation is the first and pure act from which all other acts flow and by which they are therefore determined. "Act" or "Action" derives from the Latin *agere*, "to act," which is opposed neither to *contemplari* nor to *cogitare*, but to *pati*, "to undergo"; *actio* or *actus* is the opposite of *passio*, "what one undergoes," whence the opposition "activity/passivity." On the ontological level, the agent, the act, and what is acted upon are but one: Being "is" Being, Knowledge knows itself, Light contemplates itself, and its rays create and illuminate what is created until it is finally reabsorbed in its divine Essence. This is the definition of contemplation and action in itself. This is the supreme identity of contemplation and pure Act or pure Being. To contemplate is to actualize the pure Act, it is to *be* Being, Knowledge, Beatitude.

From the *contemplatio Dei*, which is His Act, His very Being, proceeds every being, every act, all contemplation, by way of His "adaptation" matched to all levels and receptivities of existence, as Hermes Trismegistus likewise taught: "All things are brought forth from the One by the way of adaptation" of Himself to things. This is why everything should normally be in conformity with His Being, every act with His Act, all knowledge or contemplation with His Knowledge, His Contemplation. But it is not so: everything that has issued from pure Being, pure Act, does not remain united to His Presence as it descends to this lower world. Now, everything which digresses from divine Being, from his Presence, is degraded in its particular being, in its non-divine existence, in its knowledge that has become ignorance, in its action that is no longer in conformity with the divine Act or Will. Only pure contemplation and any act that is contemplative or willed by God unites with His Presence, even if in a more or less direct manner; and the being who contemplates or acts in that way is by the very fact united with the One. This is how Plotinus defines contemplation (*theoria*), as a state of the soul directly united with God through its higher part; contemplation and whatever in the soul contemplates God escapes from the degradation of doing (*prattein*) and making (*poiein*). The act of contemplation and what contemplates—to return to our own terminology—are essentially one with the pure Act, pure Being. On the contrary, what does not contemplate God and does not do His Will is—by definition—not united with Him and, having gone away from Him, is degraded and denies its own reason for being: the only Being, the single and universal Act.

Every action here below, whether perfect or deformed by man, is a manifestation of that Act, of that Being. The essence of act is Being and its immediate reason for being is the actualization, the realization of Being. Action that is not in conformity with Being, instead of actualizing Being, of realizing it, tends to stifle it, to kill it. And since such action cannot annihilate the eternal Being, it inevitably turns against the one who has acted against Him and who thereby denies and kills his own ephemeral being. Action that kills being is the sin of mankind, a sin carried to extremes by our own contemporaries. They cultivate action for the sake of action without regard to being, His Being: hence, agitation without any true aim, collective suicide, and loss of soul. Modern man preaches "progress," progress towards the abyss, and commits himself body and soul to an activity that does violence to being; he cultivates a "Tree of Science (or Knowledge)," which proves to be a "Tree of Death." He rejects contemplation as being something ineffective: men who devote their life to contemplation are considered useless, idle people, enemies of society. Countries which have remained more or less traditional are regarded as "unproductive" to the very extent that they retain signs of contemplation. Modern man has no notion that contemplation is the purest and highest form of action, and the most powerful; that it actualizes the supreme Being, the universal Act; that in contemplation the real presence of the Lord of the worlds reveals Himself, manifests Himself here below. Our contemporaries do not know that contemplation is in itself not the act of man, but of God, in face of which all actions initiated by man vanish like a mirage. God contemplates the world in Himself, and the world is. God contemplates the end of the world in Himself, and the world is finished. A man of God contemplates with God, acts with Him, and is conscious of God in himself and in all things. He contemplates the One "whithersoever he turns": "on high," where absolute Truth is enthroned; in the "heart," where His real Presence dwells; and in the "neighbor" filled with the same Presence. This man's contemplation embraces all—it is the infinite knowledge and universal love that unites all to the One.

## The Object of Contemplation in Judaism and in Islam

When one has become aware of what contemplation is—as of all the spiritual and human activity that flows from it—one knows that basically it has to do with a universal reality in which all beings endowed with intelligence participate on different levels. This reality is the pure Act, the pure and supreme Being, and the Principle of all being, all intelligence, and all action. To contemplate means to actualize the pure Act, to *be* pure Being, and to rest in pure knowledge. All of this is accomplished through the variety of modes of contemplation, and through the ways or traditions to which they belong. Just as with any activity that is essentially spiritual, contemplation in Judaism or Islam is an adaptation of these universal principles, in regard to one mode of spiritual receptivity or another, crystallized in religious form. And for the universality of contemplation—as well as for the relationship between Judaism and Islam—we will find analogies among their contemplative modes, which, the nearer they come to their object, gradually become also at one with it. In pure contemplation, all revealed ways and all true contemplators come together and are united, all being receptacles open to the One and filled with the One.

The One contemplates Himself in Himself and in His receptacles, and communicates with them according to the depth of their receptivity; this variable predisposition or receptivity is translated in this world as much by the diverse spiritual needs of humanity as by the diverse sacred modes that correspond to them and in which men worship and contemplate the only Reality and manifest His Truth and His Will in their outer action. The world of contemplation and of godlike action is His Kingdom, it is the world of the One but also the world of the One in the many, to which Israel and Islam, among others, belong. In this world of pure contemplation and godlikeness, Israel strictly signifies Judaism as such, namely the religion of Moses or the Hebrew people insofar as they follow that religion, the "holy nation," the theocracy of the Bible. In the same way, Islam is the religion of Muhammad that gives form to the Koranic revelation and to the *Sunna*, the sacred "custom," received from the Prophet and supported by his *ahadīth*, or "sayings" that have crystallized the Muslim tradition. In these two sister religions, the revealed letter is clarified by exoteric exegesis as well as by the more purely spiritual doctrine, esoterism, both of which go back, on the one hand, to Moses, and on the other, to Muhammad. As for the two esoterisms, Kabbalah and Sufism, they represent the innermost or highest interpretations and the actual spiritual realization of the divine revelations in question: the heart of Israel, and the heart of Islam. From a certain historical point of view, these two worlds of contemplation arise from the heart of Abraham and are united in his faith in the One. In the innermost depths of these two hearts there is nothing but the One (*Ehad* in Hebrew, *Ahad* in Arabic), the "One without a second" (*hu ehad we-en sheni* in Hebrew, *wahdahu lā sharīka lahu* in Arabic). Can there be two "Ones," two "Ones without a second"? One is one without any division, and One without a second is One without any associate. Such is the God of Israel: "Hear, O Israel, YHVH, our God, YHVH, is One" (*Sh'ma Israel YHVH Elohenu YHVH ehad*)

(Deut. 6:4); and such is also "The Divinity" (*Allāh*) of the Koran, who enjoins every Muslim: "Say: He, *Allāh*, is one" (*Qul huwa-Allāhu ahad*) (112:1) and who excludes every false divinity, any pseudo-absolute, by the credo: "There is no divinity if it be not The Divinity" (*Lā ilāha illā Allāh*). There is only the one Divinity, unique and universal. This is why the prophet Malachi asked the great question: "Have we not all one Father: Hath not one God created us?" (Mal. 2:10).

Judaism and Islam exoterically declare the "One without a second" to be the "only God," and this is the God who is worshiped by man; man coexists with Him as a "second." Jewish and Muslim esoterism (i.e., the Kabbalah and Sufism) pursue this monotheistic profession of faith to its ultimate conclusion by affirming the "One without a second" as the absolute One, the only Reality, who integrates all in Himself—this without falling into the traps of pantheism, which, on the contrary, integrates the Divinity into the world and which leads mentally to confusion of the Real with the unreal, of the Infinite with the finite, and of the imperishable with the transitory. According to both the Kabbalah and Sufism, what is transitory appears and disappears in the Infinite without affecting it; All-Reality, of which the eternal and the transitory are aspects, remains forever what It is. It is at once absolute Beyond-Being, causal Being, and universal Existence; It is simultaneously supra-intelligible Reality, which rests in Itself, intelligible Being, which contemplates Itself, and Existence, which goes out from Being (*ex-sistere, ex-stare*)[4] without going out from It in reality. Existence is irradiated from God's revelatory and creative contemplation; it remains linked with Him by the ray of His onto-cosmological contemplation and returns to Him in His self-contemplation. Divine All-Reality cannot be reduced to Existence, as pantheism would have it; on the contrary, it is Existence which finds itself forever integrated within the divine All, either in His Transcendence or in His Immanence. The one Reality of Existence is its divine Essence, which is at the same time transcendent and immanent, while its relative unreality is the pure expression of the creative, revealing, and unifying will of the only One: from His self-contemplation emanates the illusory appearance of an other-than-Him, so that this other may know and contemplate the fact that in reality, in essence, he is not other than Him—that in truth there is none other than Him, the One without a second. This is what the Prophet says: "*Allāh* was and nothing was with Him and

---

[4] Editor's note: Our term "exist" is derived from the Latin *ex-sistere*, which means "to come forth" or "to be manifest."

He is now just as He was." When a mirage appears or disappears in a desert, is the desert changed thereby? "The thirsty man runs towards it and there waiting for him is *Allāh*." So long as the illusory existence of the "other" lasts, this other will find nothing real, nothing positive, nothing good outside of the only real Being; and whatever this existence itself may be, perfect or imperfect, it subsists as such thanks solely to Being, the only Reality, the "One and Only Essence" (*Dhāt al-wāhidah*) of all that is. Thanks to this essential Unity or "Unity of Being" (*Wahdat al-Wujūd*), every being comes in the end to contemplate the One Being, to be that Being, to be one through the One, with the One, in the One.

While pasturing Jethro's ewes in the desert of Midian and on arriving at the foot of Mount Horeb, Moses saw and contemplated in the burning bush the real Presence of this one Essence of all that is: the Presence revealed itself to him as *Ehyeh*, the one and universal "Being," as the "Being that is Being" (*Ehyeh asher Ehyeh*), beyond and within all existence. But It also revealed to him that It is not only the Essence and Principle of existence, but simultaneously rests in Itself, in Its Beyond-Being or Non-Being—called in Kabbalah, *Ayin*, the divine "Nothingness." In fact, *Ehyeh* means not only "I am," but also "I will be." *Ehyeh asher Ehyeh* means not only "I am that I am," but also "I will be that I will be," meaning on this side of My Non-Being or Beyond-Being, of My supra-ontological and supra-intelligible Reality; and in My Being "I will be with you" (*Ehyeh 'immakh*), with all existence, with all that is born from My Being, with all My "children," the "children of Israel" and all the "children of God."

Because the only Father and God is with all His children, because "Being-and-Beyond-Being" is the spiritual Essence in all existence, the spirit of man, all of his spiritual being, is in principle capable of immersing itself not only in pure and intelligible Being, but even in the bottomless void of the divine "Nothingness," in the more-than-luminous Darkness of the supreme and supra-intelligible Principle. This is what happened to Moses at the foot of Mount Horeb in Sinai, face to face with the burning bush. He realized in secret all that he was later to reveal to the children of Israel from the summit of the same sacred mountain, when he went up step by step until he entered into the darkness of God's cloud. Then, according to Dionysius the Areopagite,

> He penetrated into the truly mystical Darkness of unknowing; there he closed his eyes to all positive knowledge, escaped completely from all grasping and all vision, for he belonged

wholly to Him who is beyond all, no longer belonged to himself, or to anything alien, but was united through the best of himself with Him who is ungraspable by any knowledge, having renounced all positive knowledge, and knowing, thanks to that very unknowing, beyond all intelligence. May we also [here the Areopagite addresses Timothy and through him all Christian contemplatives] penetrate into this Darkness more luminous than light and, renouncing all vision and all knowledge, may we thus see and know Him who is beyond all vision and all knowledge! For that is true vision, that is true knowledge, and from the very fact that one gives up all that exists, one celebrates the Supra-Essential in a supra-essential mode.[5]

This is what in Kabbalah is called *bittul ha-yesh*, the "annihilation of existence" in *Ayin*, the divine "Nothingness," implying the annihilation of human reason in "contemplation of the Nothingness." On this subject, the Hasidic[6] master Rabbi Levi Yitzchak of Berditchev (d. 1809) said:

There are men who worship the Creator with their reason, and there are other men who contemplate the Nothingness [*mistakel el ha-Ayin*], if one may express it like that; and for human reason it is not possible, but only with God's help. . . . When a man succeeds in contemplating Nothingness, his human reason is annihilated; later, when he returns towards reason, he is filled with [divine] super-abundance.

To "come down again" from "Nothingness" to "Being," from supra-intelligible contemplation to ontological and universal Knowledge not only brings with it the instantaneous reconstitution of existence, of human being, but its full illumination. The highest Contemplation itself is not—as we have just said—positive knowledge or vision; it is "being united by the best of oneself [by the pure and highest "Self"] with Him who cannot be grasped by knowledge." So it is not a question of the union of a subject with an object of positive knowledge, but of absolute

---

[5] *Oeuvres completes du Pseudo-Denys l'Areopagite*, trans. M. de Gandillac (Paris: Aubier, 1943), pp. 179–80.

[6] The mystical movement of the Hasidim, the "Devotees," was founded by Rabbi Israel ben Eliezer, known as the Baal Shem (the "Master of the [divine] Name"), towards the middle of the eighteenth century in Poland. It first spread through Eastern Europe and finally all over the world.

identity of the subject and the object in the "contemplation of Nothingness"; or, more precisely, there is in this case no subject contemplating, no object contemplated, there is only a divine "Nothingness" and a contemplation that is not contemplation, that is itself "Nothingness"; and this "Nothingness" is the Absolute, the more-than-luminous, unknowable, infinite, and unconditioned Essence of all contemplation or knowledge. Here all affirmation and all negation are surpassed, all existence and nonexistence are effaced: this is the "extinction of extinction" (*fanā' al-fanā'*) of the Sufis.

Here man is no longer a human being nor any intelligible being whatsoever: he is transformed into his own supra-human and supra-intelligible Essence, the divine Beyond-Being which reposes in itself without any exteriorization, emanation, revelation, or manifestation; this is because, from eternity to eternity, He "made Darkness His hiding place" (Ps. 18:11). This is the Obscurity of the divine Cloud, into which Moses penetrated, the "dark Cloud" (*al-'amā'*) where, according to the Prophet, *Allāh* dwells "before creating the world," that is to say beyond everything that relates in any way whatsoever to the creation. In Sufism, this more-than-luminous Obscurity is identified with *al-'adam* (or *al-'udum*), Non-Being, absolute non-Manifestation, the highest degree of divine All-Reality where *Allāh* dwells like a "hidden and unknown Treasure." He says to His Prophet: "I was a hidden Treasure, and I wished to be known, so I created the world. . . ." Wishing to be known, He descends, so to speak, from His supra-intelligible "Non-Being" to His state of self-knowledge—the state of His intelligible "Being" (*Wujūd*). Here He contemplates Himself as *Ahad*, the "One" in Itself, and as *Wāhid*, the "unique" Principle and Cause of all existence; in this latter contemplation He creates the world, and from there His "ways" are revealed in their variety as they surge out in all the "directions of the universe" and shine forth resplendent in all the possible shades of the divine "Colors" or Qualities.

From here, Islam comes down as a spiritual sword flaming with affirmation of the One, as a luminous axis linking heaven and earth, as the "straight path" (*Sirāt al-mustaqīm*) going from God to man and leading man to God. This descent of the One, this vertical hyphen, is symbolized particularly by the *Alif*, the first letter of the Arabic alphabet, whose numerical value is one. This symbol of the One and of His descent is also the initial letter of the names *Allāh*, "The Divinity," and *Ahad*, the "One," as also of the word Islam (the first letter of which is an *Alif* pronounced as "i"). This quite simple design therefore reflects the eternal archetype of Islam, the direct revelation of the One, which is the summary of all His revelations: the *Alif* contains, reveals, and reabsorbs all the other letters that come after it, just as the primordial Sound, creative, revelatory, and redemptive, which manifests all things and in which they return to the eternal silence, to the absolute non-manifestation of *Allāh*. Islam represents, from the historical point of view, the restoration of the monotheism of Abraham, which—still in the aspect of its temporal filiation—goes back to the primordial revelation of God, to the religion of Adam, to the unanimous tradition of humanity in the dawn of time. The spiritual reality of the Prophet is even prior to the first man; Muhammad said: "I was a prophet when Adam was still between water and clay." He also said that at his advent "time turned back in a circular movement to the aspect it had on the day when *Allāh* created the heavens and the earth." If the *Alif*, the vertical axis, signifies the revelation of Islam or the direct descent of the One, the said circular movement is none other than the movement of the same *Alif*, whose end comes to join again with the beginning by integrating all things in the One; this is the inner, spiritual movement of Islam, which actualizes the universal circle of the *religio perennis*. It is the primordial spirituality of man, which was due to rise again before the end of time in the form of the last religion, the one preceding the unanimous tradition of the Messiah, destined to be that of the world to come.

In other words, Islam is the "last point" of the present circle or cycle of revelations—sealed by the "Seal of the Prophets," Muhammad— the final point which rejoins the primordial Point, the One revealing Himself to the whole of Humanity. This is why the religion of Muhammad confirms all earlier true beliefs, which it represents as both the everlasting quintessence and the final synthesis. From vertical axis or straight ray of the One, Islam thus becomes the hidden circle, connecting all the revelations of the present cycle of humanity going from Adam to the Messiah of the *parousia* (the Second Coming of Christ). We find this symbolism in the letter "m" of the name *Muhammad*, the *mīm*, being circular in form. And we find this same symbol of the circle in the deep meaning and graphical development of the letters or consonants of the name *Allāh* or *Allāhu*:

$$\text{ٱللّٰهُ} \quad = \quad \text{ALLaHu}$$

One of the traditional representations of the divine Name clearly shows, by means of a certain stylization, the passage from the "vertical axis" to the "universal circle," namely: اللّٰه .[7] The axis of the *Alif* ( ا ) curves at its lower extremity and becomes the first *Lām* ( ل ), and continues to curve in the same way in the second *Lām* ( ل ), until the curve is complete and closed on itself in the *Hā* ( ه ), reappearing in the stylization of the final vowel *u* (the *dammah*, i.e., the و above the *Hā*) as purely and simply a circle ( ∘ ). In one of the variants of this representation, the name of the Prophet appears in the middle of the final circle. Now all this symbolizes the mysteries hidden in the "Supreme Name" (*al-Ism al-a'zam*), each letter of which reveals a fundamental aspect of the divine All-Reality, or of the wholly real "Divinity," *Allāh*. Among the many Sufic ways of considering these mysteries, we choose the following, which is based on the teaching of Ibn 'Arabī: The *Alif*— which at the beginning of a word always remains alone, not joined to the letters that follow it—represents the only Reality, the One without a second, "*Allāh*, outside of whom there is no divinity (*Allāhu lā ilāha illa huwa*)." The first *Lām*—in which the *Alif* bends towards itself—is the One who contemplates Himself, His pure Unity. The second *Lām* is the One who contemplates Himself through His "All-Possession," which comprehends the illusory appearances of an "other-than-He." This same second *Lām*, in passing to the second *Alif*—which is not necessarily written, but always pronounced, and with which the *Lām* forms the word *lā*, "no,"—is the eternal negation of the illusory "otherness," the reabsorption of all things in the one and only real Unity of *Allāh*. Lastly the *Hā* is *Huwa*, "He," "He who alone remains": He rests eternally in Himself, absolutely hidden in Himself; and all things rest hidden in Him, are not other than Him, this being symbolized—in the form of the circle poised over the "h"—by the final "u" of *Allāhu*. And, as we have said, the name of Muhammad is sometimes to be found in this circle—the name of the Prophet, God's Messenger, Universal Man, in whom all things rest and who, himself, rests in *Allāh*, one with the One without a second.

Thus, from the vertical axis of the One, the essential revelation of Islam, the name *Allāh*, becomes—as an actual prefiguration of the religion that issued from it—the Circle of the Absolute which integrates all in It. The man who invokes and contemplates His Name to the point of actualizing His Presence "flies off with Him"—as Ibn 'Arabī expresses it—and is integrated into His own divine Essence. For "the meaning that belongs to this Name is that it designates the supreme Essence and nothing other." In effect, we have just seen how each letter

---

[7] Let us remember that Arabic, like Hebrew, is written from right to left.

of this Name reveals an aspect of the pure Essence; first the Essence as the one Reality, total and absolute; then contemplating Itself; furthermore contemplating Itself as the unique Essence of all things and in this contemplation actualizing all things in Itself and reabsorbing them into Itself, so that It alone subsists eternally and all things subsist in It alone. But, precisely because everything is in It and because It is the Essence of all things, the Name of the Essence is also the Name of all that is. This is why the Shaykh al-Akbar adds, in his *Book of the Name of Majesty: Allāh*, that the Name *Allāh*, although it designates solely the supreme Essence (*al-Dhāt*), appears also on the different degrees of the All-Reality: it is often named when a particular Name of God is intended to refer to one of His "Qualities" (*Sīfāt*) or "Activities" (*af'āl*) characterizing His relationships with the universal existence comprised in His Essence. Thus, besides the "essential" Mysteries that are being identified in the symbolism of the letters of the name *Allāhu*, all the other Mysteries of Essence and Existence are hidden in it: "All the divine Names are contained in this Name. From it they come forth and toward it they reascend"; it is the "supreme Name," the Name and the real Presence of the highest Object of all contemplation, all invocation, all action of the *muslim*.

What Ibn 'Arabī says, in effect, is that the Name *Allāh* relates to the other divine Names as the supreme Essence relates to the Qualities It includes. Now, all of the Qualities of the Essence and the divine Activities that proceed from them and constitute the relationships between the Essence and universal Existence are summed up in the divine "Mercy" (*Rahmāniyah*); for, the Qualities and Activities, which are the archetypes of things, integrate these in the Essence. Every divine Quality or Activity is "Mercy," because it unites each thing to the One, even under the aspect of rigor, which denies all that would deny the One so that all may be one with it. While *Allāh* is the Name proper to the Essence, and to all its aspects, *al-Rahmān*, the "Merciful," is the Name proper to the preeminent divine Quality and to all the other Qualities and Activities of God that proceed from it. According to 'Abd al-Karīm al-Jīlī, the meaning of the divine Name *al-Rahmān* is "the Quality which includes all the divine Qualities"; he places it—so to speak—between the Essence (*Dhāt*) of God and His Qualities (*Sīfāt*). According to another traditional point of view—put forward notably by Ibn al-'Arabī—*al-Rahmān* belongs directly to the order of *al-Dhāt*. *Al-Rahmān* is in that case the equivalent of the Vedantic *Ānanda*, the "Beatitude," which designates an intrinsic aspect of *Ātmā*, the divine "Self." It is for this reason that it is said in the Koran: "Invoke *Allāh* or invoke *al-Rahmān*; by whatever Name you call upon Him, His are the most beautiful Names" (17:110). *Allāh*, the Name of the *Dhāt* or Essence of God, becomes, in *al-Rahmān*, the Name of the personal Divinity or of the "divine Person" (*al-Nafs al-ilāhiyah*); for it is through His *Rahmāniyah* that *Allāh* relates Himself to His creatures. Whether the created are conscious of it or not, whether they are grateful for it or not, the "merciful Lord" (*al-Rabb al-rahīm*) gives His "Life" to all that exists. His creatures exist, thanks to His Being in them; they know, thanks to His Knowledge within them; they have will, thanks to His Will within them; and they hear, see, and express themselves thanks to His "Hearing," His "Seeing," and His "Speech" in them. The true contemplative is not only conscious of this and grateful, but he never ceases, apart from the carrying out of the Law, to seek, contemplate, and actualize in his own person the Being, Qualities, and Activities of the divine Person; and when his being is filled, absorbed, and "replaced" by the divine Being and His Qualities and Attributes, his spirit as well as his spiritualized body live as the Sufis have been able to describe—as for instance 'Abd al-Karīm al-Jīlī in his book *Al-Insān al-Kāmil*, "Universal Man."[8] Then the words of *Allāh* addressed to His Prophet are fulfilled in this contemplative: "Nothing of what is pleasant to Me brings My servant closer to Me than the performance of the duties I have imposed upon him. [And] he who adores Me never ceases to come closer to Me by practices beyond the call of obligation, until I love him; and, when I come to love him, I shall be the ear with which he hears, the eyes by which he sees, the hand with which he grasps, and the feet with which he walks. . . ."[9] *Allāh* will reveal Himself to His servant in every one of his contemplations and actions and will unite him with Himself so intimately that the true name of His friend will be *Allāh*. All this He made known to al-Jīlī:

> My friend, savor Me in perfumes, eat Me in what is eaten, imagine Me in the imaginable, know Me in thoughts, contemplate Me in the objects of the senses, clothe yourself in Me! My friend, you are My aim, through you My name is mentioned and you it is who are called when I am named!

---

[8] Editor's note: See the translation by Titus Burckhardt from the Arabic, then translated into English by Angela Culme-Seymour (Beshara Publications, 1995).

[9] Editor's note: This is from a much-quoted Sacred Tradition (*Hādith Qudsī*) transmitted directly to the Prophet, though not part of the Koran itself.

Such is the revelation of the One in Islam and His descent into the man who contemplates Him in truth and acts according to His Will: it is the total union of the *muslim* with *Allāh*.

In Judaism also, the supreme Object of all contemplation and action in the end takes the place of the human subject, who contemplates Him and becomes at last His representative on earth. The "righteous" (*tsaddiq*) is so permeated by God that his whole being is finally but one with the divine Being: his activity actualizes God's Act, his thought reveals the divine Thought, and when he wishes something it is God who wishes it and makes it come true. In spite of that, the *via unitiva* of Judaism differs in form from that of Islam. The Revelation, the descent of the One into the midst of "His people" is peculiar to Israel, and is by definition the particular reason for being of Judaism. Whereas, in Islam, the One appears as a single direct ray whose flaming path traverses all levels of existence and becomes a circle integrating all things in God, in Judaism the ray of the One breaks, at the point of departure, as soon as the golden calf is worshipped in Sinai. In fact, the first Sinaitic revelation of God to His people, which united all the children of Israel with Him and was crystallized in the first Tablets of the Torah, was broken, as they [the Israelites] were, in face of this sin, this renewal of the original sin by a group of humans which the Lord had mercifully led back to the state of innocence. According to the Kabbalah, God wished graciously to bestow His Messianic Revelation on Israel, but His people were not ready for the final deliverance; the "Messiah flew away" from Sinai and the Lord had to replace the "first Tablets whose transparent stones were made of Unity without duality" or of the "Tree of Life," by other Tablets "emanating from the Tree of Good and Evil." From then on, Israel was subject to the dual Law, which veils the One; if obeyed it leads to eternal Life, but if not respected it may lead to hell. This was the institution of the Mosaic exoterism, which like a shell, enclosed the esoterism of the first revelation; purely contemplative life in the One became thenceforth a spiritual kernel hidden in the multiple forms of a religion, of an existence filled with ritual practices intended to purify man and keep him constantly attached to God. The traces of the first Revelation on Sinai, concentrated in the esoteric tradition, the Kabbalah, were reserved for a rigorously chosen few consecrated by initiation to the Mysteries of the Torah; but the followers of the Kabbalah also had to serve God by observing the Law, which, for them, signified a totality of ways for actualizing the Mysteries. This, furthermore, is why every Israelite who is faithful to God by being faithful to the Law, and whose sincere aspiration and other qualities fit him for initiation to the Mysteries, is in principle given the opportunity to become an adept of the Kabbalah.

It is true that one finds the same polarization of esoterism and exoterism in Islam, but in this case it was instituted at the very beginning and not as the consequence of a collective sin, a "break" in the ray of the One in the soul of a whole people. In Islam, as we have seen, the divine ray pierces directly through all degrees of existence, like an axis or central pivot, which links them harmoniously and bestows upon each degree what is suited to it; and we have also seen how the straight ray curves on its return and becomes a circle that brings everything back to its Point of departure: the One. Thus, passage from one degree to another and even the direct return from any point of existence to the highest, divine Degree, are mercifully made easy in Islam, the same being true, consequently, as regards the transition from exoterism to esoterism.

Indeed, initiatic adherence to Sufism, although subject to certain strict conditions, is far less difficult than entering Kabbalah, the access to which is guarded, like the lost paradise, by a fiery sword of hidden forces. That is not merely a negative effect of the "break" long ago between the Divinity really present in Sinai and the idolatrous people, but also the positive sign of the permanence of "fiery" spiritual effects going back to Sinai and actualized in the esoteric rites of Kabbalah. The dazzling Revelation of the real and intemporal Presence of the One, His direct descent onto the sacred mountain, is repeated and its effects are so powerful that only initiates who have been well prepared and tested can bear it and assimilate it. This exceptional grace of sudden illumination, ascent, and spiritual union offered to the "Chosen People" is confirmed in the Koran, where it is revealed that God "raised Israel above the worlds" (2:47). Indeed, as the Kabbalah, for its part, attests, all the souls of the Israelites were raised immediately in Sinai up to the Throne of God, so that Israel might be a "holy people" and reveal the One to all humanity. But, also in Sinai, there was the break between Israel and the One, and this break, in spite of the continuity of the "Covenant," reappeared again and again in the history of this "people" whose sole reason for being is nonetheless the One and union with Him. Israel wrestles with Him—as its very name recalls—until the day when this sacred vessel, broken by its own faults, will be finally repaired: "On that day YHVH will be One and His Name will be One" (Zech. 14:9). The ray of the One, descending into the midst of His people, will no longer be broken; the Light of the first Tablets of the Torah will reappear in its original, redemptive, Messianic Unity; the very real Presence of the One will rise up in place of the two destroyed

Temples and will fill the world with His unitive Grace; the remaining righteous of Israel will worship the One in adoration shared with the other remaining "flocks of the Lord"—affirmation and contemplation of the only Reality will be unanimous, just as it already is for the contemplatives of all authentic ways. *Al-tawhīd wāhid*, "affirmation of the One is itself one," say the Sufis.

There have always been groups of Jews who have sought to prefigure this ideal state in the midst of their own community; their endeavor has been to carry out the divine Will as perfectly as possible, to sanctify themselves in the image of the Most-Holy One and thereby contribute to the advent of the Messiah. This elect was not confined to the restricted circles of the Kabbalists, but radiated outward to create a living passage between the domain, so difficult to enter, of the Kabbalah and the domain of public or exoteric study and application of the Torah. The Truth of the One, His divine Wisdom, the Wisdom of the Kabbalah, had to be given back to the body of the people of Israel, who always had a tendency to backslide, if not toward loss of faith or a superficial observance of the law, at any rate toward a sterile and congealed formalism barring the path to real union with God. This was already the chief aim and mission of the prophets of Israel: they came to break up from within—through their revelations and their example of a godlike life ruling the whole of man's existence—the dark incrustations formed again and again around a Torah neglected or taken literally, which then left no opening for the heart and spirit of the divine Speech and Presence.

A last echo of this repeated effort to spiritually renew Israel resounded in Polish Hasidism, which arose towards the middle of the eighteenth century, and in whose midst one can find more than one analogy with certain aspects of Sufism: for example, the insistence on total attachment to God and to the spiritual master, on fear and love of the Lord as inescapable conditions of knowing Him, and on all the spiritual and human virtues. But the characteristic element in Polish Hasidism—whose followers are still to be found today in Europe, in America, and notably in Israel—is the love of God, of His people, and of all creatures. This is a love that is filled with fear and knowledge of God. It integrates all existence into spiritual life: it is the joy of meeting the Omnipresent in everything. It is the happiness of freeing His sparks that have fallen into the darkness of this world and of raising them toward Him. This comes about thanks to the power to rise which is natural and proper to the soul so that, when praying with unbounded fervor, it springs up towards Him and unites with Him.

Hasidism is an emotional and collective mysticism everlastingly fed by the memory of the Only One, the Well-Beloved; it explodes in sacred songs and dances and is demonstrated in the extraordinary intensity of common prayer; it is seen in the radiant faces at holy meals eaten together, in the extreme recollection of all those gathered around the master while he is teaching,[10] and in their study together of the sacred Doctrine. It does not exclude silent contemplation, or prayers, or meditation in solitude; but apart from the purely esoteric exercises performed in secret and reserved for the elect, the initiates, the Kabbalists, who form the nucleus of Hasidism—a nucleus of actual or potential masters—the way in Judaism revolves here around the pivot of spiritual integration of all the elements of life, soul and body, of compassionate conversion of all earthly darkness, of all evil, which is merely a degradation or inversion of good, hence of the affirmative and unitive absorption of the whole of this lower world in the Highest. And this way is open to every Jew, however humble and ignorant, to the simpleminded who, not knowing how to articulate a prayer, cry out to God—with cries that tear asunder the veils of the world, open the doors of Heaven, causing the Father's heart to incline towards His unfortunate creature. In these aspects of pure universal love, Polish Hasidism is distinct from earlier movements which, like it, formed a bridge between esoterism and exoterism, but were founded rather, like German Hasidism in the thirteenth century, on ascetic practice. However, in the latter also we find an extreme manifestation of the love of the neighbor, just as one finds the communal life, with all goods shared, in the midst of that other group of Jews who, more than a thousand years earlier, attempted to embody the wisdom and holiness of Israel at the cost of an ascetic discipline of the highest degree, namely the Essenes. What characterizes these and other similar eso-exoteric movements which have marked the course of Jewish history, can be summed up in the affirmation of a contemporary descendant of a Polish Hasidic family, who is not interested to know "that two and two make four, but that God is one—that man and God make one—the secret is in the *Alef*, in the One."[11]

---

[10] For genuine Hasidic teaching translated into English, see *Liqqutei Amarim* (Collected Essays) by Rabbi Schneur Zalman of Liadi, trans. Dr. Nissan Mindel (Brooklyn, N.Y.: Kohet Publication Society, 1962).

[11] Elie Wiesel, *Celebration hassidique* (Paris: Ed. Seuil, 1972). (Editor's note: The translation into English is titled *Souls on Fire: Portraits and Legends of Hasidic Masters* [New York: Simon & Schuster, 1982].)

**An Example of Contemplation: The Symbolism of Letters**

We have seen that Sufis contemplate the only Reality, the All-Reality, in the *Alif*, amongst other things, and Kabbalists do the same in regard to the *Alef*, the first letter of the Hebrew alphabet. Like the *Alif*, the latter has the numerical value of one and symbolizes the One Himself, but here the One is He who reveals Himself to Israel. In other words, the *Alef* represents all of the following: the One Himself; the One who descends into the midst of His children; His single Light or His pure straight Ray, which is broken in Sinai before the golden calf; and His first Tablets, made of His Unity and broken by that sin. (This initial break is repeated throughout the history of Israel in betrayals leading to the destruction of the two Temples and the dispersion of the people all over the world, where they are persecuted and almost exterminated.) All this, as well as the return of Israel and of all peoples to the One, is written eternally in the *Alef* (**א**) which is not, like the Arabic *Alif*, a simple straight line, a lightning bolt from the One falling straight from the heavens and symbolizing what we have said of it above, and more. Instead, the *Alef* is a broken shaft, a wavering light, a flame flickering in all directions to reveal the eternal Archetype and the earthly destiny of Israel, and above all (1) the "Point (or Center) above" ( ' ), representing the Supreme Principle, the transcendent Divinity, or the "Holy One, blessed be He"; (2) the "line of Union" between divine Transcendence and divine Immanence, which is the slanting line—stylizing the letter *Vav* (ו)—itself symbolizing the "Son," the "Messiah descending" as from the mountain top onto Sinai where he is received by Moses as the Light and Word of the Torah; and (3) the "Point (or Center) below" ( ◦ ) representing the immanent Principle, divine Omnipresence revealed as real Presence, or the *Shekhinah* which is the *corpus mysticum* of Israel and which at the same time cares for all people "as a mother does for her children." The "lower Point" ( ◦ ) is like an inversion of the "Point above" ( ' ); it looks above on its own transcendent Essence, which is united with it; this is the "union of the Holy One, blessed be He, with His *Shekhinah*" and this very union, implying the union of all creatures with the Creator, is symbolized by the "line of union" ( \ ); thus we see the "Union of all" in the One: **א**.

But that is only one way of contemplating the *Alef*, which in truth encloses all the Mysteries of the One and of His descent into the midst of the children of Israel. We shall only touch here on a small portion of these mysteries as they enter the context of our subject.[12] There is,

---

[12] For instance, the Kabbalah interprets the oblique stroke of the *Alef* not only as a

for instance, another way of contemplating the *Alef*, a variation on the same theme of the Transcendence, Descent, and Immanence of God, which is the contemplation of the ten fundamental Aspects of the One that are also the ten supreme Archetypes of all things, the ten *Sefirot* or synthetic "Enumerations" of the Infinitude of the divine Realities. In Islam, and particularly in Sufism, every reality whatsoever is tirelessly and directly brought back to the One; however, in Judaism, and above all in Kabbalah, all things are constantly related to their ten supreme Archetypes, the ten *Sefirot* or fundamental Aspects of the One. This is His tenfold Unity which is reflected in the whole Mosaic Revelation: it is reflected first of all in the Ten Commandments, as well as in the "sacred Community of Israel," which is ritually valid only in the presence of ten Jewish men. Here the absolute Unity of God is contemplated at the apex of contemplation of His tenfold Unity, the indivisible Unity of the ten *Sefirot*. This is because the absolute One is the very first and highest *Sefirah*, the "Supreme Crown" (*Keter Elyon*), the pure Essence of the nine others that emanate from It in the ontological plane.

The first Emanation is *Hokhmah*: His eternal "Wisdom," His own Knowledge, the Knowledge of His infinite Unity. In Sufi terminology, this is the degree of divine Unity (*Ahadiyyah*) or of the first "Irradiation" (*Tajallī*) of the One (*Ahad*) in Himself and received by Himself alone. This receiving of knowledge of the One by Himself constitutes the third great degree of divine Essence; however, this degree includes the principle of all other reception of the only Reality, and thus the principle of all His "receptacles," namely of the eternal archetypes of things and the things themselves. Here, the One is revealed as the single Essence of all things, and so this degree is called by the Sufis the degree of the "Unique" (*Wāhid*), whereas in Kabbalah it is called *Binah*, the onto-cosmological "Intelligence" of God, and also *Imma*, the supreme "Mother" of all things, the generative Receptivity of the "Father," *Abba*, who is none other than *Hokhmah* in eternal union with *Keter*.

Just as, according to the Koran, *Allāh* is *Ahad* (*Allāhu Ahad*) and *Wāhid* (*ilāhun wāhidun*, "one and only divinity"), so *Keter*, *Hokhmah*, and *Binah* are one and the same God, namely (1) the Essence in Itself, (2) the Essence as it contemplates Its own Unity, and (3) the Essence as It contemplates all reality in Itself. It is one and the same divine Es-

stylization of the *Vav*, but in a certain respect also as that of the letter *Nun*, that is, the final *Nun*: ן , which symbolizes itself the Archetype of man or Universal Man. Now the latter is identified with the "Son," whose image is the *Vav*: ו ; it will be noticed how similar these two letters are, the final *Nun* having the appearance of a *Vav* prolonged downwards.

sence, *YHVH*, considered under three fundamental aspects. This supreme Trifold-Unity is revealed in the *Alef* (‫א‬) in the form of its "upper point" ( ' ), identified with the letter *Yod* ( ' ). The fine upper point of the *yod* itself signifies *Keter*, its thick stroke *Hokhmah*, and its fine lower point *Binah*. From this "supreme Point" with three aspects descend the seven "Sefirot of cosmic construction," the seven fundamental aspects of God the creator, revealer, and redeemer, and of His universal Immanence. The oblique stroke of the *Alef* (‫\‬)—identified with the *Vav* (‫ו‬), which has the numerical value six—symbolizes the six active *Sefirot*, namely *Hesed, Din, Tif'eret, Netsah, Hod*, and *Yesod* (Grace, Judgment, Beauty, Victory, Majesty, and Foundation). To this is added the "lower Point" ( ‹ ), which represents the *yod* directed upwards, symbolizing the last *Sefirah*, named *Malkhut* (Kingdom) or *Shekhinah* (divine Immanence). The latter therefore receives the real Presence of all the other *Sefirot*, constituting with them the divine Decad, which is symbolized by the numerical value ten, the value that belongs to the *yod*. This last *Sefirah* is the whole of Divinity present "below" (in the "lower *Yod*"), which is called *Adonai*, "My Lord." This is the personal God who is immediately accessible to each creature, the God who dwells in all hearts.

In the *Alef*, the One descends from His highest degree to the terrestrial degree, amid His people, to be Himself the *corpus mysticum* of the latter—to be contemplated, known, and realized by Israel. This sacrosanct body is at once that of God, His "sefirotic Body," and that of Israel, the Spirit of Israel, which carries out the Ten Commandments—the ten Acts of the *Sefirot* or of the tenfold One—on earth. The child of Israel who obeys His Will, causes the "divine Body" to act in his human body and is united with Him; whereas if he sins, "he sins against the very Body of the divine King." Thus the history of Israel is thereby the very history of their God here below; it is eternally written in the *Alef*, inscribed in the One, whose descent calls forth from Israel—which is YHVH's own "portion"—either reception of Him and union with Him, or negation of Him and fall, the destruction of the receptacle.

The spiritual way of the Jew traverses the body and the history of Israel, its body at once ethnic and spiritual. By his permanent identification with Israel, by his every observance of the Law of Moses, and by his contemplation of the *Sefirot* and the invocation of their divine Names, the Jew becomes, in reality, "YHVH's own portion (or part)" (Deut. 32:9): he is united with the *corpus mysticum*, with the *Shekhinah* (which is the "final *H*" of *YHVH*), His Immanence. YHVH in His Transcendence is represented by the *Yod* (or by *YH* = *Yāh*) and YHVH in His Immanence by the final *He*. On the other hand, the *Vav*—situated between the two *He's*—signifies the descent of the Transcendent into the realm of the Immanent. Now Israel, although fallen from its first and highest degree (symbolized by the *Yod*), has remained inseparable, at its lowest degree, from the "*He* below," that is, from the *Shekhinah*. The latter has accompanied the children of Israel in their dispersion throughout the entire world and is what will bring them back to "Zion," to the One. But, for the Kabbalists, the "final *He*," the *Shekhinah*, means more than just the *corpus mysticum* of Israel with all its sacred institutions, laws, teachings, and rites—in short, the whole Torah. Beyond this, adepts of the Kabbalah seek to unite with this "final *He*" through every door which has been opened by the many means of grace deriving from the Torah, so that they might rise, starting from this last "letter" (i.e. the directly accessible reality of YHVH) toward the higher "letters" or degrees, and finally to the "highest Point," to the *Yod*, to YHVH-Transcendent. At the summit of all his observance of the Law, of all his study of the Torah, or of all the steps of his exegesis of the scriptures, the Kabbalist rises, through the initiatic means of Jewish esoterism, to the *Vav*, the immediate descent of the Transcendent. He receives the direct inflow of the *Yod* (or of *YH* = *Yāh*) and, thanks to this inflow, it is given to him to actualize the last spiritual ascent to the "highest *Yod*," to the "supreme Crown" (*Keter Elyon*), which is none other than the "God Most High" (*El Elyon*). Thus the attained Kabbalist is not only "YHVH's own portion (or part)," thanks to union with the "final *He*," but he comes to be one with the highest Archetype of the whole of humanity and of the universe, with the Archetype of Archetypes.

Such is the object and the aim of the Judaic *via contemplativa*. The aim is the One.

## Judaic and Islamic Modes of Contemplation and Action

In Judaism and Islam, God is worshipped, contemplated, invoked, and served, not through some image drawn from one or another of the four terrestrial kingdoms, and not through a human or angelic mediator, but through His Name or His Names; His Name or His Names designate respectively His Essence, and His Qualities and Activities. It is true, however, that in these two non-iconic ways the image of man reappears, if not as a figurative symbol, at least in the indirect anthropomorphism characterizing the Names of the onto-cosmological Attributes and Activities of God and even of certain intelligible Aspects of His pure Essence as revealed in the Torah and the Koran. The evident reason for this anthropomorphism is that the Infinite, in order to establish relations with man, to make Himself understood and known by man, must necessarily enter the latter's field of vision: He must, so to say, espouse the form of man and of his universe and speak in human language. In other words, the Infinite reveals Himself to man through the eternal human archetype reposing in Himself as a mode of His own receptivity, as a receptacle, in which He gives Himself to Himself and receives Himself, taking on—according to an expression of the Sufi al-Junaid—the "color of His recipient." But it is not His Essence as such which assumes the "colors" of the receptacles: the Essence is eternally "beyond what they attribute to Him" (*ʿammā yasifūn*). It is the infinite Perfection or "Quality" belonging to the Essence, which, being revealed, is translated first into the essentially single multiplicity of Its ontological Qualities, then, in the midst of the Cosmos, into the effective multitude of Its manifested Qualities and Activities. Thus it is that the Infinite takes on in the eternal human receptivity the "color," the principal form of man; in other words, the eternal archetype of man is the Infinite which makes Itself anthropomorphic, so that the form of man is theomorphic and by becoming conscious and fully realizing his deiformity the human recipient may, even in this lower world, find again his divine Content, both in Its Perfection and in Its Essence.

Man realizes his likeness unto God by conforming his acts to the Will of God—which itself is manifested through the activity and the whole of human existence—and by imitating with all his faculties the divine Perfections, of which the human qualities and virtues are the terrestrial reflections and vehicles. When this likeness comes to maturity, it produces, according to Sufism, the *fanā' al-afʿāl*, the "extinction of (human) activities" in the divine Act, and the *fanā' al-sifāt*, the "extinction of the (human) qualities" in the divine Qualities. Thereby the human being reaches *fanā' al-dhāt*, "extinction of the (individual) essence" in the universal and divine Essence, which corresponds, in the Kabbalistic way, to the *bittul ha-yesh*, the "annihilation" of individual existence and its transformation into "Being-and-Beyond-Being." The supports for this spiritual realization in Judaism and Islam are by definition all the traditional modes of human existence, the many sacred forms of the outer and inner activity of man and, in particular, those of contemplation. Now here we shall not go into the traditional or ritual practices belonging to the exoterism of these two religions, which are sufficiently well known. We propose to look briefly, beyond the religious prescriptions, at the esoteric domain, which in no way implies that the contemplatives in the two ways would neglect the observance of these prescriptions; for them, all outer activity, every application of

virtue, every manifestation of faith, faith and virtues themselves, prepare, sustain, and rejoin the innermost activity, pure contemplation,
the *unio mystica* itself. While exoterists remain attached to their domain simply as a point of departure for gaining a salvation correlative to a posthumous paradisial coexistence with God, the esoterists
start every day from that same domain in order to rise to their own
sphere of spiritual activity, that of pure Truth, of the One without a
second. Every exoteric activity becomes for them a mode of contemplation, beginning with the purifying ablutions, the canonical prayers,
the prescribed fasts and almsgiving, met with in both of the religions
in question, and to which can be added, for the Muslims, above all the
pilgrimage to Mecca and, for the Jews, the prescriptions and prohibi-
tions of which there are as many as 613 in all.

The elite in both of these ways thus respond affirmatively to the
truth expressed in the divine saying quoted above, where God declares: "Nothing of what is pleasant to Me brings My servant closer
to Me than the performance of the duties I have imposed upon him";
furthermore, they actualize the following: "He who adores Me never
ceases to come closer to Me by practices beyond the call of obligation,
until I love him. . . ." Now, these practices can be summarized as all
modes of study or exegesis of the sacred Scriptures and the spiritual
realization of their content, starting from initiation to the "Wisdom of
the Kabbalah" (*Hokhmat ha-Qabbalah*), which is in essence—to make
use of a Sufic term—the "divine Wisdom" (*al-Hikmat al-ilāhiyah*), the
Knowledge proper to God Himself and in all things. This divine and
universal knowledge is in principle the end result of "study of the Torah" (*Talmud Torah*) or of the Koran, and initiation to "Mysteries of the
Torah" (*Sithre Torah*) or to the divine "Truths" (*Haqā'iq*); this means
initiation to the Mysteries or Truths of the "Name" of God (*ha-Shem*
or *al-Ism*), which comprises all reality and all revelation. Indeed, the
divine Name takes on the highest importance in the contemplative life
of Judaism and of Islam; and it is not only a mnemonic or ideographic
support for contemplation but also—and above all—the support for
invocation of God, of His real Presence. While concentrating on His
Presence, while meditating on His qualities, contemplating the Light—
or the more than luminous Darkness—of His Essence, the Kabbalist,
like the Sufi, calls upon His Name, whether pronouncing it with the
mouth, or formulating it mentally, or actualizing its informal reality
in the heart.

In Judaic esoterism, the simultaneity of meditation and invocation
as supports for contemplation appears, amongst other things, in the

combination of the "way of the *Sefirot*" (*derekh ha-Sefirot*) and of the "way of Names" (*derekh ha-Shemot*). In other words, divine Names are invoked which correspond to the *Sefirot* that are being contemplated. This, incidentally, represents only one of the many combinations of the "contemplative Kabbalah" (*Qabbalah iyunit*) with the "operative Kabbalah" (*Qabbalah maasit*). The characteristic modes of Jewish esoterism, the combination of "contemplative Kabbalah" and "operative Kabbalah," is also met with in the various methods of the science of letters (*Gematria*)—which is also the science of numbers—since the letters of the sacred alphabet express, as do the proper names or the divine names of the *Sefirot*, the fundamental archetypes of all things. More precisely, the twenty-two letters of the "celestial alphabet" represent the eternal relationships between the *Sefirot*, that is to say, between the unchangeable Aspects and Qualities of the divine Essence; and these relationships are at the origin of all the acts, or revelatory, creative, and transforming movements, of God: they are the eternal agents of the sefirotic Decad, the immediate principle of the divine Activity. Each of these "eternal letters" is by itself alone a Name—a particular determination—of God, and their innumerable combinations are in turn so many divine Names or Words, actualizing their eternal content in the midst of the Cosmos. The revealed Scriptures (i.e. the Torah, the Prophets, and the Hagiographs) are none other than the scriptuary actualizations of the transcendent letters of the eternal relationships between the *Sefirot*. These letters, combined differently in Names, Words, or Truths of God, all operate in the midst of the world and of man: they carry out the whole of the divine work. The man who goes deeply into the letters and their combinations through the four degrees of sacred exegesis, and who meditates on them, contemplates them, recites them, chants or invokes through them, the man who prays by uniting the letters in formulas of worship or of supplication, he who arranges them in different ways according to the "Science of (their) combinations" (*Hokhmat ha-Tseruf*), cooperates with God. With the Lord, man actualizes in himself the "Letters" that God "writes" in eternity, and man unites them till they become God's "one and only Name"; for "YHVH is One and His Name is One." Thus the servant finally unites all things in himself and unites himself with the One by actualizing God's real Presence, which dwells in his heart and in the holy Name.

Now, this unitive work begins with the study and application of the revealed letters as such, which is the first step, at once exoteric and esoteric, of traditional exegesis and activity. The "simple" or literal interpretation (*Peshat*) of the sacred Scriptures leads, in the first place, to the perfect carrying out of religious practice—of the "Law"—in all the prescribed modes. Then a man can rise to the second step or degree of exegesis, which is still common to the exoteric oral Doctrine, the Talmud, namely the public "study" of the Torah, and to the esoteric oral Doctrine, the Kabbalah. Having reached this degree, called *Remez*, "allusion" to the many meanings hidden in each phrase, word, letter, sign, and point of Scripture, a man passes from the domain of chiefly external activity to that of inner activity, mental and spiritual, to reflection, meditation, contemplation, Here, the Talmudist, like the Kabbalist, no longer proceeds simply by means of elementary reasoning, but examines carefully the truths enclosed in the literal expressions in the Scriptures; he begins with the overall symbolism of a whole section that relates to a particular event in sacred history, and he then proceeds to a closer reading. This is now on the scale of a sentence, a phrase, a letter, all of which are symbolic, as is each revealed vowel, sign, and point. In his study in depth of the Scriptures he may use, among other things, the Science of the combination of letters or numbers, whose best known methods are the *Gematria* (which involves the numerical value of letters), *Notarikon* (which involves the initial, middle, and final letters of words), and the *Temurah* (which is based on the permutation of letters). Mastery of the two fundamental degrees of exegesis, *Peshat* and *Remez*, as well as of all the Talmudic modes of interpreting the Torah, allows the Talmudist to pass to the third degree, called *Derash*, the homiletic "exposition" of the doctrinal truths, by way of anagoge, which moves from the literal or exoteric interpretation of the Scriptures and rises up to their exegesis on a spiritual level. The Talmudists come up to this third degree, but without approaching its "fine upper point," the esoterism which alone constitutes the fourth degree of exegesis, called *Sod*, the "Mystery," to which only the Kabbalists accede: this is the domain of initiation to the pure *Hokhmah*, the divine "Wisdom" hidden in the Scriptures and called, in relation to the teaching, *Hokhmat ha-Qabbalah*, the "Wisdom of the esoteric Tradition."

This fourth method has as its object the "Mysteries of the Torah" (*Sithre Torah*). It consists essentially of the exegesis and spiritual realization of the first chapter of Genesis (*Maaseh Bereshith*, the "Work of the Beginning"), and of the first chapter of Ezekiel's Prophecy, namely the vision of Man on the divine Throne and of the Throne itself, which is like a "Chariot" (*Merkabah*); hence this chapter is called the "Work of the Chariot" (*Maaseh Merkabah*) and the name given to initiates who carry out this work is *Yorde Merkabah*, "those who come down into the Chariot" hidden in their heart, the descent being in reality their ascent through all the heavens up to the divine Throne. But apart from these revelations from the Scriptures relating to the emanation of the divine Principle and reintegration in It, the whole of the Torah, the Prophets, and Hagiographs serve as a point of departure for the exegetic and operative methods of the *Sod*. The ten *Sefirot* play the part of fundamental supports of contemplation, while the divine Names here represent the essential operative means; along with all the other means of union given, they lead the Kabbalist through the four degrees of *PaRDeS* (the word in which we find the initial letters of the names of these degrees themselves, namely, *Peshat, Remez, Derash, Sod*, and which signifies "Paradise"): they lead him beyond even this Paradise of Knowledge to the supra-intelligible realm, to the "Nothingness" which is the Absolute.

The other means or methods of spiritual realization in Judaism represent for the most part variants or combinations of those previously cited. In all these ways, a great *kawwanah* is required, that is to say, a theocentric "intention" which, in conformity with its sacrosanct object, calls for the greatest "attention" from the contemplatives, total "concentration" of his mind on the Principle contemplated, and the "recollection" of his whole being in the only Truth and only Reality— these being some of the many possible translations of the term *kawwanah*, to which can be added the one formulated by Rabbi Moshe of Kobryn (d. 1858): "To direct the heart toward God." This essential and universal way of all contemplation, this necessary condition of all spiritual realization, is founded in Scripture on the commandment: "And thou shalt love YHVH, thy God, with all thy heart, with all thy soul, with all thy strength"—this fundamental commandment being itself inseparable from another that in particular must be carried out in external activity: "Thou shalt love thy neighbor as thyself." For God is all in all and it is necessary to contemplate Him and inwardly unite oneself with Him in order to see Him and approach Him in all things; as the Kabbalah testifies: "In all things there is a 'drawing near' [to God] for him who understands how to accomplish the union [with Him] and to worship [or contemplate] the Lord. . ." (*Zohar, Tetsaveh*, 181b).

This is why the Kabbalah never ceases to stress the absolute necessity that he who prays, invokes, meditates, and contemplates should do so with "all his heart and all his intelligence to the point where all his limbs and organs are associated with these" so that his whole being thereby penetrates more and more into the realm of the Spirit and finally is absorbed completely in its own spiritual and divine Essence which is the Essence of all things.

Happy is the portion of whoever can penetrate into the mysteries of his [divine] Master and become absorbed into Him, as it were. Especially does a man achieve this when he offers up his prayer [or invocation] to his Master in intense devotion, his will then becoming as the flame inseparable from the coal [the spirit], and his mind concentrated on the Unity.
. . . Whilst a man's mouth and lips are moving, his heart [the spirit which dwells in it] and his will must soar to the "Height of Heights" [the supreme Principle], so as to acknowledge [in truth] the Unity of the whole in virtue of the Mystery of mystery in which all ideas, all wills, and all thoughts find their goal, to wit, the Mystery of the Infinite [*Ein Sof*] (*Zohar, Vayakhel*, 213b).

The ultimate aim of all modes of contemplation and of action in Judaism is *Ein Sof*, the Infinite, the Unity of Being (*Ehyeh*) and Beyond-Being or Non-Being (*Ayin*). Now, all the fundamental Judaic modes of "union" (*yihud*), the various *kawwanot* or ways of concentrating on the One, the permanent "attachment" (*debekut*) to Him, all modes of "prayer" (*tefillah*), of "invocation" (*qeriyah*), of "meditation" (*hirhur* or *hitbonenut*), of "contemplation" (*histaklut*), all "fervor" (*hitlahabut*) or intense love for the Only One and all "fear" (*yirah*) of nonconformity with Him, in a word, all "service" (*abodah*) of God and of one's neighbor, the performance of the *mitsvot* or "commandments"—all that is to be found again in other forms revealed by *Allāh*, in Islam, and in particular in its esoteric or contemplative domain, Sufism.

The immediate aim of Sufism, to which we come back once more, is *Haqīqah*, pure, supreme, universal "Truth," whereas the immediate object of the majority of Muslims is the carrying out of the *Sharī'a* or Koranic "Law" and sacred customs going back to the Prophet. (The practice of the *Sharī'a* is to Islam what the practice of the *mitsvot* prescribed by the Torah and its Talmudic interpretation is to Judaism.) What is in question are outer actions, but actions which normally are motivated by the faith of those who perform them. There are many degrees of this faith, from the seeking for a posthumous paradise to the pure love of God, the pure knowledge of Him, by which the works of the *Sharī'a* are transformed into as many modes of contemplation.

In Islam, the spiritual elevation of one's being, starting from outer activity and rising to the inner contemplative act, takes place by three fundamental steps which are: (1) *al-islām*, "submission to the divine Will," and thus effective observance of the Law; (2) *al-īmān*, "faith," defined as true belief in *Allāh*, His angels, His books, His messengers, and the Day of Judgment; (3) *al-ihsān*, preeminent "virtue," which implies the purely spiritual element in all religious practice and in faith itself, thus the "vision of God," the contemplation of Him, whether luminous or obscure. "*Ihsān* consists in worshiping God as if you see Him, for even if you do not see Him, He sees you." If our contemplation is not filled with His Light, it must be filled with our faith in Him—the "believing without seeing"—and with our works willed by Him. These three degrees of the Islamic Path are found in its esoterism in the analogous triad *makhāfah* (fear), *mahabbah* (love), and *maʿrifah* (knowledge) of God. Here, "fear" consists above all of *al-furqān*, theoretical and practical "discernment" between the true and the false, between the only reality, *Allāh*, and unreality (the "I" and the "world"); "love" is the direct and permanent aspiration to the only Truth and the only Reality, to the one and only well-Beloved; and "knowledge" is none other than contemplative union with the "One without a second." These are the three fundamental degrees of *tawhīd*, of the Sufic affirmation of the One, and these degrees are repeated again in other analogous triads, such as that which starts from the idea that man is above all an *ʿabd*, a "servant" of God. Regarded in this way, the spiritual way becomes the threefold service of the Absolute, beginning from *al-ʿibādah*, the rigorous or ascetic "service" of all the faculties of the being who submits to the spiritual exercises; then *al-ʿubūdiyyah*, "servitude," which is the central idea of the present triad and gives it its global significance—all the patience, all the endurance required by the search, often of long duration, for the spiritual Goal; lastly, *al-ʿubūdah*, total "enslavement" of the servant to his Lord, his complete "extinction" (*fanāʾ*) in Him, the "loss of the awareness of his servitude in contemplation of Him who is served." But on coming back to himself, "the servant remains the servant," submitted (*muslim*) to the Will of the Lord with the submission (*islām*) with which he set out on his quest of the Absolute and which played its part in the spiritual exercises of his *ʿibādah*.

In Muslim exoterism as in Muslim esoterism, man is *ʿabd*, the servant of *Allāh*, but in esoterism he becomes a true "poor man before his Lord" (*faqīr ilā Rabbihi*). *Al-faqr*, "poverty" or spiritual receptivity in face of the only Truth and the only Reality, is his fundamental way of existence from the day when he ceases to lead the illusory existence of a "second" beside the "One without a second"; from that day on he follows a spiritual "path," *tarīqah*, thanks to the initiatic "blessing" (*barakah*) received from a "Master" (*murshid* or *shaykh*, lit. "old man"). Thenceforth he is a *murīd*, an "aspirant" to Truth, linked by the "pact" (*al-bay'ah*) of an initiation to an esoteric "chain" (*silsilah*), which goes back to the Prophet. From then on, the *Sharī'a* or exoteric "law" represents for him a totality of modes of spiritualization. This starts with the first of the "five pillars," or fundamental obligations of Islam, the *shahādah*, the creed or "attestation" of the One God and of His messenger Muhammad. By affirming that "there is no divinity if not The Divinity" (*La ilāha illā Allāh*), the *faqīr* renounces himself as being a false "divinity" (*ilāh*), and by adding that "Muhammad is the messenger of the Divinity" (*Muhammadun rasūl Allāh*), he affirms his exoteric and esoteric imitation of the Prophet, who is the model of all believers, whether they be those who follow just the *Sharī'a* or those who are also *fuqarā'*. As for the second of the five "obligations," prayer, for the *faqīr* it is not limited to the prayer that has to be made at least five times a day: it is continued in other forms, such as the recitation of the Koran or of the Rosary, and above all in the form of the *dhikr*, the permanent "remembrance" of *Allāh* in its various and often simultaneous aspects of the "invocation" of a divine Name, of the "meditation" (*tafakkur*) of a truth or of an aspect of He who is invoked, or of the "contemplation" (*mushāhadah*) of His Presence (*hudūr*); the sacred song and dance also play their part—insofar as they are true "means of union"—in the *dhikr*. The third "obligation"—the fast in the month of Ramadan, in which the descent of the Koran took place—is often carried on beyond that period by the *faqīr*, particularly when he is in *khalwah*, the spiritual "retreat" devoted to the *dhikr*; but in a still deeper sense, he who is "poor in spirit" (i.e. the *faqīr*) abstains to the greatest extent possible from all psychic food, even thought itself, in the permanent and non-discursive concentration of his spirit on the supreme and universal Principle— and this in fact is the essential meaning of fasting: the *vacare Deo* into which He sends down His Presence, His Light, His Word, the Koran. The same applies to the fourth "obligation," almsgiving, which, in the eyes of the *faqīr*, is the gift of oneself to God in the neighbor; his almsgiving or tithe is not limited to the legal percentage to be withheld from one's revenue: he gives himself to those who have need of him. Lastly, there is the "fifth pillar" of Islam, the pilgrimage to Mecca, which retraces here below the journey of the soul to the Throne of *Allāh*. For the *faqīr*, this takes place every day and everywhere: each day he makes his pilgrimage to Mecca in his heart, to the universal Center hidden in himself, where *Allāh* dwells in all His Majesty and Beauty.

This daily inner pilgrimage of spiritual man, his search for the Absolute, is his gradual "approach" (*taqarrub*) to God, which implies partial inner liberations from the "I." These are the stations (*maqāmāt*) of his growing poverty on the way to his complete extinction in God. This gift of oneself to All-Reality calls for virtues and cognitive efforts which together constitute all aspects of spiritual poverty (*al-faqr*), a synonym of the "unitive way" (*al-tawhīd*). Among these virtues figures above all the "struggle against the soul" (*mukhālafat al-nafs*), insofar as the soul, through its ignorance and its passions, masks the pure and divine Self of man; this negation of the "I" implies not only every kind of renunciation (*al-zuhd*) or abstinence (*al-wara'*), but also every virtue which affirms the Reality through a positive symbolism, such as love of God (*al-mahabbah*) and confidence in Him (*al-tawakkul*), gratitude (*al-shukr*) and contentment (*al-ridā*) in regard to what He grants us, patience (*al-sabr*) or hope (*al-rajā'*) concerning what He has not yet given us, truthfulness (*al-sidq*) and purity (*al-ikhlās*), which manifest the Truth present in us. The warfare (*al-mujāhadah*) of man against his ego is not waged solely because of the divine Self immanent in him but in view of the Presence of the Self in all things: man also meets his divine Self in the "other-than-I" around him and it is likewise by affirming the latter through altruism (*al-ithār*), generosity (*al-sakha'*), chivalrous spirit (*al-futūwwa*), and courtesy (*al-adab*) that he fights and overcomes the ego. Apart from these virtues which relate to the divine Omnipresence, there are others which derive above all from the unfathomable distance between the "I" and the Transcendent, or from the (relative) absence of God: these include "fear" (*al-khawf* or *al-taqwa*), "sadness" (*al-huzn*), and humility (*al-khushū'*). Finally all the virtues are summarized in "servitude" (*al-'ubūdiyyah*) towards God, submission (*al-islām*) to His Will, faith (*al-īmān*) in Him, and worship of Him "as if you see Him, for even if you do not see Him, He sees you" (*al-ihsān*). As for the initiatic way of he who is "poor," it presupposes his spiritual conversion (*al-tawbah*) and consists of the initiatic pact (*al-bay'ah*) with the (spiritual) Master, inner "attachment" (*al-suhbah*) to him, spiritual retreat (*al-khalwah*), invocation (*al-dhikr*), meditation (*al-tafakkur*), "observation" of the Omnipresent (*al-murāqabah*), etc. All these virtues and all these spiritual efforts, to which one could add many others, are crystallized in *tawhīd*, that is, in permanent concentration on the One, which implies the "effort of actualization" of His Presence (*al-istihdār*) intended to lead to "realization of the Essence" (*tahqīq al-Dhāt*)."

We have just seen that besides the attitudes, stations, or spiritual degrees characterized by the virtues, there are some which refer more directly to knowledge. The cognitive ladder which begins in *islām* and ends in pure *tawhīd* starts with the literal assimilation of the Koran and goes on to the exoteric and esoteric exegesis of the Koran, the latter being concretized in the spiritual actualization of the revealed Truth, the "realization of the (divine) Essence (itself)." Now, from the point of view of Sufism the whole of the Revelation of the Essence, of the Truth, of the divine Qualities and Activities, and of the Revelation of the All-Reality in the Universe and in the Koran, all this is nothing other than the descent of the Supreme Name of *Allāh* and of all the divine Names comprised therein. This is why in Islam (as in Judaism, where the whole of the Torah is nothing but the multiform revelation of the Name of the One) the sanctification of the divine Name by invocation, meditation, or contemplation is of capital importance; it is also why here, as in the sister religion, we find a veritable science of the divine Names starting from the "Names of the Essence" (*Asmā' Dhātiyah*), the highest of which is *Allāh* and amongst which are to be found *Huwa*, "He," *al-Ahad*, "the One," *al-Samad*, "the Independent," and *al-Quddūs*, "the Most Holy"; then descending towards the "Names of the Qualities" (*Asmā' Sifātiyah*) such as *al-Rahmān* (the Merciful), *al-Salām* (Peace), and *al-Karīm* (the Generous); and on towards the Names of the divine "Activities" (*al-Af'āl*), such as *al-Muhyī* (He who gives life) or *al-Mumīt* (He who gives death). The various categories of these Names—which also include the *Shahādah*—are actualized above all by the *dhikr* (contemplative invocation) with its various methods or techniques which often differ from one *tarīqah* or Sufi brotherhood to another and of which we cannot here draw up a complete list.

All these initiatic techniques of contemplative invocation, like every esoteric science of the divine Names and of the Letters of the sacred alphabet, enter into the general category of knowledge that the Sufis call *'ilm al-yaqīn*, the "Science of Certainty." This is a degree of *furqān* (discernment) acquired thanks to the teachings of one's spiritual master. To assimilate it demands from the disciple *muhādarah*, the "presence of the heart" or of the "intellect" (*al-'aql*) that dwells in it; the latter grasps the teachings through their intrinsic proof (*burhān*), a logical—and deeply ontological—proof which reveals the truth in discursive or rational mode. In fact, *al-'aql*, the intellect, is first of all regarded here in its peculiarly human or mental aspect: reason, which assimilates Truth by reflection or meditation (*tafakkur*) of the discursive order. But, while there is a discontinuity between this rational order and the purely spiritual and non-discursive realm of contemplation (*mushāhadah*), it is not absolute: the discontinuity hides a continuity which is none other than the universal Logos relating human logic to ontological, divine Reality. This is *al-'ilm* in the universal sense, divine "knowledge" or "omniscience" which, in the midst of discursive meditation, discovers the Truth or Reality that is its object; reflection by means of the reason is suddenly absorbed by intuition or inspiration, by the direct vision of the cognitive Object which has no need of rational proof. When the "eye of the heart" ('ayn al-qalb) opens, looks, and sees, the disciple is raised to the degree of knowledge called 'ayn al-yaqīn, the "Source" or "Eye of Certainty." This is the degree where sacred thought, or methodical meditation, becomes a key to mukāshafah, the direct "unveiling" of the Object of meditation; al-bayān, the "evidence" of the cognitive Object, is found instead of logical proof, and al-'ilm, the divine "omniscience" dwelling in the pure spirit of man, acts in place of his reason (al-'aql).

Now, the true object of all spiritual searching, hence of all doctrinal reflection and methodical meditation, is none other than the "One without a second," in which the "second," the one who searches, reflects, and meditates has to be effaced and integrated. And indeed the "evidence" of the sole Reality finally becomes so strong that all human thought, even all human being, is extinguished as the shade of night vanishes at sunrise: there is no longer anything but the divine Sun, the luminous Eye of Allāh infinitely open in the midst of the heart. There is no longer anything but Him looking at Himself and contemplating Himself in His servant; yet, at the same time the servant is indeed truly in Him, like a spark indistinctly included in His boundless Clarity. This is the entrance to the highest cognitive degree, called the "Truth of Certainty," haqq al-yaqīn; this is the degree of mushāhadat al-Rububiyyah, "the Lord's own Contemplation" in the servant who, on coming back to himself, is an 'ārif bi-Allāh, a "knower through Allāh."

When the soul of the servant is reduced by its extinction to what it was in the beginning, a divine spark, it becomes again what it is in truth and in eternity: the Infinite. And when the servant comes down again from eternity into time, he finds his terrestrial body in its primordial beauty. His earthly body is filled with Light from above, with the Presence of "God, the Light of the heavens and of the earth." In the middle of his invocation the servant became silent because the sound of the divine Name, its whole articulation, was transformed into pure Light. The invocation became silent contemplation of the single Light above, around, and within the human and individual light. The Essence of the servant is light, his spirit, his soul, and his body are light, even though, from the outside, one sees a man, a body. His head no longer thinks, for it is open to the Infinite and filled with light; his heart desires nothing, for he has become a source of light which radiates in all the directions of the universe toward the Infinite. His being is but one with the pure Being, his act one with the pure Act, the Act of Being and of Knowledge. To be Being is to be infinitely happy, it is to be conscious of the Plenitude of Being, it is to know oneself as infinite Light. To be the Light is to be the Clarity of all knowledge, it is to have no further need of thinking or of acting unless the Light wishes it. Then the Light which is pure Being manifests Itself as pure Act, as divine Will, and with this Will, Life comes down from on high like a beatific stream. It fills the terrestrial body which before that was full of suffering and the body becomes a paradise of light. Then the whole of the soul, the whole life of the body is light; and it is with this light that the servant contemplates God in all things, the Light of the heavens and of the earth. "For with Thee is the fountain of life: in Thy light shall we see light" (Ps. 36:9).

Existence is suffering. Being is bliss. To exist is to go out from Being, it is to leave happiness behind. To act is to actualize either Being or existence, either Light or the *chiaroscuro* of transient life on earth. Contemplation is the pure act by which one passes from all action and from existence itself to Being, to eternal Life, to infinite Light. If all men were immersed in contemplation of the only Truth and only Reality, where would the problems of humanity be? And if all those who have become incapable of such contemplation were to pray, if they were to serve the contemplatives and follow their advice, where would their difficulties be? Heaven would send them its blessing and the earth would give them its fruits in abundance; it would no longer be an "accursed soil" but a paradise, and mankind would rediscover the happiness of Adam before his fall. For, the true destiny of man is contemplation: it is to contemplate the One, to pray to, to call upon, and to serve the One and thereby to be united with the One. Outside of the One, there is no salvation, no peace, no grace, no light, and no happiness; apart from the One, there is only dualism, struggle, suffering, and death.

See, I have set before thee this day life and good, and death and evil; in that I command thee this day to love the Eternal, thy God, to walk in His ways and to keep His commandments and His statutes and His ordinances, that thou mayest live. . . . But if thine heart turn away, so that thou wilt not hear, but shalt be drawn away, and worship other gods [the false gods fabricated by man, the *idola mentis*] and serve them, I denounce unto you this day, that ye shall surely perish. . . . Choose life, that thou mayest live. . . . (Deut. 30: 15–18, 19).

# GLOSSARY

*Adam ha-rishon* (Hebrew): "first man"; in the Kabbalistic interpretation of creation, *Adam Qadmon*, after his manifestation in heaven, is "created" and "shaped" as the "first man," *Adam ha-rishon*, in the earthly paradise.

*Adam ilaah* (Hebrew): "Transcendent Man"; see *Adam Qadmon*.

*Adam Qadmon* (Hebrew): "Principial Man"; in the cosmology of the Kabbalah, this is the celestial, immaterial human prototype whose "body" is then made of the primordial ether (*Avira*) and is coextensive with the entire corporeal universe, still being one with God's Essence and His ontological possibilities. *Adam Qadmon*, after his manifestation in heaven, is "created" and "shaped" as the "first man" (*Adam ha-rishon*) in the earthly paradise.

*Adonai* (Hebrew): "my Lord"; the personal God who is immediately accessible to each creature; the God who dwells in all hearts.

*Amoraim* (Hebrew, sing. *amora*): "orators" or "interpreters"; teachers and interpreters of the spoken Doctrine who were active in the centuries following the compilation of the *Mishnah*.

*Ānanda* (Sanskrit): "bliss, beatitude, joy."

*Anokhi* (Hebrew): "I"; God's "I-ness," proclaimed and thus given to the Chosen People on Mount Sinai.

*Arabot* (Hebrew): the seventh heaven.

*Ātmā* or *Ātman* (Sanskrit): the real or true "Self," underlying the ego and its manifestations; in the perspective of *Advaita Vedānta*, identical with *Brahma*.

*Avira* (Hebrew): "Air," "Ether"; the undifferentiated Ether, the "pure and imperceptible air" of the eighth heaven, descending from the *Shekhinah*.

*Ayin* (Hebrew): "Nothingness," "Non-Being," "Beyond-Being."

*Binah* (Hebrew): "Intelligence," "Understanding"; the third *Sefirah*; the cosmic "Intelligence" of God which originates from *Hokhmah*; *Binah* is the Divine Mother who then gives birth to the seven *Sefirot* below Her.

*Bittul ha-yesh* (Hebrew): "annihilation of existence"; the spiritual action of extinguishing the limitations of human reason in the contemplation of the Divine "Nothingness" (*Ayin*).

*Bodhisattva* (Sanskrit, Pali): literally, "enlightenment-being"; in *Mahāyāna* Buddhism, one who postpones his own final enlightenment and entry into *Nirvāna* in order to aid all other sentient beings in their quest for Buddhahood.

*Brahma* or *Brahman* (Sanskrit): the Supreme Reality, the Absolute.

*Brahmā* (Sanskrit): God in the aspect of Creator, the first divine "person"; to be distinguished from *Brahma*, the Supreme Reality.

*Din* (Hebrew): "Judgment," "Power"; the fifth *Sefirah*; the rigor which emanates from *Binah* leads to *Din*, which results in the principle of concentration, distinction, and limitation, allowing for the emergence of evil; *Din* is the left arm of the divine "body," which balances *Hesed*; also called *Gevurah*.

*Ein Sof* (Hebrew): literally, "without end"; the Infinite; the Essence of God inasmuch as it is beyond the limits of human knowledge and thus of the *Sefirot* themselves.

*Fanā'* (Arabic): "extinction, annihilation, evanescence"; in Sufism, the spiritual station or degree of realization in which all individual attributes and limitations are extinguished in union with God.

*Fiat lux* (Latin): "Let there be light" (cf. Gen. 1:3).

Great Synagogue (or the Great Assembly): in Jewish history, instituted from the so-called Persian period, a period that is not historically clear. Ezra may have been the leader of the Great Synagogue during his time. The "Men of the Great Synagogue" instituted many benedictions and prayers, and the traditional view is that the entire liturgy was given a definite form during this period. It appears that they were also active in canonical codification and masoretic studies. Tradition associates the Great Synagogue with events recorded in Nehemiah 8–10.

*Hesed* (Hebrew): "Love," "Kindness," "Grace"; the fourth *Sefirah*, the outpouring of divine Mercy, Grace, and Blessing within manifestation; *Hesed* is the "right arm" of the divine "body," balancing out *Din*, God's justice and power.

*Hod* (Hebrew): "Majesty"; the eighth *Sefirah*; working along with *Netsah*, *Hod* is the source of prophecy.

*Hokhmah* (Hebrew): "Wisdom"; the second *Sefirah*; *Hokhmah* is pure and redemptive wisdom, which must be pursued by the seeker of Kabbalah.

*Kawwanot* (Hebrew): "intention," "devotion"; in Kabbalah, ways and methods of concentrating on the One.

*Keter* (Hebrew): "Crown"; the first, supreme *Sefirah*; *Keter* designates Beyond-Being, the Absolute, the "Nothingness" of *Ayin*; it is the Divine in Itself, before any of the "determinations" or manifestations of the lower *Sefirot*.

*Malkhut* (Hebrew): "Kingdom"; the tenth *Sefirah*; the divine emanations that have flowed through the upper *Sefirot* then flow through *Malkhut* into the material worlds; it is also known as *Shekhinah*, and is associated with the Holy Spirit.

*Merkabah* (Hebrew): "chariot"; associated with mystical ascents, such as the ascent of Elijah to heaven. For spiritual seekers, it symbolizes the transparent vehicle of the Spirit, which is hidden in one's heart.

*Metatron*: in Jewish esoterism, an angel-like presence between the immaterial and material worlds. In the *Zohar*, it is the "form" or "universal body" of the *Shekhinah*, which is itself supra-formal and infinite; *Metatron* is responsible for revelations to humanity (i.e., to the prophets and the saints) and can take the "likeness of an appearance of a man"; *Metatron* is associated with the glory or immanence of YHVH.

*Netsah* (Hebrew): "Endurance"; the seventh *Sefirah*; *Netsah* is the right thigh of the divine "body"; it is the grace of God flowing down into existence, the "victory" of His unity amidst all duality of creation; along with *Hod*, *Netsah* is the other source of prophecy.

*Nirvāna* (Sanskrit): "blowing out, extinction"; in Indian traditions, especially Buddhism, the extinction of the fires of passion and the resulting, supremely blissful state of liberation from egoism and attachment; see *fanā'*.

*Philosophia perennis* (Latin): "perennial philosophy."

*Sat-Chit-Ānanda* or *Sachchidānanda* (Sanskrit): "being-consciousness-bliss"; the three essential aspects of *Apara-Brahma*, that is, *Brahma* insofar as it can be grasped in human experience.

*Sefirot* (Hebrew, sing. *Sefirah*): literally, "numbers"; in Kabbalah, the ten emanations of *Ein Sof* or divine Infinitude, each comprising a different aspect of creative energy.

*Shekhinah* (Hebrew): "settling," "indwelling," "presence"; the indwelling of the Divine Presence in manifestation; the Divine Immanence; also, the tenth *Sefirah*, called *Malkhut*.

*Sophia* (Greek): "wisdom"; in Jewish and Christian tradition, the Wisdom of God, often conceived as feminine (cf. Prov. 8).

*Tasawwuf* (Arabic): a term of disputed etymology, though perhaps from *sūf* for "wool", after the garment worn by many early Sufis; traditional Muslim word for Sufism.

Tetragrammaton (Greek): "Name of four letters"; the Tetragrammaton refers to "*YHVH*," the "lost word" that was above all others the "saving" Name in the tradition of Israel; it is known as *Shem ha-Meforash*, the "explicit Name," the one whose every consonant reveals and symbolizes one of the four aspects or fundamental degrees of divine All-Reality; it is the holiest and most powerful of all divine Names, also called the "complete name" and the "synthesis of syntheses," because it includes all the other divine names, each of which, by itself, expresses only one or another particular aspect of the universal Principle.

*Tif'eret* (Hebrew): "Beauty"; the sixth *Sefirah*; *Tif'eret* is the central *Sefirah* in the "Tree of the *Sefirot*" (see Figure 1 on p. 137), harmonizing the other *Sefirot* around it; it is the trunk of the divine "body," and thus the masculine principle of creative emanation, partnered with the *Shekhinah*.

*Torah* (Hebrew): "instruction, teaching"; in Judaism, the written law of God, as revealed to Moses on Sinai and embodied in the Pentateuch (Genesis, Exodus, Leviticus, Numbers, Deuteronomy).

*Tsimtsum* (Hebrew): "contraction," "restriction," "retreat," or "concentration"; a Kabbalistic doctrine introduced by Isaac Luria to describe the divine mystery on which creation depends. It involves God's withdrawing His Light from one part of Himself, leaving a void to allow "room" for cosmic expansion. It concerns the part of the divine Essence in which the light was weakened to allow the existence of souls, angels, the material worlds, etc.

*Yesod* (Hebrew): "Foundation"; the ninth *Sefirah*; the procreating "foundation" of God's creation, or the procreative organ of *Adam Qadmon*, it channels the divine emanations from above to *Shekhinah*.

*Yoga* (Sanskrit): literally, "yoking, union"; in Indian traditions, any meditative and ascetic technique designed to bring the soul and body into a state of concentration.

For a glossary of all key foreign words used in books published by World Wisdom, including metaphysical terms in English, consult: www.DictionaryofSpiritualTerms.org.
This on-line Dictionary of Spiritual Terms provides extensive definitions, examples, and related terms in other languages.

# LIST OF SOURCES

Chapter 1, "Some Universal Aspects of Judaism": In *The Unanimous Tradition*. Edited by Ranjit Fernando, article translated by Malcolm Barnes. Colombo, Sri Lanka: Sri Lanka Institute of Traditional Studies, 1991, pp. 57–75.

Chapter 2, "The Meaning of the Temple": *Studies in Comparative Religion* (Autumn, 1971), pp. 241–246.

Chapter 3, "The Mission of Elias": *Studies in Comparative Religion* (Summer-Autumn, 1980), pp. 159–167.

Chapter 4, "The Sinaitic Theophany According to the Jewish Tradition": *Studies in Comparative Religion* (Summer-Autumn, 1984), pp. 214–234 and (Winter-Spring, 1985), pp. 45–58.

Chapter 5, "Torah and Kabbalah": *The Universal Meaning of the Kabbalah*. Translated by Nancy Pearson. Hillsdale, NY: Sophia Perennis, 2005, Chapter 1.

Chapter 6, "Creation, the Image of God": *The Universal Meaning of the Kabbalah*. Translated by Nancy Pearson. Hillsdale, NY: Sophia Perennis, 2005, Chapter 3.

Chapter 7, "The Great Name of God": *The Universal Meaning of the Kabbalah*. Translated by Nancy Pearson. Hillsdale, NY: Sophia Perennis, 2005, Chapter 8.

Chapter 8, "The Worldview of the Kabbalah": Translated by Gerhard Giesse. Paper presented at "Oetinger-Symposion," Stuttgart, Germany, September 30, 1982.

Chapter 9, "Contemplation and Action in Judaism and Islam": In *Traditional Modes of Contemplation and Action: A Colloquium held at Rothko Chapel, Houston Texas*. Edited by Yusuf Ibish and Peter Lamborn Wilson. Tehran: Imperial Iranian Academy of Philosophy, 1977, pp. 365–400.

# BIOGRAPHICAL NOTES

**LEO SCHAYA** (1916–1986) was a prolific author and editor of works on comparative religion, esoterism, and the Perennial Philosophy (or Traditionalism). Following in the current of earlier authors such as René Guénon, Ananda K. Coomaraswamy, Frithjof Schuon, and Titus Burckhardt, Schaya's work was unique in its focus on the Semitic monotheistic traditions, and particularly on Judaism.

Schaya was born in Basle, Switzerland. His given Hebrew name was Aryeh Lev Schaya. Of his family, who were originally from the Polish town of Wieruszow, he wrote that they "were all fervent Hasidim." However, after the family's emigration to Switzerland in 1913, they no longer practiced the religion as their forefathers had. Leo's attraction to spirituality would develop during his teen years through his reading and meditation upon primary and secondary texts from Judaism and other major spiritual traditions of the world. The young man's insight into these often complex and mystical texts, and his personal inclination toward the truths found in them, indicated a far-ranging intellect and an intense spiritual yearning that would emerge in his later work. In the areas of philosophy, theology, metaphysics, comparative religion, and non-European languages, Leo Schaya was almost entirely self-taught during his formative years.

He had a strong inclination to his own religious tradition of Judaism, but also developed an interest in such wisdom traditions as neo-Platonism, Sufism, and Advaita Vedanta. In 1935 a friend took him to the lectures given by Frithjof Schuon in Basle on the "transcendent unity of religions." At the end of the series of lectures, Schaya introduced himself to Schuon, and thus began a close intellectual association and friendship, as well as an extensive correspondence of many years, which lasted until Schaya's death. Following World War II, Schaya moved to Lausanne for several years and from there in 1952 to Nancy, France, where he lived for the rest of his life.

For many years, Schaya utilized his business and administrative skills in several positions in his native Switzerland and France, but in 1979 he turned entirely to his real interest, the writing and editing of works on comparative religion. However, in those same years after his retirement, he also maintained numerous relationships with friends in many countries centered around the spiritual life.

Schaya's intellectual gifts were put to good use from 1977–1984 as editor-in-chief of *Études Traditionnelles*, a French journal which published many compelling articles on the spiritual traditions of humanity and on various aspects of the *philosophia perennis* for much of the twentieth century. Following this, Leo Schaya founded and was the editor of another French journal, *Connaissance des Religions*, a position he filled till his death in 1986.

Leo Schaya's own published writings include dozens of articles published in various journals and several books. Prior to this volume, the only book of Schaya's to appear in English has been *The Universal Meaning of the Kabbalah* (Sophia Perennis, 2005; first edition, London: George Allen & Unwin, 1971). In that book in particular, and in many of his articles, he explored in unparalleled depth universal aspects of metaphysics and spirituality found in Judaism—particularly in the Kabbalah—but also in other great spiritual traditions of humanity. Schaya's writings have also gained notice for their attention to the treatment of esoterism and symbolism, and for the intense sense of the sacred that pervades them.

Although his mother tongue was German, Leo Schaya published his books primarily in French. These include (with the years of their initial publication): *L'Homme et l'absolu selon la Kabbale* (1958), *La Doctrine soufique de l'Unité* (1962), *La creation en Dieu: À la lumière du judaïsme, du christianisme et de l'islam* (1983), and *Naissance à l'Esprit* (1987). Only the first of these has been translated in its entirety into English and published.

Besides his work as an author and editor, Leo Schaya also delivered several papers at prestigious conferences. Two of these are represented in this volume: "The Worldview of the Kabbalah," from a symposium on Friedrich Christoph Oetinger in 1982, and "Contemplation and Action in Judaism and Islam," from a colloquium titled "Traditional Modes of Contemplation and Action," in 1973.

Although little has been published in English on Schaya's work as a thinker and author, one can find more biographical details, some insightful observations on his body of work, and an extensive bibliography of Schaya's writing in an article written by Robert G. Margolis, "At 'The Meeting of the Two Seas': An Introduction to Leo Schaya and His Writings," in the journal *Ajames* (no. 13, 1998. pp. 389–418). In addition, Jacob Needleman's "Foreword" to *The Universal Meaning of the Kabbalah* explains Schaya's central theses very well. Finally, the "Foreword" by Patrick Laude in the present volume adds another dimension to our understanding of this devotee of the One.

**ROGER GAETANI** is an American editor, educator, and translator. Gaetani was born and formally educated in the United States (at Syracuse University and Indiana University), but spent a number of years in Morocco and Saudi Arabia as a teacher. While there, and in travels through other countries in Africa and Asia, he gained an appreciation for traditional cultures, thought, and art. He co-edited, with Jean-Louis Michon, *Sufism: Love and Wisdom* (World Wisdom, 2006). Gaetani also directed the DVD compilation of highlights of the 2006 conference on Traditionalism, *Tradition in the Modern World: Sacred Web 2006 Conference*, and edited the book *A Spirit of Tolerance: The Inspiring Life of Tierno Bokar* by Amadou Hampâté Bâ (World Wisdom, 2008). Gaetani's most recent publication is the translation, from the original French, of Éric Geoffroy's book *Introduction to Sufism: The Inner Path of Islam* (World Wisdom, 2010).

**PATRICK LAUDE** is a French philosopher, author, editor, and educator. He has been on the faculty of Georgetown University since 1991. Since 2006 Dr. Laude has taught theology and humanities courses at the Georgetown University School of Foreign Service in Qatar. His scholarly interests lie in contemplative and mystical traditions, particularly in their relationship with poetry, as well as in Western representations and interpretations of Islam and Asian religions. Patrick Laude is the author of the following books in English: *Frithjof Schuon: Life and Teachings* (co-authored with Jean-Baptiste Aymard, SUNY Press, 2004), *Singing the Way: Insights in Poetry and Spiritual Transformation* (World Wisdom, 2005), *Divine Play, Sacred Laughter, and Spiritual Understanding* (Palgrave Macmillan, 2005), *Pathways to an Inner Islam: Massignon, Corbin, Guénon, and Schuon* (SUNY Press, 2010), *Louis Massignon: The Vow and the Oath* (The Matheson Trust, 2011). Laude is also the editor or co-editor of the following volumes: *Music of the Sky: An Anthology of Spiritual Poetry* (co-edited with Barry McDonald, World Wisdom, 2004), *Pray without Ceasing: The Way of the Invocation in World Religions* (World Wisdom, 2006), *Universal Dimensions of Islam: Studies in Comparative Religion* (World Wisdom, 2011), and *Understanding Islam: A New Translation with Selected Letters* (World Wisdom, 2011) by Frithjof Schuon. He has had articles and book reviews published in numerous collections and journals, and has presented papers on a wide variety of subjects at dozens of conferences all over the world.

# INDEX

## Other Titles in the Perennial Philosophy Series by World Wisdom

*The Betrayal of Tradition: Essays on the Spiritual Crisis of Modernity,*
edited by Harry Oldmeadow, 2005

*Borderlands of the Spirit: Reflections on a Sacred Science of Mind,*
by John Herlihy, 2005

*A Buddhist Spectrum: Contributions to Buddhist-Christian Dialogue,*
by Marco Pallis, 2003

*A Christian Pilgrim in India: The Spiritual Journey of Swami
Abhishiktananda (Henri Le Saux),* by Harry Oldmeadow, 2008

*Emir Abd el-Kader: Hero and Saint of Islam,*
by Ahmed Bouyerdene, 2012

*The Essential Ananda K. Coomaraswamy,*
edited by Rama P. Coomaraswamy, 2004

*The Essential René Guénon,* edited by John Herlihy, 2009

*The Essential Seyyed Hossein Nasr,*
edited by William C. Chittick, 2007

*The Essential Sophia,*
edited by Seyyed Hossein Nasr and Katherine O'Brien, 2006

*The Essential Titus Burckhardt: Reflections on Sacred Art, Faiths, and
Civilizations,* edited by William Stoddart, 2003

*Every Branch in Me: Essays on the Meaning of Man,*
edited by Barry McDonald, 2002

*Every Man An Artist: Readings in the Traditional Philosophy of Art,*
edited by Brian Keeble, 2005

*Figures of Speech or Figures of Thought? The Traditional View of Art,*
by Ananda K. Coomaraswamy, 2007

*A Guide to Hindu Spirituality,* by Arvind Sharma, 2006

*Introduction to Traditional Islam, Illustrated:
Foundations, Art, and Spirituality,* by Jean-Louis Michon, 2008

*Introduction to Sufism: The Inner Path of Islam,*
by Éric Geoffroy, 2010